LIVING LIFE SIDEWAYS

THE COMPLETE SERIES

MICHELLE SEGREST

NAVIGATE CONTENT, INC.

LIVING LIFE SIDEWAYS: The Complete Series

True Story of Heart-Pounding Adventure & Heart-Wrenching Survival

By Michelle Segrest

Content Editor: Bo Segrest

Copy Editor: Emily Britt

Cover Design: @germancreative

Cover Photography: Bethany Womack

Paperback ISBN: 979-8-9898475-0-1

Copyright ©2023, Navigate Content, Inc., Birmingham, Alabama, USA www.navigatec
ontent.com

This book is a personal memoir and a work of nonfiction. It reflects the author's present
recollections of experiences over time. No names have been changed, no characters
invented, and no events fabricated, however, some names have been omitted, some
events have been compressed, and some dialogue has been recreated. This is a book of
memory, and memory has its own story to tell. But I have done my best to tell a truthful
story. I stand by every word.

The conversations in the book all come from the author's recollections, as well as from
detailed journals written throughout the journey by the author. Still, they are not written
to represent word-for-word transcripts. Rather, the author has retold them in a way that
evokes the feeling and meaning what was said, and in all instances, the essence of the
dialogue is accurate.

Neither the author nor the publisher assumes or hereby claims any liability to any party
for any loss, damage, or disruption caused by errors or omissions, whether such errors
or omissions result from negligence, accident, or any other cause.

DEDICATION

For my children, Shelby and Bo. Nothing will ever stop me from seeing your faces staring back at me.

For my dear mother, Patti Lambert, thank you for the gift of your adventurous spirit and for teaching me that I deserve to be with a man who will honor me.

CONTENTS

LIFE ON A
20-DEGREE
TILT

LIVING LIFE SIDEWAYS SERIES
BOOK 1

MICHELLE SEGREST

Chapter 1

BATTLING THE BALTIC

Anticipation and excitement swelled in sync with the Baltic Sea waves.

After almost six years of dreaming about the adventure, intense planning, budgeting, and preparation, the departure date was set. On Sunday, August 19, 2018, at 09:00 we would set sail from Stralsund, Germany to Gulf Shores, Alabama on a worldwide voyage that included an Atlantic Ocean crossing.

The bright orange sailing vessel, *Seefalke*—a 43-foot steel ketch that was built by Dutch designers specifically for the heavy, harsh conditions of the brutal North Sea—was undergoing final preparations for the 6,000 nautical mile journey.

The captain, a stoic, matter-of-fact German, had been sailing more than half of his 41-year life. He taught himself to sail on small dinghies on German rivers, then gained critical experience aboard a destroyer in the German navy. But it was his experience day-sailing the small 24-foot Flying Tramp, *Toja*, in the Baltic Sea for the past decade that had inspired him to seek more challenging waters and longer voyages.

As the first mate, I had minimal experience, but had caught the sailing bug quickly. Even though I was ten years older than the skipper, I got a late start. I went sailing for the first time with my longtime friend, Yvi Habermann. When we were in high school, she was a German exchange student who lived with my family in Decatur, Alabama. We remained close friends through the years.

While in Hamburg in 2013 for business, she took me sailing one afternoon. I was hooked. I'll never forget that day because that's when she told me about how she sold everything she owned and embarked on an 18-month voyage in a small 7m, wooden sailboat.

Yvi's stories of freedom inspired me as she spoke about how she had abandoned her 9-to-5 job and left land life behind for unexpected adventures in faraway lands I had never even heard of at that time. I imagined the courage it would take to embrace such an adventure—and the bravery needed to actually make it happen. My head began to spin with thoughts of what an adventure like that would look like for me. I questioned whether I had the guts to embark on such a life-changing odyssey, but nevertheless, I began dreaming of an escape from the ordinary.

A week later, while still traveling through Germany on business, I met the skipper on a work assignment. Perhaps my thoughts of Yvi's adventure clouded any rational reasoning. As he told me of his own sailing adventures and dreams of a life at sea, I became enamored with his passion.

The skipper was tall, slim, and charming, with an electric personality, bright smile, and deep aquamarine eyes that twinkled in contrast with his latte-colored skin. His look was very exotic, and it was hard to pinpoint his ethnic background. I later learned that because he had been adopted as a baby, his origins were also a mystery to him. He simply considered himself German.

I had never thought of myself as pretty. With a thick, athletic build, I wasn't fat but still never felt comfortable in my own skin. All my life, I wanted to be petite. My blue eyes, and long, sandy hair were generally features that men liked, but the skipper told me quickly that he was not usually attracted to blondes. He also told me I wore too much makeup, but he would soften the insult by saying, "I can't see your face with all that paint." He had a way of looking at me that made me feel beautiful even though he never said the words.

After aggressive pursuit on his part and without too much resistance on mine, we began a romantic but often tumultuous long-distance relationship.

I frequently traveled to Germany and other parts of Europe to spend time with him, and he traveled to the U.S. to steal time with me. Our extra efforts made the relationship feel like a fairy tale at times as we whisked away to enchanting lands for the occasional romantic rendezvous. It was difficult living 5,000 miles apart. The seven-hour time difference made it even more harsh. We also had the obvious language and cultural challenges. It was not easy, but we felt it was worthwhile as our connection deepened with time.

Through our many relationship obstacles, we always found peace at sea. I had developed my own passion and was determined to learn the art of sailing. At every opportunity, we sailed aboard *Toja* on the Baltic Sea.

A couple years later, I purchased a small 15-foot, open-hull, wooden day sailer, *Protagonist*, that I kept moored at my home on Plash Island in Gulf Shores. With the luxury of year-round tropical weather on Alabama's Gulf Coast, I wanted the opportunity to sail when I was home and not just when I traveled to Germany to visit the skipper.

There is a great quote from the movie, *Wind*, that became my mantra: "Big boats get the glory, but small boats make the sailor." *Protagonist* was the perfect boat for learning to sail, for building my confidence, and especially for fine-tuning my skills. With no instrumentation, no automation, and no autopilot, *Protagonist* forces the helmsman to hold the tiller and maneuver the boat manually.

Since I only sailed with the skipper about once every two months, mainly due to the distance between us, I enlisted the help of other sailors like Bob McDonald, one of my neighbors. Sailboat Bob, as he is affectionately called by all who know him, is an 80-something-year-old salty sailor who has sailed his entire life. We would take a day sail on *Protagonist* or on his 34-foot ketch,

Windy City, and we always took along my two beagles, Cap'n Jack and Scout.

I absorbed Sailboat Bob's sailing experience and knowledge like a sponge and loved hearing his stories. I watched him as he artistically handled the ship. He suffered from the early stages of Parkinson's, which caused his hands to tremble uncontrollably while trying to complete simple tasks like operating a smart phone or cooking. Even while walking, his body shook. His voice often trembled as he struggled to find the right words.

But when he was on a sailboat, the trembling stopped. Sailboat Bob could hoist the sails and tie the most intricate knots. He could repair mechanical systems, trim the sheets, manage the wheel, and tack with ease.

Sailing was, literally, more natural for him than walking, talking, or breathing.

For me, sailing seemed so mechanical and deliberate. I had to study and focus, and I worked hard to apply the lessons I was learning. Sailboat Bob was a much more patient teacher than the skipper, who became easily frustrated with my many questions and inability to pick up skills quickly. The language and cultural barriers didn't help. The skipper would scream at me in German and slowly strip me of my confidence with each insult. "Why can't you get this?" he would bark at me. "It's so easy."

But it was different with Sailboat Bob. It was okay with him if I failed or if he had to explain something a second or third time. He never yelled at me—not once—even though I made many mistakes along the way. He always encouraged me and made me believe I could become a true sailor.

As time went on, I began to get the *feel* for the sails, the wind, and the movement of the air and water, and I began to understand how they all are interconnected. The physics of sailing started to make sense, and I began to feel more comfortable with the wooden tiller in my hand.

I continued to be inspired by the possibility of having a grand adventure just as Sailboat Bob had dreamed of one day sailing out to sea and leaving land life behind.

During the months of our detailed planning, the skipper and I decided to bring Cap'n Jack and Scout along on the voyage. We couldn't bear the thought of leaving them at a boarding facility or even with family or friends for such a long time. But it wasn't easy to transport them to Germany.

Flying from Atlanta to Frankfurt, they had to travel in kennels in the cargo while I sat on pins and needles in my economy seat for the nine-hour trek. I realized it would be much less stress to take them across the Atlantic by sea rather than by air. They are true traveling dogs who now have experience traveling by trains, planes, boats, and automobiles.

The beagles, who were 18 months old at the time, had been sailing with me since the day I brought them home when they were only four months old. I'll never forget that day. Cap'n Jack jumped out of the car before I could get the leash around his neck. He sprinted straight to the marina and leaped onto *Protagonist* from the pier. Scout, his ever-faithful little sister and the runt of the litter, ran after him. But she was too small to make the jump into the boat. I helped her onboard, and we took a quick sail on Bon Secour Bay.

As the neighborhood dolphins approached our small wooden boat, the beagle puppies howled with glee, their tails wagging energetically and noses twitching in the air as they took in all the new smells. It was official. They were born to be sailing dogs. And while I will always take them sailing with me, I'll never again put them on an airplane.

Now that my dream was becoming a reality, the skipper and I checked off our final departure lists and frantically took care of the many details in Stralsund. Thilo, our superb electrician and mechanic, completed his final tasks and cleared the refurbished electrical systems as ready to set sail. We made one last provision run, and I did some chores. There were clothes that needed washing and two pups who were in need of a bath.

I secured all the items in the cabin that could be tossed and thrown during rough conditions. I had no experience on overnight passages and had never prepared a cabin for offshore sailing. But by necessity, I learned quickly.

We took one last opportunity to take a proper shower—*Seefalke* didn't have one. We had rigged a small 5-gallon solar water bag on the mast so that we could catch rainwater at sea and shower on deck. At the mooring in Stralsund, we needed to walk a mile to the marine machine shop to use the mechanics' shower. It was greasy and oily, but the water was hot.

I was already missing my children, Shelby and Bo. I FaceTimed with them and knew that the most difficult part of the journey would be the time spent away from them on an adventure that we assumed would take about eight months. After all, the original plan was to transport *Seefalke* from Stralsund to Gulf Shores, where we would live together permanently instead of continuing the challenge of living 5,000 miles apart.

Since my children were young adults (both in their early 20s) with their own lives and independence, I could justify that they didn't need me every day. I always wondered how the skipper could leave his younger children (ages 15 and 9 at that time) for such a long voyage.

Departure from Stralsund

SUNDAY, 19 AUGUST 2018
  Departure 09:00
  The skipper bounced out of bed at 05:30, long before any alarm. I tried to squeeze in the last 30 minutes of sleep, but it was useless. I fed and walked the dogs, and we prepared the boat for departure. It

was just minutes before 09:00 and our celebration flags were flying high. The seadogs were secured in their life vests and tethered safely in the sunken, 4-foot-deep center cockpit. The weather was clear and sunny without a single cloud in the cornflower sky. We toasted the journey and gave Neptune a shot of whiskey to ensure a safe voyage—an old sailor's superstition.

The bridge began to rise, and we coasted through the narrow opening into the Baltic Sea—waters we know very well. We hoisted the main sail, then the genoa, and were cruising along nicely for about four hours.

I can't effectively describe what it feels like to experience the beginning of a dream that has been on the bucket list for so many years. I looked at the skipper. He held the wheel and stared hypnotically at the open sea. I knew this was his destiny.

It was his lifelong dream to live aboard a boat and sail the world. It had only been my dream for about five years, and sometimes I wondered if my dream was less about the sailing adventure and more about wanting to be loved by this man and to be with him every day. Maybe giving him his dream would, by default, make my dream come true, too.

After six years of a relationship that was separated by brutal distance and time, I thought about all the challenges and what it had taken to get to that point. I thought about his multiple infidelities that broke my heart over and over again. I thought about how the affairs had shattered my confidence and how my low self-esteem was probably the reason I continued to forgive his indiscretions. I remembered the loneliness of being apart, the torture of the unknown, the neglect, and the secrets he kept hidden on his phone.

There were unanswered questions that still haunted me. But I convinced myself that if he was willing to bring his precious sailboat to Alabama, then he must finally be serious about starting a faithful and honorable life with me.

There was no doubt that living together every day on a small boat would be the ultimate test for our relationship. Would it be a blessing or a curse, I wondered.

Lost in my thoughts and without warning, the waves began to roll and swell to about 2 m high. We began to fight against the current and the wind. I safely secured Cap'n Jack and Scout in the cabin below. As *Seefalke* began to rock and roll, the skipper and I both took seasickness medicine.

We pushed heavily against the wind, and the current was attacking us—pushing us back farther and faster than we could move forward. It was a battle of nature against man and ship. And while *Seefalke* was holding her own, nature seemed to be beating the humans by a landslide.

It's in moments like these that you forget how soothing the sea can be, and you remember its power and force.

We continuously adjusted the sails—switching back and forth between the genoa and a smaller jib—as the swirling wind and cold rain pounded us. We reefed the main sail and continued to battle the Baltic, which clearly did not want us invading her waters on this day.

I felt queasy but told myself to fight it.

Look at the horizon. Ignore the motion that is slamming us. Stay busy. Think of something else.

I worked hard to convince my brain that I didn't feel the harsh effects of the roller coaster that was once the Baltic. The harder I tried to convince myself I wasn't getting seasick, the more the uneasiness took over.

I felt the color drain from my skin. I told the skipper that I was about to lose it. Within 15 seconds of making that statement, I leaned over the port side deck outside the cockpit and spewed the foul-tasting cereal and yogurt from the morning's breakfast onto the stern.

At first, I felt okay after emptying my belly. *I've been seasick before and this was not as bad as that last time. I just fed a few fish. I'm really okay.*

But as the ship continued to sway back and forth, and up and down, my body finally gave in and let the Baltic win. I got comfortable in my position over the side of the boat, strapped myself in, and hurled for a couple of hours.

It didn't take long for my belly to empty completely, but the contractions and heaving continued until I was throwing up only stomach acid and possibly pieces of my stomach lining. It was so forceful that I lost control of my bladder. I was embarrassed, but the skipper gave me a reassuring grin and told me it was going to be okay. He was also feeling the harsh effects of *mal de mer*.

I worked my way into the cabin below to find some clean panties and discovered that I had done a terrible job securing the cabin items. Almost all of the cabin's contents were in piles of disorganized rubble.

It looked like someone had shaken *Seefalke* like a cup of dice and thrown its contents into the belly of the boat. I somehow made it through the messy maze to the head, cleaned myself, and changed my clothes. But I couldn't make it back to the cockpit. I dropped to my knees, wrapped my arms around the toilet, and didn't move a muscle.

I finally felt well enough to lie on the hard wooden floor, lifeless, for about another hour, completely paralyzed and unable to get up from that spot. Seriously, if someone held a gun to my head and told me to move one inch, I would have just had to let them pull the trigger. I was helpless.

At one point, I looked at the puppies sitting so sweetly in their little bed in the cabin saloon, all cuddled up with each other, safely secured and behaving so well. I could tell they were worried about me, and perhaps a bit afraid themselves, but fortunately, they seemed fine.

I managed to rise to my shaky feet, grabbed a trash bag to hopefully catch anything else that might want to exit my body and worked my way a few steps toward the cockpit. But I could only make it about three feet to the table bench in the saloon before I collapsed.

I apologized to the skipper, and he reassured me that it was okay. The pressure of not pulling my own weight was making it worse for me. I wanted to help him sail the ship. But I couldn't.

After 12 hours, the waters began to calm, and we decided to anchor for the night. As soon as the motion stopped, so did my misery. That is the amazing thing about seasickness. When the motion ends, the sickness ends. I felt just fine cruising along on the calm waters.

I helped the skipper drop and secure the anchor and then walked the pups on the deck—back and forth from bow to stern, stern to bow. I knew they probably needed some exercise. We were still in the progress of potty training them onboard. Since the dogs generally searched for grass when it was time to potty, the skipper had built a small wooden 1m x 1m box from a few pieces of lumber. We added soil and seedlings and were trying to grow a natural grass patch for them. It was positioned on the bow with a fake grass mat underneath.

We had sailed for 12 hours in brutal conditions. By the time we got the ship secure, it was around 23:00 and we all crashed immediately and fell into a deep sleep.

Trouble at Anchor

MONDAY, 20 AUGUST 2018

At 03:30, the skipper bolted out of bed. "The anchor is dragging," he said. He is an experienced sailor and can *feel* things that others can only see or hear. I sprang to my feet, too, and we both leaped onto the deck in our skivvies.

The water was no longer calm—2 m waves rolled us and provided a cold saltwater shower as they crashed onto the bow. The heavy wind chapped our faces and pushed all of *Seefalke's* 11 tons. We turned on the engine and tried to retrieve the anchor, but the chain got jumbled inside the windlass and completely jammed it. It wouldn't drop down, and it couldn't be retrieved. The anchor was dangling from the bowsprit, and we feared it would strike *Seefalke* and rip into her hull. We tried to retrieve the anchor manually, but it wouldn't budge.

We fought and tugged with all our might. Finally, we were able to attach a line and leverage our weight to pull up the anchor and secure it. By that time, it was 03:45 and we had no choice but to move forward. We didn't even try to put up a sail. Instead, we cranked the motor and forged ahead. We both took more seasickness medicine and prayed it would help.

It was pitch black dark.

Seasickness is an interesting phenomenon. For some reason, when you can't see the motion, your body tells you it's not there, even though you can feel it. I've studied seasickness extensively. It involves the balance of the inner ear, the sinuses, blood flow, heart rhythm, hydration, and many psychological factors including nerves, excitement, and fear. Different parts of your body send different signals to your brain. The wires get tangled and the confusion of all those crossed signals to the brain can cause uneasiness.

As the sun began to rise, so did the empty insides of my belly. The skipper recommended that I go down below and sleep for two hours. I did. The boat rocked the entire time I was below deck, but I felt okay lying flat on the bunk in the middle of the boat.

I returned to relieve the skipper, and he said he would try to sleep for two hours. I took my shift, but honestly, I basically just strapped myself in the cockpit and held on for dear life for 120 straight minutes.

The skipper returned as promised, and I went below to rest another two hours. That was when I made a crucial mistake. I should have stayed in the fresh air where I felt steady. I sat down on the bunk and felt it all set in again. I could feel something rising in my throat and ran to the head as fast as I could...just in time.

Then I hugged the toilet for the next couple hours. There was zero food in my belly, so it was unclear to me what was coming back up. But something was. At one point, the skipper checked on me because he saw my lifeless body sprawled out on the floor and thought I was passed out. Or dead.

If you've never been seasick, let me try to describe it for you. Imagine the worst hangover you've ever had, combined with the worst possible food poisoning. Then throw in a nasty case of Type A flu complete with vomiting, chills, cold sweats, and a pounding, throbbing headache. Then, feeling all of that simultaneously, put yourself inside a washing machine and turn on the spin cycle.

Next, hop onto the fastest, most topsy-turvy roller coaster you can find. It is complete disorientation. Bile boils in your stomach and throat, ripping through your innards. You experience gut-wrenching heaving that can be felt in every part of your body. It jerks your body from your waist as if it were attached to a hook on a crane.

Then imagine all your muscles starting to cramp as the dehydration paralyzes you. Some people see visions, and others completely black out. I can remember sailing from Rönne, Denmark to Karliskrona, Sweden a few years before this trip. The captain had to D-ring strap me to the boat to keep me from falling out...or from throwing myself out, because that is what I wanted to do.

The misery doesn't stop until the motion stops.

We cruised into Rostock around 16:00, and just as soon as we were on calm waters, I felt fine. I was able to jump up on the deck, secure the mooring lines, secure the fenders, and help moor *Seefalke*. I took the dogs on a long walk and cooked dinner. I felt well enough to clean the entire boat and re-organized all the items that had scattered all over the cabins. We went to bed early and got some much-needed sleep.

Assessing the Damage

TUESDAY, 21 AUGUST 2018
  Hohe-Düne Marina
  We awoke to assess the damage. It was severe.

We knew the anchor windlass was broken, but we didn't know that all the bolted down wooden boards of the bowsprit had been blown away. There was nothing there—not even a splinter of wood or a stray bolt. The Baltic apparently ate them for dinner—a nice entrée after the appetizer of my belly's contents.

We also realized that one of the sheets of the genoa had gotten tangled underneath *Seefalke* and chewed up inside the motor of the bow thruster. It reminded me of when you roll your vacuum cleaner over a cord and the cord gets sucked up into the mechanism and cannot be retrieved.

The skipper, a pump engineer by trade, tore apart the cabins that I had so carefully organized and worked on the repairs. He discovered that the anchor windlass needed a new fuse, but he had to completely empty the bow cabin to find his fuse supply, discovering he didn't have a spare in the correct size.

I set out on a hunt for supplies. Hohe-Düne is a gorgeous marina. However, it's a bit fancy and "high society" for my taste. It seemed like the kind of place where huge yacht owners moor their vessels and leave them for someone else to repair while they go stay in a five-star hotel.

There were no marine shops to be found. I took a 15-minute ferry ride into Warnemünde and searched for supplies there. After about four hours of searching, I returned to *Seefalke* empty handed. A failed mission. Again, I felt the disappointment of not being at all helpful for my captain.

The skipper dove underneath the boat and disengaged the mangled line from the bow thruster. He had to cut the line to get it out, so that added another sheet to the list of supplies that I had already failed to find. The good news was that we only had to replace the line and not the bow thruster. It now worked just fine.

We decided to go into Rostock to continue the search for the fuse and boards. We took the ferry back into Warnemünde, then took a train into downtown Rostock. The pups loved all the new smells as they always do when we stop at different ports.

We walked 2 km to the marine shop. They didn't have the boards we needed or the correct fuse voltage, but we found a fuse that would work. When we returned to *Seefalke*, the skipper quickly fixed the anchor windlass, and then I spent the next two hours putting everything back into its proper compartments and securing all our belongings...again.

We showered in the marina facilities and went to bed early, looking forward to another day of rest. I planned to do laundry the next day and catch up on some work for my clients. But the Baltic had something different in mind.

CHAPTER 2

MEAN GIRL

BALTIC SEA PASSAGE (PART TWO)

WEDNESDAY, 22 AUGUST 2018

There is a popular saying for those who sail the Baltic Sea: "If you don't like the weather, wait an hour."

The Baltic is the largest body of brackish water in the world. It is about 1,600 km long with a maximum depth of about 1,500 ft. Its salinity is much lower than ocean water, which results from an abundant freshwater runoff from the surrounding land. In winter, the Baltic Sea becomes a block of ice over roughly half its surface area. In late spring and summer, the ice melts and sea temperatures rise rapidly.

The weather changes on a dime.

I can remember sailing on the Baltic one spring afternoon in 2016 when our port side was sunny and calm with blue skies that reminded me of a warm sunny day in Alabama. To the starboard side, the skies were black, and high waves swelled and charged toward us—complete with thunder and heavy rain. It was that different to the right and to the left of us.

We awoke in Hohe Düne to a gorgeous sunrise, calm waters, and favorable winds. The skipper went to the washroom to shave his bald head and decided we needed to take advantage of the conditions, prepare the boat, and set sail around 10:00. I adjusted my mindset quickly. That wasn't the first time our sailing plans changed. And I knew it wouldn't be the last.

I unleashed the dogs to play on the beach for about half an hour so they would be well exercised and a bit worn out for whatever the Baltic had in mind for us that day.

The skipper meticulously finalized the passage plan. The detail and specificity of his preparation had always impressed me. I knew he would never take unnecessary chances.

I purposefully collected seasickness medicine, crackers, water, bananas, and ginger tea and organized them in a handy place in the cockpit—a seasickness station, just in case. This time, I would be prepared.

We left the marina and remembered why we love sailing on these spectacular waters so much. As bitter as the Baltic had been on our first two days at sea, on that day she was as sweet as pumpkin pie!

Under a perfectly sunny, royal blue sky, we sailed at about 3.5 knots along the sea that was now welcoming us into her nurturing arms. It was so calm we were able to do a little work. I am a journalist, and the skipper has an industrial consulting business, so we were both able to work remotely—an advantage that made the voyage possible financially.

I took the first shift at the helm, and we hoisted four sails and with calm seas. We sailed 43.4 nautical miles in 14 hours into Großenbrode, and the four of us enjoyed a glorious sunset from *Seefalke's* bow. As the sun began to kiss the water and melt away, filling the sky with color, I found comfort in the skipper's arms. It had been weeks since we had taken the time to relax together. Cap'n Jack and Scout joined us and cuddled close. We talked about the freedom and serenity that comes from sailing. I missed my children and my family, but the homesickness was quelled by the gratitude I felt for the opportunity to have this grand adventure.

It was midnight when we approached the Heiligenhafen Marina. We had never been in that marina and it was pitch black with no lighted buoys, so we decided to anchor for the night right outside the entryway.

Oh, how we needed that day to enjoy the sailing and *not* be seasick! It reminded me why we do this.

A Day of Rest and Preparation

THURSDAY, 23 AUGUST 2018
*Heiligenhafen (*Großenbrode*, Germany)*
A day of rest, recovery and real work was needed. Boat repair and boat maintenance are simply a part of the reality of the sailing lifestyle. It's not all bikinis and martinis as you might imagine if you watch a lot of YouTube videos. We were both productive, and as a bonus, I got to connect with my friend, Yvi, who drove to the marina to visit us for the day.

Having been on a journey like this a few times herself, Yvi gave me great advice and confidence that I could do it, too. We talked about seasickness and how to fight it. She recommended either standing up or lying flat when the sickness sets in. She also said one of the best things to do is stay busy and perhaps even stand up and take the wheel. It helps to focus on the horizon, and it also gives you a sense of control of the motion, she said. I was grateful for her wisdom.

She confirmed the notion that seasickness can be psychological. Back when she had been a sailing instructor, she told students that if they held a potato in their left hand, then they wouldn't get seasick. The mind-over-matter trick worked for most of them. I had some potatoes on board and was willing to try anything. I added one to my seasickness station.

We prepared to make the final move toward Kiel the next morning. We estimated it was about 30 nm away, but we could face heavy currents the second half of the day and would most likely deal with cold and rain—perhaps even thunderstorms. I had a celebratory bottle of champagne chilling in our very small cooler and was ready to toast the first milestone of our trip.

But I could never have anticipated what the Baltic had in mind for us the next day and what I would have to do to earn it.

The Baltic Sea—She's a Mean Girl

The Baltic Sea is a bitch.

She's like the queen of the mean girls in high school. You know the one ... beautiful, talented, engaging, and alluring. She's the girl who every boy wants to date and every girl wants to be. Everyone loves her, and everyone hates her.

When she's nice, she can make you feel like the most important human on the planet. But rub her the wrong way or catch her in a bad mood and she will make you pay! You won't see it coming. It will blindside you and leave you wondering what you did to get on her bad side.

I am in love with the Baltic. I learned to sail on the Baltic and have been sailing her beautiful waters since 2013. She is alluring and engaging, and I thought I was her friend. I'm not sure why she decided to turn on me.

Let me make one thing clear. I am the girl who doesn't care if the mean girl likes me or not. I generally just admire her from afar and find other friends in other circles. I'm not interested in the drama. But I'm also the girl who will not get beaten up or beaten down without a fight. At least that's been my heartfelt belief for the past five decades.

The last few days sailing the Baltic forced me to question that belief. The mean girl had gotten the best of me. I spent two days of utter misery over the side of *Seefalke* fighting a mean girl who did not want me on her turf. She had mercy on me for one day, reminding me why I love her so much. But was that just her way of manipulating me to come back for more abuse?

We had only one more day on the Baltic. I was determined to face her and defeat the mean girl who was torturing me. It was a rainy and windy morning when we left the marina in Heiligen-hafen. The weather report called for heavy winds and currents against us. It was cold. But we forged ahead anyway.

I was nervous and afraid. I wasn't afraid of the weather, conditions, or the sailing. My fear was fighting the seasickness that had crippled me so many times on the Baltic. I gave myself a pep talk and tried to stay busy with preparations. I told myself that I wouldn't let the Baltic Sea beat me down again.

After feeding and walking Cap'n Jack and Scout, I bundled into my cold-weather gear and helped prepare *Seefalke* for the voyage. Staying busy quelled my fear. We departed with the rain and wind, but it was not bad at all—at first. We got the four-legged crew settled down below and hoisted the smaller jib and main sail. We double-reefed the main sail ahead of time in preparation for the inevitable heavy wind.

I was fighting to keep my eyes open, so I decided to take a short nap. That would also help me to relax, I hoped. The puppies hopped onto the bunk next to me for some extra cuddles.

Probably an hour or so later I awoke to a rocking boat. I could hear the skipper rushing around on the deck above and caught glimpses through the upper hatch windows of him adjusting the sails. The boat began to tilt and a few of my well-secured items went flying across the cabin.

Then the pups and I began to slide off the bunk as if we were on a slippery block of ice. I didn't know it at the time, but we were in the middle of a heavy gale with winds whipping us at 38 knots! We were on a 36-degree tilt … and the skipper was having the time of his life!

I lay flat on my back on the bunk. My right leg was stretched out straight and propped against the board that generally kept the pups secure in their bed. My left leg was bent and upright, blocking the pups from flying across the cabin with the various items that were still not secured. I couldn't move to secure the pups in their bunk. I could only hold on to keep them safe as we were practically vertical at that point. They were barely fazed at all, but I was using every muscle in my body to stabilize myself, and them, in that awkward position.

I think it was what yoga is supposed to feel like—holding one unusual, uncomfortable position as long as possible while your muscles flex and spasm.

I called up to the cockpit to be sure I wasn't needed on deck. The skipper looked down at me and had the biggest, silliest grin on his face. I thought to myself, sarcastically and with a bit of agitation, *What are you smiling about?* A seasoned sailor, he was loving the challenge of fighting the storm. "Just keep holding on," he said.

Then an alarm sounded.

It was coming from the bilge. That meant water had gotten in and risen to a level that would trip the alarm. The skipper told me to check it out. *What? Are you kidding me? How will I get out of this position without slamming into the other side of the cabin?*

First, I had to secure the pups. I somehow got them settled and surrounded them with three sleeping bags to give them extra padding. They were now in their usual barricaded bed, which stabilizes them in a confined space and keeps them from moving around in the boat. They curled up and went right back to sleep. *Why can't I be that relaxed?*

Then I needed to get to the bilge, which meant pulling up the floor covering and opening the two hatches that led down below to *Seefalke's* stomach. I was doing all of that on a 36-degree tilt during gale-force winds. I felt like I was in one of those old black-and-white movies where the room spins and the actors dance around on the walls and the ceiling.

There was a little water in *Seefalke's* belly but not enough for concern. I closed the hatches and plopped back down on the bed, this time with both legs giving me leverage.

It was a forceful squall, but a short one. Soon, we were back on some sort of evenness, and I could see through the upper hatch window that the skipper had pulled in the jib. It was flapping just a little on the edge. I asked if everything was okay, and he again looked down with a ridiculously happy grin, so I knew I was okay to just stay put. He was fine.

I wanted to go back to the cockpit. But I was afraid.

In fact, I was paralyzed. Paralyzed with fear.

I didn't feel queasy at all, but the fear of getting sick again was keeping me from returning to the cockpit.

I lay there for what seemed like hours, just staring blankly through the hatch window at the flapping jib. I was hypnotized. I don't know why. I learned to sail on the Baltic. I had spent the past five years sailing on the Baltic. I love the Baltic Sea! She's my friend. *Why was she kicking my ass this time?*

I knew it was the last time we would be sailing on her during this trip. Once we made it to Kiel, we would sail through the Kiel Canal and then meet the challenging North Sea on the other side. *I'm wasting my time down here when I should be up there sailing the Baltic!*

I remembered a wise old saying: "The brave one is not the one who has no fear. The brave one is the one who has fear, but does it anyway."

Then I snapped out of it. I got up and said to myself, *If I get sick, I get sick. I need to be out there.*

The boat was still rocking, but it was manageable. I could see the high waves through the portholes. I put on my life vest and walked up the four wooden plank stairs to the cockpit. The skipper was standing on the cockpit bench, wind in his face, wearing the biggest smile I've ever seen. *How could I possibly be afraid? I have a captain who lives for this shit!*

He was not going to let anything happen to us. He was happy in his element—facing the sea and the storm with absolute joy! I stood up on the bench, too, and let the cold wind chill my face and blow my hair. It was exhilarating. I had wasted seven hours in the cabin below fearing something that usually makes me so happy. And in that moment, I remembered why.

We can battle the sea or we can embrace it. Sometimes she will be sweet and sometimes mean as a snake. But either way, this is her turf. We must embrace the experience and trust that we will get through it. *If I get sick, I get sick.* But I'm out here, and I have this opportunity to challenge myself. I may not beat the Baltic, and I can't expect to, but I will NOT beat myself!

We still had four hours to Kiel, and I knew that the dreaded North Sea was waiting for us on the other side. But in that moment, I just enjoyed the Baltic. She was breathtaking. *Seefalke* surfed on the 2 m waves like she was performing a choreographed dance for a mesmerized and appreciative audience. We were all flying.

Yes, the Baltic Sea is a bitch. But I love her.

Our next mission was to venture through the locks of the Kiel Canal—the Panama Canal of Europe. It's a 98 km freshwater canal that is considered to be the most heavily-used seaway in the world with 90 to 130 ships transiting through it each day.

Then we would meet the North Sea for the first time.

If the Baltic is the mean girl you love to hate but can't help but love, then the North Sea is the schoolyard bully.

I had heard tales about the monster that lives beneath the North Sea. I had read about the water's powerful and unforgiving tides that have challenged sailors for centuries.

What I didn't know yet but was about to discover was that facing the North Sea monster would require facing the monster that lies within us all.

CHAPTER 3

A SAILOR'S WORK IS NEVER DONE

After a grueling Baltic Sea passage, I realized that this voyage didn't resemble anything I had seen on the YouTube sailing channels. As I bundled in my heavy winter coat, scarf, ski pants, and snow boots, I wondered where were all the crystal blue waters, playful dolphins, and endless cocktails with tropical views? Where were all the bikinis and martinis?

We only had a couple of days to recoup from our battle wounds before forging ahead through the Kiel Canal on our way to the North Sea. I had expected that we would have opportunities to explore new ports, immerse ourselves into new cultures, and eat exotic food. I wondered why we couldn't just take a beat and enjoy the journey and the exciting destinations along the way.

Generally, a schedule is a sailor's enemy. Staying on a schedule can force you to take unnecessary risks. As a result, dire and sometimes fatal mistakes can be made. However, it was essential for us to at least keep one eye on the calendar.

We needed to outrun winter.

It was cold in northern Europe and getting more frigid by the day. The last place we wanted to be in winter was the North Sea, the English Channel, or the dreadful Bay of Biscay.

A break for rest and repairs was needed, but it had to be a short one. There was no ignoring that the ship and crew were in need of attention, and I learned the hard way that a day of rest requires a lot of work.

A Balancing Act

SATURDAY, 25 AUGUST 2018
Laboe Hafen, Kiel
There is never nothing to do when you live on a boat.

Boat maintenance was a priority, but so was our day jobs. It was tough trying to work while sailing. Many people who take a voyage like ours either have taken a sabbatical from work, or they quit their jobs and sell everything they own to finance the long-term holiday. Some folks have the means to quit. For us, it was a financial necessity that we both continue working.

Even with remote jobs, it's not as easy as it sounds. We didn't have to report to an office or have regular office hours, but the work had to get done. While at sea, we were generally unable to work at all except for maybe handling a few emails and the occasional phone call. The weak internet and cell service at most marinas was an obstacle. It was a challenge, but we were lucky and grateful, even though when other sailors were going to the beach, seeing the sights, or eating at local restaurants, it was difficult for us to stay focused. That was the trade-off, and for us, it was worth it.

After such an eventful voyage through the Baltic Sea, it was important to get *Seefalke* ready for our next passage—a motor sail through the Kiel Canal. I swabbed the deck, re-organized, and secured all that was mangled and shifted from the storms the day before. The wooden dog yard the skipper had built for potty training Cap'n Jack and Scout had received an unfortunate burial at sea during the 38-knot winds that flanked us. Only two crushed boards and some black soil remained on the deck as a reminder of the failed potty experiment. It was a dramatic indication of the need to better secure all the gear on deck so it wouldn't be so vulnerable to heavy winds in the future.

Meanwhile, I removed the water from *Seefalke's* stomach that had crept in during the storm. It was only about two inches deep, but it was enough to require removal to prevent mold and other problems. Upon investigation, I realized it was coming in from the anchor chain box in the bow.

I crawled inside the bilge. When standing on the bottom of the bilge, the saloon floor was about thigh-high to my 5-foot-7-inch body. The opening was about 18 inches wide and perhaps 4 ft long, but there were metal support beams that created a row of "boxes" just to add an extra element of difficulty for completing the task.

The water was not deep enough to bail with a bucket or a manual pump. Instead, I used three large sponges to slowly soak up the water and then wring it into a bucket. It was a simple, but tedious project—made difficult only by the awkward positions required of my body to get down in there. When you work on a boat, you must learn to make repairs in a twisted pretzel position.

I filled and emptied four and a half buckets, sponge by sponge.

We completed the projects and then took a break to take Cap'n Jack and Scout into the small village for a long walk and some exploring. They enjoyed the fresh air and exercise, and so did we. There was an outdoor market in the village, so we bought some fresh fruit and vegetables and enjoyed the atmosphere, even though there was a slight misty drizzle.

Adjusting to Living on a Sailboat

When you live on a sailboat, you begin to appreciate the little things that are often taken for granted in normal, everyday life—like a shower, for example. Whenever we were in a marina with proper shower facilities, we would take full advantage. It generally cost 2 Euros for four minutes of water flow at most European marinas.

We didn't have a regular shower on board (just a solar shower bag that we could use on the deck). We never really knew when our next shower opportunity would come, so when we were moored at a marina with facilities, we always took advantage—whether we needed it, or not. Of course, we usually needed it.

While shaving my legs I noticed all the many bruises, cuts and scrapes that seemed to have tattooed my limbs—battle scars of a true sailor that were telling the story of my journey. At times, my body looked like Rocky Balboa's face after his first fight with Apollo Creed.

I remembered how just a few weeks before, when the pups and I first arrived in Stralsund and began living on *Seefalke*, I was constantly banging myself against everything as I tried to maneuver my way around the tight quarters. That was another casualty of living on a boat that you just have to get accustomed to with time.

In the beginning, I felt like *Seefalke* was beating me up all the time. I noticed new bruises and scrapes every day. One day I sat on the head and when I stood up, there was blood all over the seat. I realized I had several cuts on the backs of my thighs and later identified that they were from climbing over the sea rail and scraping my flesh against the trimmed zip ties that we used to attach the dogs' safety sea fence.

After our first passage, I realized that *Seefalke* wasn't beating me up. She was making me tough. It became obvious to me that when a forceful wave slams you at sea and you get thrown to the other side of the cockpit, you really don't have time to worry about the mark it left or the pain it caused. I learned quickly that if you nurse every wound you get on a sailboat, you will spend all your time nursing wounds. It's best to just blurt a four-letter word and keep going.

As the bruises began to heal and fade away, so did the memories of how they got there.

As I continued my chores, I realized I was also sore from using muscles I was not accustomed to using every day. It was a good sore—the kind you feel after a good workout. I was learning that my body must adjust to boat living as much as my mind.

My body was slowly learning all the small nooks and crannies of the boat and eventually, I quit hitting my head on that low ceiling or banging my knee against the last step into the cockpit.

I had recently written an article for a client about drones being used in manufacturing. They fly through facilities and learn where to duck and swerve to avoid slamming into all the heavy machinery. I could relate. I felt like my body was learning its way around *Seefalke* just like the industrial drone learns and then remembers the map of the facility. And I didn't really mind all the cuts and bruises—I was proud of my battle scars.

First Leg of the Kiel Canal Sailing Passage

SUNDAY, 26 AUGUST 2018

We awoke with plans to cross the Kiel Canal, but it was still unclear whether we would cross all the way in one day into the fierce Elbe River at Brunsbüttel or find a safe mooring within the canal that connects the Baltic to the North Sea.

While I tended to Cap'n Jack and Scout's morning routine, the skipper studied the weather reports and built our strategy. The wind howled in Laboe Hafen, and nasty weather was forecasted for the next few days.

I often accused the skipper of over-planning. He is the "planner" and I'm the "doer." I am the definition of impatience and don't generally take the time to plan. I don't preheat the oven before cooking—I turn it on and throw in the food. I don't create an outline before writing an article—I start writing. I don't warm up for a tennis match—I just start swinging.

On days like this, it was nice to know that our crew had balance. If it wasn't safe to go to sea, we would not take the chance. Period. It was important to take all the time necessary to plan and prepare. But when it's time to go, you must be ready.

Sailors Beware of the North Sea Tides

When considering a passage through the Kiel Canal, you must consider the ever-changing tides on the other side that make the North Sea unique ... and dangerous. Considering the tides of the North Sea is as important as deciphering the wind and weather.

The Elbe River dumps into the North Sea, but experienced sailors say you will feel like you are offshore before you ever make the transition into the North Sea.

There is a legend among North Sea sailors about the power of its tides. It goes something like this....

There is a monster living beneath the North Sea, and it is forcefully breathing in and out. Each inhale and exhale lasts six hours. The six-hour breath in is a low tide. When the monster releases the breath out for six hours, high tide is created. Sometimes the monster has a hiccup, and that is called a spring tide.

There was a harbor city in medieval times called Rungholt that in 1634 became the Atlantis of the North Sea. It was totally sucked away and now sits at the sea's bottom thanks to these powerful and unforgiving tides.

The legend says that because the people of the city were too sinful and arrogant, the monster decided to suck the city right off the face of the earth. One myth says you can still hear the church bells ringing below the waters while sailing over the lost city on a calm night.

We had a plan of attack, but I was infatuated with the legend and dreamed about the monster every night.

The ideal situation for us was to enter the Elbe River with southeasterly winds and leaving tides (in between high water and low water). For perfect conditions, we needed to get to the other side of the Kiel Canal within the following three days.

Because there was then a low tide and an incoming storm front, we decided that we would go about a third of the way through the canal to Rendsburg and find a spot in safe harbor to moor *Seefalke* and wait out the storms.

Often called "The Panama Canal of Europe," the Kiel Canal is an architectural marvel. It took 9,000 workers eight years to dig, and after its opening in 1895 it had to be widened again to accommodate Germany's new generation of battleships. The 98 km waterway slices the head of Denmark from the body of Europe and, as a result, saves Baltic shipping a 460 km detour.

Crossing the Kiel Canal would save us that same detour.

The locking-in procedure at the canal's entrance is more complicated than I had imagined. We approached the entrance of the canal along with about 10 other sailboats and huge ships. There are two entrances—one for large ships and one for small leisure craft—but the smaller one was closed so we needed to enter with the big ships.

The canal has lighted signals. One red flashing light means the lock is closed and no ships can enter. A white blinking light means smaller boats can enter. There are other signals, but these were the two that were important for us to know. Verbal approval is required from the lock master by radio on Channel 12.

Even though we were motoring toward the entrance at a slow, relaxed pace on a bright, beautiful morning, I was stressed. The unknown can often cause anxiety.

I readied the mooring lines on the bow and the stern, then positioned the fenders very low and on both sides. But because of the floating piers, I was forced to adjust them several times to be sure they were floating on the water's surface. We received radio confirmation that we would moor *Seefalke* at the lock on the port side.

It was my job to jump off the bow onto the pier and secure the bow line first. It was a normal mooring procedure for us. The skipper would toss me the stern line, and I would secure it before adjusting the spring lines. I wasn't prepared for just how low the pier was positioned. I had the port bow line in one hand and held onto the sea fence with the other. *Seefalke* already sits high on the water—about 3 m above the surface. The low pier made it feel even higher.

I am not a petite woman, but I have tiny baby hands. Sometimes I had trouble handling a long, thick line with one hand. I anticipated the possibility of getting completely tangled in the line and crashing hard into the pier ... or worse, falling between the ship and the pier. As I was trying not to tangle the line, pieces of it slipped from my hands, and it was getting completely twisted and unorganized—just as I had feared.

When we got close enough, I jumped. I landed on the wooden pier with a loud BOOM and almost lost my footing. I struggled to get the tangled, knotted line through the mooring ring while the captain yelled forcefully in German for me to get it secured quickly so we wouldn't crash into the boat in front of us. It's a simple procedure, but my nervous energy combined with the fear of angering the skipper made it all extremely chaotic.

It was messy, but we were safely locked in. I waited on the pier for the signal, and despite the scolding from the captain, I felt like a badass sailor.

We waited about 15 minutes, got the signal, and then untied the lines. I climbed back onboard, and we went through the lock passing the smiling crews of the gigantic container ships who were waving to us. I like to think they were impressed with us and not at all laughing at my clumsiness.

Then we had to moor again at a pier on the other side of the canal so we could pay our 18 Euro passage fee. Wouldn't it seem more efficient to have a guy on the floating pier at the lock to collect our money? At that second mooring, *Seefalke* suffered a minor injury when her hull scraped against a metal cleat on the pier. It was fortunately just a deep scratch on her steel surface that chipped her bright orange paint. We added it to our list of repairs.

Once we were safely inside the canal, we could relax and motor through. Raising sails inside the canal is not allowed unless you also have the motor running. We were against the wind, so it didn't make sense for us to use the sails. Another rule is that you can go no faster than 15 km per hour through the canal. We cruised along and were amazed at all the huge ships that passed.

The canal is 98 km long, but only about 100 meters wide—basically the length of an American football field. That may seem like plenty of room, but it seemed especially tight when sharing that space with massive ships that have dinghies that are larger than the 43-foot *Seefalke*. These were only the feeder ships and not the huge container ships that are sometimes a half mile long.

I took the helm. I was still getting accustomed to steering with a wheel after mostly using a tiller for the past five years. It was more comfortable now. I needed to be aware of the wash and wake that were created when the larger ships would pass us. We also needed to watch the depth when we got close to the shore to let a big ship pass, but we remained at a very safe 11 m. There are a few spots where ferries usually crossed, so it was important to pay attention to the timing at those intersections.

We moored in Rendsburg and settled into our safe harbor.

Struggling to Find Balance

MONDAY, 27 AUGUST 2018
Rendsburg Marina (Inside the Kiel Canal)
It was raining the next morning, so we opted for another day of work and rest. As always, we performed some boat maintenance. We worked on *Seefalke* every day, but that day we did less work on our sailboat and focused more on our paying jobs.

I completed an article for a client, but continued to struggle with the routine of working while sailing. It was difficult to find a good rhythm that balanced work with daily life at sea.

The skipper also struggled to find balance. He would never admit it, but I could see how the pressure was wearing on him. He slowly released some of the responsibilities to me, but I could tell he was not truly comfortable trusting me with important tasks—especially when we were at sea. It was important to build my own confidence so that he would have confidence in me.

When it comes to sailing experience, there is a big difference in a few years and half a lifetime. In fact, five years is minimal when sailing heavy offshore voyages. I wanted the skipper to teach me more, but he struggled to find a way to transfer all that tribal knowledge. He could feel things and sense things that my system didn't respond to innately yet.

He reinforced my theory that one can be a great sailor, but not a great teacher. That made me think of Sailboat Bob, and I wished I could call him. He always gave me so much confidence and encouragement. I needed it badly. As I continued to feel the skipper's pressure, I placed more pressure on myself. It was essential for me to find ways to do more so he could do less.

I worried about the heavy traffic we would face sailing through the North Sea and inside the English Channel. Not only would we have tides, winds, weather, and waves to consider, but there were traffic separation schemes, huge cargo ships, other leisure craft, and offshore oil platforms to maneuver around.

The open sea is one thing—there is room to make a small mistake and recover. When other obstacles are in the way, you must be more aware and more armed with knowledge and skill—and experience.

While I continued to get that experience, I focused on the things that I could do well. I could organize the lockers and the cabins. I could take care of the dogs. I could manage all of the cooking, cleaning, laundry, and of course, upgrade my boat maintenance skills.

I was grateful that my stepdad, Doug Lambert (we call him Pops), taught me how to handle tools and fix things when I was younger. That was long before HGTV and DIY videos. I've valued those skills all my adult life, but they were especially important while living on a sailboat.

Sometimes we had to fix things while the boat was at sea and in motion. That was a new challenge that even Pops, who can fix anything, would appreciate.

Second Leg Sailing Through the Kiel Canal

TUESDAY, 28 AUGUST 2018

We departed early to complete our voyage through the Kiel Canal. Our weather window for entering the North Sea was the next day, so we had a full day for the light cruise. We had five or six hours before approaching Brunsbüttel, a port at the end of the canal just before the locks that exit the canal and feed into the Elbe River.

The wind and tides were perfect. It was early afternoon, so rather than moor at Brunsbüttel as originally planned, we locked out of the canal and cruised forward to Cuxhafen, another port about 20 nm along the Elbe River close to the mouth of the North Sea. It required another two hours but would give us a head start for the next morning's departure to the island of Helgoland.

We went through the locks with little drama and entered the mighty Elbe River.

The Elbe is one of the major rivers of Central Europe. It rises in the Krkonoše Mountains of the northern Czech Republic before traversing much of Bohemia, then Germany, and flowing into the North Sea at Cuxhafen, 110 km northwest of Hamburg. Its total length is 1,094 km.

Experts believe that without the Elbe River, Hamburg would not be the economic power it is today. The Elbe has been the city's gateway to the world, at least since the days of the Hanseatic League. It's safe to say Hamburg owes its multicultural vibe and worldly character to this mighty river.

It doesn't feel like what anyone would consider the definition of "river." It feels like open ocean. Many sailors say it's difficult to tell where the Elbe ends and the North Sea begins.

I marveled at the difference in the scenery. Inside the Kiel Canal, there were warm, bright colors with intimate villages along its banks. As we entered the Elbe, everything seemed to turn from vivid color to black and white. The temperature instantly dropped about 20 degrees and, of course, there was much more movement in the air outside the wind shadow of the canal. It was eerie, but spectacular.

Conditions were calm, so I cooked dinner while we were still cruising. It was not normal sailing conditions with a tilt or heavy wind gusts. But nevertheless, I was proud of myself for cooking a full dinner while in motion. I chopped fresh vegetables, cooked sausages and potatoes, and made a yummy, hearty stir-fry that warmed our chilled bones.

We arrived in Cuxhafen in the early evening and prepared for an extremely early departure toward Helgoland the next morning.

I focused on what was ahead—my first ever meeting with the North Sea and the monster that lies beneath its surface. This would be, by far, the most challenging body of water I had ever sailed at that point.

The skipper lacked experience in the North Sea as well, which contributed to my anxiety. I wondered if I would rise to the occasion or if my low confidence level would affect my ability to handle the unknown. I worried about how I would manage maneuvering through the heavy traffic without putting the ship and crew in danger. I wondered how I would handle my first-ever night watch.

I was terrified and just one night away from learning the hard way how quick decisions at sea can have catastrophic consequences.

CHAPTER 4

BUMPER CARS WITH AN OFFSHORE BUOY

NORTH SEA PASSAGE (PART ONE)

29 AUGUST 2018

We planned to leave Cuxhafen with the high tide that would essentially blow us out to sea. With a favorable wind forecast, we scheduled a 05:30 departure so the North Sea monster's deep exhale would push us toward Helgoland. I had not been seasick since the first two days of our voyage, so didn't feel nervous about that anymore. I was earning my sea legs.

The ideal conditions did not go unnoticed by the other sailors in the harbor. When I awoke at 04:00 to feed and walk Cap'n Jack and Scout, sailors were preparing their boats for the moonlight morning departure. A line of white mast lights slowly filed out of the harbor, one by one.

I filled a thermos with coffee and another with hot ginger tea for easy access. I organized all the seasick supplies in a bin I had firmly stabilized with velcro on the cockpit credenza. We prepared *Seefalke*, settled the seadogs in their secure cabin, and departed with the high tide pushing us out into the Elbe River right at the mouth of the North Sea.

We hoisted the main sail, then the genoa, then the mizzen. The wind was heavy, and the waves were already swelling at about 1 m. It was much more comfortable to have the current and wind in our favor rather than pushing against us like it did in the Baltic.

At sunrise, we were cruising at about 6 knots—a speedy pace for our heavy ship. I enjoyed the ride and soaked in the open ocean beauty of my first meeting with the North Sea.

About two hours from Cuxhafen, I felt relaxed. I told the captain I needed to close my eyes for just a little bit. I stayed in the cockpit enjoying the fresh air and the smooth ride. Then I ever so slightly drifted off to sleep.

About 30 minutes later ...

If you've never heard the sound of steel on steel, let me describe it for you. Imagine the sound of a freight train skimming alongside a metal wall. There are no nails on a chalkboard that can compare with that screeching sound. I was awakened immediately to discover that *Seefalke's* bow had slammed head-on into an offshore buoy.

While I was sleeping, the skipper saw the buoy and tried to avoid it. But he underestimated our speed and the pushing current. He tried to adjust the sails but couldn't maneuver *Seefalke* quickly enough.

Steering an 11-ton sailboat is nothing like driving a car, in which you can slam on the brakes and stop quickly. A car can swerve to miss an obstacle in the middle of the road. You may end up in a ditch, but quick adjustments can generally be made to change directions quickly. It's not at all like that on *Seefalke*. You must look way ahead for obstacles because the vessel cannot make easy adjustments. Quick stops are impossible.

I always thought that buoys were made of some sort of hard industrial rubber that a boat would just bounce off like a bumper car. But I learned through this experience that they are made of steel. In fact, they are small steel boats floating with anchors. If we had been in a fiberglass or wooden boat, it's possible we would be at the bottom of the North Sea right now.

The skipper sprinted to the bow and bent over the sea rail so far that his waist was the only part of his body touching the boat. He kept his cool, but the concerned look on his face gave me chills. I asked him what happened, even though I wasn't sure I really wanted to know.

"It's bad," he said matter-of-factly.

I was afraid to look. I took the wheel as he scrambled. I remained as still as a statue and waited for orders from my captain. He told me to go down to the bow cabin and empty everything out of all the lockers. I did.

Then I took the wheel again as he went down to determine if he could see any damage from the inside. He returned after what seemed like an eternity but was probably only about 60 seconds. He couldn't find the point of contact.

I asked again, "How bad is it?"

He told me to go look. I did.

I clipped the cantilever of my safety strap to the steel sea rail and balanced my body over the side—just as the skipper had done a few minutes before. That's when I saw what I really didn't want to see. There was a dent in *Seefalke's* steel hull that was about a foot wide. It looked like a deep cut, perhaps more than just a flesh wound. *Seefalke's* bright orange paint was completely scraped away at the point of contact, revealing the naked, gray steel underneath.

My childhood training from Pops kicked in. I grabbed the measuring tape from the toolbox and measured the distance from the front of the bow to the dent. Then I measured from the top of the deck down to the dent. To find the damage from the inside we needed a point of reference. We couldn't safely lean over the sea rail far enough to see the full extent of the damage from the outside. Was there a hole in the boat? Was water coming in? We would only be able to tell from the inside.

All of this was happening in the middle of the open ocean while sailing at 6 knots with an extremely heavy current.

The skipper went back into the bow cabin. He ripped apart the thin, decorative plexi-wood wall that separated the cabin from the steel hull. He couldn't find the dent. He told me to try again to find it. This time I measured from the top hatch (a point of reference I could identify from inside the cabin) to the dent and then went back down. I ripped apart more of the wall and finally found *Seefalke's* dented hull from the inside. The skipper went down to check it. We could finally definitively confirm that it was indeed only a dent and not a hole. No water was seeping inside. *Seefalke* was injured, but she was fine. And so were we.

It's in times like these that we have to remember that the sea is a hostile environment for humans. People are not meant to live at sea. We must rely on our floating homes to protect us. I said a prayer and thanked God for giving us the intelligence to choose a steel boat for the voyage. It made me cringe to think what could have happened otherwise.

Fair Winds and Following Seas

It was an otherwise perfect afternoon—the definition of "fair winds and following seas" as we cruised along smoothly with the magnificent North Sea current.

We made it to Helgoland in eight hours, moored *Seefalke*, and then assessed the damage. There was no doubt that the original confrontation with the buoy applied the harshest injury to the boat. However, we bounced off that thing like a pinball machine about four times after the initial hit, leaving several marks and missing orange paint along *Seefalke's* starboard side. From outside, we could also confirm that the flesh wounds were, thankfully, completely cosmetic.

I finally felt totally confident and helpful. No one can fix something with paint like I can. I pumped up the small, red, inflatable dinghy, climbed in, and performed the surgery. I used the electrical sander to smooth out the damaged paint edges. There was nothing we could do about the dent. Then I applied some rust-protective primer and several coats of bright orange paint. While there, I touched up some other spots along *Seefalke's* hull.

While I was productive with the repairs, the skipper was licking his wounds. He was beating himself up for his mistake with the buoy. He went over it and over it—in his mind and out loud. He said he could see the buoy that seemed farther ahead in the distance, and he did all he could to avoid it. I believed him and did not blame him. I reinforced much I believed in his abilities. But he emphatically rejected any compliments or words of encouragement.

He told me about an article he once read in a yacht magazine in which experienced sailors confessed some of their mistakes at sea. He remembered one of them talking about slamming into an offshore buoy. The skipper is an experienced sailor. But he is human, after all.

Seefalke's former captain called and calmed the skipper, reminding him that mistakes are just lessons that need to be learned. The mistake was not fatal. Sometimes, for a sailor, that's enough. They discussed how fortunate it was that we had the power of steel to protect us.

Getting Creative with Puppy Cranes

Meanwhile, we had another challenge. We were moored at a floating pier next to a massive wall with a ladder leading to the top of the pier—easily accessible for humans. It was a different story for canines.

When we first arrived at Helgoland, the tide was high, and the top of the ladder was about 10 feet from the floating pier. So, I climbed to the top of the ladder and the skipper (who is about six-feet tall) easily handed me Cap'n Jack and then Scout. We walked them and let them play and explore. No problem.

But remember those deep breaths the monster beneath the North Sea takes? We returned to *Seefalke* and finished our painting project. Then it was time to take the pups out for their evening walk. But by that time, the monster had taken in another deep breath. It was low tide and now the ladder was at least a 25-foot climb. It was no longer manageable to make the puppy handoff.

We had an idea. The pups' life jackets are very secure and have handles. They are designed so that if the pup falls overboard, you can grab the handles and pull them in (or you can grab the handles with a boat hook). When the dogs are strapped into the life jackets, they are velcro'ed and secured with clamps. There is no way the jackets will come off of them unless you take them off, and sometimes even that is a challenge.

The skipper rigged a long line with a pulley to create a fairly sophisticated doggie crane. He climbed to the top of the ladder.

Another sailboat was rafted next to us in our mooring. The skipper of that ship expertly tied the knots at the end of the homemade crane onto the handles of Cap'n Jack's life vest.

Then, using the homemade crane, Cap'n Jack was lifted up to the top of the ladder—safely and securely—using the rigged pulley system. We repeated the maneuver with Scout. Before we get beaten up for this from all the animal lovers, we want to assure you the system was safe and secure, and we would never do anything to put the dogs in danger.

Exploring the Island of Helgoland

Safely on land, thanks to the puppy crane, the four of us explored the island and climbed to the top of the red rock mountain to see the observatory of the migrating birds and enjoy the breathtaking view.

Helgoland is on a major migration route for birds crossing the North Sea. For centuries, the birds—those on migration and those breeding there—were an important source of food for the islanders. In the early 19th century Helgoland also became a source of bird specimens for collectors and museums.

Ornithologist and artist Heinrich Gätke first visited the island in 1837 and moved there permanently in 1841 as secretary to the British Governor. He began collecting specimens of rarities for both artistic and scientific purposes. He spent most of the next 60 years studying the birds.

The dogs seemed hypnotized watching the thousands of birds swarm the edges of the massive cliffs. We continued to explore and found a huge field where we unleashed the hounds for a while so they could run and play.

When we returned to our mooring I did some laundry and decided to take a much-needed shower, which was always a race-the-clock event at some of the marinas due to the time limits of water flow. In most of the marina shower facilities throughout Europe, it generally cost 2 Euros for a four-minute shower. Sometimes, I would splurge and take an eight-minute shower for 4 Euros. I managed to get it down to a science.

First, I would get everything organized so when I hit the button and the water started, I was ready. Then, I would strip down to my birthday suit. I would lay out my supplies and make sure everything was handy. I didn't want to waste a second or a single drop of water. Then I turned on the water and started the clock. I spent 30 seconds shampooing my hair, then 30 seconds rinsing out the shampoo. It required another 30 seconds to apply conditioner, and then I spent one minute washing my body. That left 90 seconds to rinse off my body and rinse all the conditioner out of my hair. Then the water would shut off. Done.

When I splurged and took an eight-minute shower, I had time to shave my legs and relax underneath the soothing warm water. Those extra 240 seconds seemed like a luxury.

As I crawled into the bunk, it was apparent that the North Sea buoy mistake was weighing heavily on the skipper's mind. I wanted to comfort him, but he was not interested in conversation or intimacy. In fact, he had not been interested in intimacy since before we set sail from Stralsund.

That night, he wasn't interested in human contact of any kind. In fact, it seemed that he preferred I was not even there. The silent treatment was common for the stoic German. It's something that I had always tolerated, but never understood.

Pure silence—no response whatsoever even when I asked him a direct question. He looked right through me as if I were invisible. No words. No expressions. Nothing. It happened often. Whether I was calm and loving, or if I screamed and cried uncontrollably, he had the ability to completely ignore me. It's a cold form of neglect that left me feeling bitterly lonely.

The skipper deployed the cruel silent treatment torture throughout our relationship. I had witnessed him punish his own children the same way a few times. I would always try to give them an understanding look or take them for a walk—something to distract them from the cold, quiet burn. It broke my heart every time he ignored them because I knew exactly how it felt. I struggled to understand it and found it impossible to justify.

I needed some comfort, too. I needed to know that we were in this together. I was frightened and a bit unnerved about what was waiting for us the next morning.

Would the North Sea continue to challenge us? I wondered if we would have good weather and conditions, or if we would meet the North Sea monster that haunts my dreams. I remembered our challenges battling the Baltic Sea mean girl. I wondered if we were destined to confront the schoolyard bully the next day.

What I could never have anticipated was what it would actually take to tackle the challenge of sailing that mighty sea—or what I would have to endure to battle the monster that lived within me.

CHAPTER 5

THE NORTH SEA BULLY

NORTH SEA PASSAGE (PART TWO)

After battling the Baltic Sea mean girl, my fear of the North Sea bully had intensified.

With two decades of experience, not much rattles the skipper when it comes to sailing. He is confident, seasoned, and skilled. In typical German fashion, he rarely shows emotion. To show any form of it would be an admission of weakness, in his opinion. By contrast, I am the overly emotional, highly excitable American girl who had been sailing for only six years at that time. My sailing mentality had ranged from I-can-conquer-the-world, superhuman powers on a good day to confidence-crushing fear on a bad day.

Searching for a strategy, I asked myself, "How do you tame a bully?" The answer was clear. You stand up to her and face her—head on.

Or you catch her in a good mood.

Of course, it doesn't hurt to have a big orange bodyguard with an iron fist and a steel jaw to protect you. *Seefalke* was built in the North Sea by Dutch designers who carefully constructed her specifically for those brutal conditions. She had spent 43 years of her 45-year life sailing the North Sea. Rest assured, *Seefalke* and the North Sea are old friends. They get along just fine.

Even with favorable conditions, a voyage across the North Sea is never easy.

Day 1

31 AUGUST 2018

Our original plan was to sail a short first leg from Helgoland to Den Helder in The Netherlands. It required sailing through the night and deep into the next day. That meant I would experience my first night watch—double anxiety when combined with my first-ever North Sea passage. I was terrified, but I didn't tell the skipper. I put on a not-too-convincing brave face.

Since there were only two of us, the watch schedule required that we rotate from the helm to the bunk every four hours.

When we departed Helgoland at 05:00—90 minutes into high tide—it was cold and dark, and there was a slight drizzling rain. As we crept into the black opening of the North Sea, the skipper took the first watch while the pups and I took cover in the cabin below.

My internal clock woke me at 08:45–15 minutes before my shift. I emptied my bladder, washed my face, brushed my teeth, and made some coffee. I could see the huge waves crashing against the small porthole windows from inside the cabin. We were already being pushed by the heavy current and 15- to 20-knot winds that put us on a nice 25-degree heel. We were sailing smoothly at 4.5 to 5 knots.

The skipper briefed me about what to expect, but with less detail than I probably needed. My main objective was to stay on course, dodge any traffic or buoys, and adjust the sails if the wind shifted. But we also had to deal with a traffic separation scheme (TSS), which are common along busy waterways, especially in areas like the North Sea where there are gigantic ports with hundreds of huge oil tankers and container ships passing through.

A TSS works kind of like driving on a highway or expressway. There is an invisible "median," which is a no-go zone. On the navigation chart, they are indicated in pink. Unlike driving on a highway, there are no lines in the middle and no grass in the median. Those sections can only be identified by looking at the charts. The purpose of a TSS is to separate the huge ships from the smaller leisure craft, like *Seefalke*. To cross a TSS, you must do it at a 90-degree angle and only if all traffic is clear.

It was smooth sailing, at first. The waves seemed HUGE to me—about 3 m high. Occasionally, a high wave would splash against *Seefalke*'s beam and give me a shocking, cold, saltwater shower. I was facing the bully head on, enjoying the ride, and burying my fear under a thin blanket of nervous anxiety.

A couple hours into my shift, I looked down into the cabin and saw the captain sleeping, all nestled with the pups. That meant he was relaxed and had confidence in me, which gave me confidence in myself.

Sometimes, confidence is a bad thing.

About 30 minutes later, something suddenly awakened him. Sometimes experienced sailors feel things that simply don't trigger the senses of novice sailors like me. He sprinted to the cockpit in his underpants and stocking feet, pushed me out of the way, and took the wheel. Somehow, I had managed to drift over into the TSS. We were flanked by three gigantic ships.

I couldn't understand what I did wrong.

Apparently, the current had pushed *Seefalke* over into the no-go zone. Even though I was on the correct heading I had still managed to drift into the TSS. It's easy to underestimate the force of those currents. It was an extremely dangerous mistake, and it's also illegal. The skipper took control and turned the ship around, dodging the massive freighters. Soon, we were back on track.

I was beating myself up over the mistake, and the skipper's disappointment in my inability to handle the situation was even more upsetting. The thought of taking the helm again paralyzed me with fear. I tucked my tail between my legs and moped into the far corner of the cabin, trying unsuccessfully to repair my wounded pride.

We had dinner around sunset, and then it was time for another briefing about the night shift. I was still dealing with my confidence crisis after the TSS fiasco. Not only did I have to think about all the watch responsibilities, but I now had to do it in the black of night. The captain took the first shift—20:00 to midnight.

At 23:30, after barely any sleep and filled with a mix of anxiety and determination, I strapped on my life vest and slowly climbed the four wooden steps to the cockpit. The skipper was exhausted after maneuvering through the heavy traffic during the previous four hours. He briefed me, but again assumed I knew more than I did. Then he went down to sleep.

For some reason, looking through binoculars always gave me a headache. At night, I had even more trouble seeing through the lenses. I saw all the lights around me, but I had trouble determining if that blob of lights was a ship or a buoy or an offshore rig. *Ok, that's a ship, but is it moving, or is it anchored?*

I was also struggling with depth perception. *Is that ship right in front of me or is it two nautical miles away?* I couldn't tell the difference.

Frustrated, my anxiety intensified. All I knew for certain was that I was failing miserably at what I call "the night watch video game."

This is how the video game works. It's totally black but there are glowing and blinking lights in various shapes, sizes, and colors. All the lighted objects are coming toward you or going away from you in all directions and at various distances and speeds. You are moving. The water beneath you is moving. Most of the lighted objects are moving. Some of the lights are blinking in sequences that are significant. You have no ammunition, and you cannot fire at a target. You can only play defense. You must dodge all the lights, avoid slamming into anything, and manage to also avoid shallow water areas.

Most important, in the night watch video game, you only have one life. Literally.

48

All the stationary objects are identified on the paper charts. The plotter screen shows the ships that are within one or two nautical miles, but only if they are connected to the Automated Identification System (AIS). When they are in your path within a certain range, their icons start blinking and an alarm begins to screech.

On the screen, it looks like the other ship is right on top of you, even though it may be half a mile away. It shows where the other moving ships will be in six minutes, but it doesn't show you where *Seefalke* will be in six minutes.

I looked behind me. I looked to the right. I looked to the left. I tried to focus on the various objects through the binoculars and through my own eyes. Lights continued to blink on the screen.

The alarm continued to squeal. I saw a ship on the screen, but I was unable to see it when I searched the perimeter. *Where is it?* On the screen, it looked like it was sitting on my stern. *Arrrrggggghhhh-hhhhh. Help!!!!*

Why is this so hard? Why can't I do this?

Suddenly, the lights in front of me were getting bigger and brighter. They were moving but in no particular direction that I could interpret clearly. There was nothing on the screen that helped me to identify the lights. There was nothing I could see clearly through the binoculars and nothing on the chart.

What seemed like only an instant later, two distinct shapes came into focus as clearly as if I was looking at them through a magnifying glass. I could now clearly identify them as two fishing ships connected to each other by an enormous fishing net.

It's important to reiterate that steering an 11-ton sailboat is nothing at all like driving a car. You can't just swerve out of the way at a moment's notice to avoid a collision. It is not possible to slam on the brakes and stop instantly. You must maneuver long before you approach a dangerous object.

I tried to steer *Seefalke* away from the boats and the net that could become tangled with our keel, but the strong current continued to push us directly toward them. I panicked and screamed for help from the captain. He bolted to the cockpit, again in his underpants and stocking feet, grabbed the wheel, turned on the engine, and steered us clear just as we were about to slam into the two fishing boats.

When we were clear of danger, he stared at me with an obvious look of confusion and disappointment and asked me how that could have happened.

"I really don't know," I told him. He asked if I was using the binoculars. I told him that I was, but explained that I was having a hard time seeing through them.

I wasn't trying to make excuses.

Then I realized something to myself as I said it out loud: "Even if I see the danger, it doesn't mean that I know what to do about it."

He was silent. The look on his face showed me that he was trying to figure out how to teach me—how to make me *feel* what he innately knows. He couldn't find the words to comfort me or to teach me, so he remained silent.

He stayed with me for a little while longer until we were out of the heavy traffic zone. By that time the sun was rising, and I could see better. The skipper went back to bed, and I just held my breath and gripped the wheel with clenched fists, trying with all my might to mentally make it through the rest of my shift.

While I was feeling battered and beaten by the beastly bully, the captain returned to the cockpit at 05:00 and calmly took the wheel as if nothing had happened the night before. I waited for him to scold me or lecture me on the two near-fatal mistakes of the previous day.

He said nothing.

Nothing derogatory. Nothing encouraging.

Just silence.

My disappointment in myself bubbled to the surface, and I burst into tears. I felt completely defeated and incompetent. I didn't think I deserved to be sailing that magnificent ship on such a formidable body of water. I wanted to look at him, but my eyes could only find the cold, steel cockpit floor as I hung my head in shame.

"I think we need to have a serious conversation about whether I'm ready for this," I told him.

Then, without letting him respond, I went below, collapsed on the bunk, and cried myself to sleep.

Day 2

1 SEPTEMBER 2018

I awoke two hours later, made breakfast, and slowly forced myself to join the skipper in the cockpit. The air was crisp, cold, and refreshing. The sapphire sea was spectacular. The water looked as though 50 shades of blue had melted together to form one brilliant hue that was created for our eyes only.

The skipper was laser focused. He had spent the morning hours studying the weather and wind forecasts. Without any mention of the day before or any casual morning salutations, he matter-of-factly stated, "I think we should just keep going and skip Den Helder."

The conditions were perfect, he explained, and it was important to take advantage of the strong easterly winds that are usually rare for the North Sea. I trusted his decision.

The bully was tame. She was in a good mood. She and her buddy, *Seefalke*, were having a great time, and we decided to let them keep playing.

But my confidence was at an all-time low.

This time my eyes found the skipper's as I reminded him of my last words before going to bed. "I may not be ready for this," I repeated, this time more emphatically. My confidence was totally shot. My captain needed a more capable sailor to help him.

He couldn't do everything. And I was beginning to believe that I couldn't do anything.

Then the skipper admitted he had done a poor job of teaching me and preparing me. I could tell how hard it was for him to admit it. I understood that it is difficult to transfer half a lifetime of knowledge and experience to someone else. I understood that when something comes so naturally to someone, it's often difficult for them to break it down into details and teach someone else how to do it.

Experienced sailors don't have to think about how to sail. They draw from their years of experience and just sail. At some point, it becomes muscle memory.

I thought again about Sailboat Bob and wished I could talk to him. He was such a patient teacher who gleaned so much happiness from helping me learn. He would know what to say to me. I needed my Yoda in that moment, and I think somehow the skipper knew it wasn't him. But he dug deep inside himself and said something that shocked me.

"I haven't been a good teacher," he admitted. "I guess we've been sailing together for so long I didn't realize you had never taken a night watch all by yourself."

He reminded me that he often makes mistakes, too. Then he glared his aquamarine eyes directly into mine and said something I'll never forget.

"You just need experience, and this is how you get it."

Then he said, "Michelle, I have confidence in you. If I was going to battle, I would want you with me. You would be the first person I would pick to be on my team. You can do this."

He talked me down from the ledge, something I needed so very badly.

In that moment, I thought about my other sailing mentor, Yvi. She once told me a story about when she was on her 18-month sailing trip with her husband. He was seasick for three straight days while they were sailing the North Sea. They didn't have good conditions. The bully was in full force and knocking them all over the playground.

She took the helm of their 7 m boat for three straight days and nights without a break. She told me that it's in times like those that you find out what you are truly capable of doing.

I snapped out of my pity party and asked the skipper to teach me. I focused on asking good questions and not relying on him to remember to teach me every detail. I took responsibility for my own education.

I was on a mission. I practiced for my night watch all day long. The skipper challenged me and quizzed me with each oncoming vessel. He showed me how to measure the distance and how to tell if a ship was coming or going. I was determined.

A smart and strategic skipper, he then re-organized the watch schedule. He no longer based it on time intervals. Rather, he based it on the situation. He would take the difficult, high-traffic shifts. I would take the longer, easy, open-ocean slots while he rested. Instead of switching at a pre-determined time, I would wake him when I got to a specific waypoint, and we would assess the situation together to determine whether I should keep going or if he should take over.

That night, the skipper took an early shift and got through another TSS. Then he woke me and spent about half an hour briefing me.

"There are two key contacts right now," he said. "Tell me what they are." I looked through the binoculars and performed a perimeter check. I identified every light. "That's a buoy. That's a ship that's not moving, so it's anchored. That's a huge wind park."

I began to see things clearly.

"That's a sailing boat under motor that's going away from me. I know this because there is a white light on the mast, and I see the green navigation light. Green is on the starboard side and it's moving to the right of me. It's going away."

I made similar calculations with every single light in the perimeter. Then I identified the two key contacts and articulated my plan of action. I felt confident. The skipper went down to sleep, and I carefully performed my checks every 10 minutes. I checked my eyesight against what I saw through the binocular lens. Then I checked the paper chart to see if the object was already identified.

At 04:00, everything was clear. I was so wide awake I wasn't even blinking. I had safely made it through dozens of obstacles, and now there were none. Not one.

Seefalke and I were all alone on the open water.

I looked down into the cabin. The skipper was all cuddled with four velvety beagle ears in his face, sleeping soundly. I let him sleep and extended my shift. Around 05:30, the North Sea began to wake up, so I woke up the skipper. He told me he had finally gotten some deep sleep, and I was proud. I had done my job. I kept us safe.

Day 3

2 SEPTEMBER 2018

We took advantage of the weather and favorable winds and kept on going rather than moor in any of the many ports along the way. I practiced for my night watch, trying not to exhaust the captain too badly with my barrage of questions.

I was beginning to feel like a real sailor and not just a random first mate tagging along for the ride.

We passed some of the largest shipping ports in the world—Amsterdam, Rotterdam, and Antwerp. I was mesmerized by all the gigantic freighters and oil cargo ships. In Rotterdam, we saw the famous *Marit Maersk*, one of the world's largest container ships. It's almost 400 m long and 59 m wide. With 100,000 horsepower, it hauls 10,150 containers, and each one of them is larger than *Seefalke*.

Our course was now set for Dunkirk, France, the last port in the North Sea right at the entrance of the English Channel.

The remainder of the passage would be complicated. We needed to maneuver through traffic separation schemes, tons of buoys, large busy ports, and as a bonus, some areas with low water levels. It would be a long night for the skipper if he took all of the heavy load. I took my shift at 18:00 and continued through to the first waypoint.

Rather than fear the night watch, this time I decided to embrace it.

There is something special about that moment when the sun disappears behind the horizon. It's not yet dark, but it's not daylight anymore either. Some of the anchored ships begin to light up like Christmas trees and others look like ghostly shadows in the distance. The only sound is the waves.

I performed my checks, surveying the perimeter every 10 minutes. I identified every light. Most of the time I went clockwise, but just to be sure, sometimes I switched it up and went counterclockwise. It's an old editor's trick. Sometimes when you read an article so many times you just don't see the words anymore. If you edit the article backward, starting at the end, you can see things in a different way and catch the mistakes.

Soon, everything was black.

When you are floating on the water, you don't really see the world around you fade to black. For a while, you see all the colors left over from the sunset—orange, pink, red, yellow. The water changes color, too. At first, it's a brilliant blue. Then it softly fades to a silvery grey.

At some point it becomes black as coal—like the sky. It is so black that sometimes it's difficult to see where the sky meets the water. But you can still hear the waves. On that night, millions of stars were lighting the way.

It was so quiet and peaceful I could barely remember why I had been so afraid.

At times, *Seefalke* would talk to me. A sail would flap. Her bones would creak a little—a sound kind of like when someone steps on a loose wooden floorboard. I heard the waves lapping against her body and echoing throughout her steel hull.

I like to think she was letting me know I wasn't alone. She was there to protect us—our bright orange bodyguard. I felt as safe as a baby in her mother's womb.

"Don't be afraid," she whispered to me. "I've got this."

In return for her protection, we keep her in deep waters. We steer her away from obstacles. We show her the way home, and she takes us there—safely and securely.

Day 4

3 SEPTEMBER 2018

The skipper took over at midnight and sailed us into the morning. He had a tough night with hundreds of obstacles to maneuver around. I wished I could help more. But this was the plan, and it was working.

As the sun began to rise after our last night shift in the North Sea, we made our approach and safely moored at Dunkirk. Then I understood what the skipper had told me about earning the experience.

To get it, you must face the bully head on.

I didn't know it at the time, but the beating I took from the North Sea bully would later help me through even tougher battles in the Bay of Biscay and on a three-week Atlantic Ocean crossing. I can look back now and thank her for the lessons, the experience, and the scars that will stay with me forever.

You just need experience. And this is how you get it.

We made it through the North Sea, but our challenges didn't end there. Next, we needed to fight even more traffic on the busiest shipping waterway in the world—the English Channel. That's where I got my first lesson in what it really feels like to live life sideways.

CHAPTER 6

WORLD'S BUSIEST WATERWAY

ENGLISH CHANNEL PASSAGE (PART ONE)

TUESDAY, 4 SEPTEMBER 2018

We were so exhausted after the intense North Sea passage it was useless to make any significant sightseeing efforts in Dunkirk. While walking the dogs, we passed many lovely French restaurants but opted for a burger joint instead. I craved the protein that only red meat could provide.

With the satisfying burgers on our bellies, the skipper and I crashed early. I don't think I moved an inch the entire night. The soreness from the last passage had set in. My neck and shoulders were particularly sore, perhaps the result of not being accustomed to wearing the heavy life vest. I was sure the extremely tense and stressful sailing conditions also contributed to the ickiness I felt.

It requires excessive energy and muscle activity to stay balanced on a moving sailboat for four straight days. We had some hours of calm seas, but for the most part, our bodies were active even while relaxing.

While living on a sailboat, nothing is ever perfectly still. Even when moored, the boat moves. As our voyage continued, I felt my arm and leg muscles tightening—getting stronger and leaner. It was odd considering I hadn't exercised for many weeks.

My brain was constantly working, too, and I felt mentally exhausted. Any off-shift time was spent sleeping, if I was lucky. When awake, it was essential to remain acutely aware of the conditions, traffic, boat chores and maintenance, navigation, weather, and regular work activities.

Upon arrival in Dunkirk, I was too exhausted to shower, so I found the marina facilities first thing the next morning. At first, the water was like ice, and I had to think really hard about just how badly I wanted to get clean. But it eventually heated to a tolerable lukewarm and felt great to wash away the stress and excitement of the past four days.

We considered another straight, nonstop voyage across the English Channel, but I was not a fan of that idea. There were many lovely spots to see along the northern French coastline, and I felt a strong sense of wanderlust. But the skipper preferred to forge on in good weather without stops than have a single day trip with severe and challenging conditions. I couldn't really argue with that reasoning.

We got into an onboard rhythm while crossing the North Sea and were able to find a system for sailing 24/7 that allowed us to maintain some sense of normal. Well, it was a sense of a "new normal." But honestly, I was exhausted from the North Sea trek and craved a break in the action.

Thanks to the favorable North Sea easterly winds, we were close to being back on track with our original schedule, even though we were almost three weeks delayed with the original departure. It was important for us to outrun the harsh northern European winter.

We decided to depart the next morning for the small French coastal port of Saint-Valéry-en-Caux—a port that Yvi recommended. We planned a voyage straight there that would require sailing a first leg of about 100 nm.

We calculated that at an average speed of 4.5 knots, it would take us about 24 straight hours. If we departed around 09:00, we would likely arrive at high tide the next morning. At that port, it would be impossible to enter at low tide—a new challenge to consider.

We learned that an ugly storm front would be forming a few days later, so we planned to arrive at Saint-Valéry-en-Caux and then hunker down in its protected marina until the storm passed before continuing through to the other end of the English Channel.

Departure from Dunkirk 08:50

WEDNESDAY–THURSDAY, 5–6 SEPTEMBER 2018

The night before departure, I didn't sleep well. Hurricane Gordon was on a path toward my home in Gulf Shores. I texted with my friend, Trisha, who also lived in my condo community. She graciously prepared and secured my home. Another friend, Lynn, transported my car to a safe place. I missed my friends and family. Fortunately, the storm was a Category 1 and caused only minimal damage.

I was excited about sailing through the English Channel, but I also knew that with the heavy traffic, traffic separation schemes, and heavy currents, it would be a difficult passage. We carefully planned the watch schedule for another all-nighter. Again, I was scheduled for the open ocean, lower-traffic opportunities while the captain scheduled himself for the areas that required more skill and experience. The captain took the first shift while I cuddled with the pups and went straight to sleep, hoping to catch up on the lost sleep from the night before.

Dunkirk is the last stop in the North Sea. It dumps into the English Channel just before the narrow, difficult-to-maneuver Strait of Dover. After about three hours of restful sleep, my internal clock woke me, and I went to the cockpit even though it was at least two hours before my shift. The wind was whistling at about 15 to 20 knots. *Seefalke* was gliding like a downhill skier along the 2 m waves at an average of 6 to 7 knots, unusually fast for our heavy steel ketch.

Within 30 minutes, we entered the narrow Strait of Dover, marking the boundary where the North Sea ends and the English Channel begins. Many huge ships crowded the narrow path on that cloudy, gray, hazy day. It was chilly, but not unbearable, with no sun in sight. The water was a silvery gray, and the eerie sky was full of billowy gray and black clouds. Just like when we left the Kiel Canal and entered the Elbe River, everything seemed to turn to black and white with many shades of gray but no other colors.

We were on about a 25-degree tilt—close to my threshold for comfort. We sailed through the Strait of Dover and felt the difference in speed from *Seefalke's* normal 4.5 to 5 knots. We raced through the water, *Seefalke's* bow slicing through the waves like a hot knife through butter.

We saw Cap Gris-Nez near Calais in the distance. Once we passed the cliffs, we tacked to the port side and made our turn to the southern part of the channel toward Saint-Valéry-en-Caux. I took the helm, and we charted a southerly course toward our destination with favorable currents, as predicted.

The wind was perfect. The currents no longer worked against us, and we maintained the amazing average speed of around 6 to 7 knots.

The skipper went down to sleep, and I settled into my watch. There was not much traffic the farther we sailed away from the main TSS in the English Channel. For me, it was a relatively easy shift. The water was deep, with perfect winds, and a respectable-but-tolerable 20 to 25-degree tilt at times.

Sometimes, when heeling on a sailboat I would get nervous. I have always feared capsizing. But I was less afraid while sailing on *Seefalke*. Her keel is almost as long as her 43-foot frame and is about 1 m wide. Her 11-ton body provides significant balance. *Seefalke's* cockpit is extremely safe—almost 4 ft deep on all four sides. Sailors are completely protected inside that cocoon in the center of the boat.

I've seen sailboats that have the cockpit in the stern with an open back and no pocket to stand in. There is nothing to protect the sailors from heavy waves crashing in. And there is nothing to protect the sailors from flying out backward. I was grateful that was not the design of our boat.

My only problem with the cockpit was that I was not quite tall enough to see over the top of the front hood. I was forced to stand on my tippy-toes, which was not always easy while trying to stay balanced. When the boat was rocking in all directions, it helped me to spread my legs about body width apart, bend my knees, and allow my legs to bend and move to cushion the movement.

It was kind of like doing lunges and squats at the same time to the rhythm of the waves—kind of like the motion you need to make with the lower part of your body to maintain the twirl of a hula hoop. That was not easy to do on my tippy-toes.

My shift was relatively easy and actually enjoyable. I didn't have much traffic for almost six hours. The waters calmed significantly within the first three hours—enough that I was able to let Cap'n Jack join me in the cockpit. He curled up on the bench next to me and rested his head on the credenza while Scout slept comfortably in the cabin.

For the last two hours of the shift, I felt completely alone in the world. I saw no land or other ships around the entire perimeter. Nothing. There was only the sea and the sky and the horizon that connects them in my full 360-degree view.

I never saw the sun that entire day, but as the day turned to evening, the water changed from silvery gray to seafoamy-turquoise. It was an interesting shade of green that I couldn't compare or relate to any other object. I don't think I had ever seen that color before.

The skipper was scheduled to take over at 20:00, and like clockwork, he popped up out of bed before I could wake him. I was drowsy from the lack of sleep the night before, and even though my shift was uneventful, I needed rest.

But first, I wanted to cook a hot dinner. I knew the next shift would be tough as the night was turning black and the empty horizon would soon begin to glow and sparkle with the lights of fishing ships, buoys, and traffic coming in and out of several ports—a zillion moving lighted objects to interpret and maneuver around.

The waves rocked us heavily again, so the dogs went below with me. The galley was a dangerous place in those kinds of conditions. We had a gas stove/oven that was lit with a match. We had a semi-cardanic hinged stove, which means it would swing with the motion of the boat keeping the surface even with the horizon.

I decided to make something easy—a bacon-egg-cheese omelet. Cooking on the boat was like walking through a fun house maze at the local fair. My legs were spread well beyond my body width, and I was unconsciously doing my lunge/squat/hula-hoop motion with the rhythm of the waves.

I had one hand firmly grasped to the counter while the other hand coordinated the ingredients and utensils. I sliced bacon strips and began sizzling them in the pan. Then I carefully broke four eggs into a bowl and began to whisk them. I wanted to add salt and pepper. Out of habit, I sat the bowl on the counter to reach for the seasonings. That's when I was reminded that the counter was not cardanically hinged and definitely did not swing with the motion of the boat to keep the surface even.

The bowl immediately slid across the counter, dumping about half of the whisked eggs all over the galley floor. I managed to cook the remaining eggs, although we had to settle for scrambled rather than a neat omelet.

I cleaned the galley and then cuddled with the pups for some rest before my 01:00 shift. I was on my back, and Cap'n Jack was wedged between my legs with his head resting on my tummy. Scout was curled in the fetal position inside my left armpit with her head resting sweetly on my shoulder. We rocked safely inside *Seefalke* and drifted into a deep sleep.

I awoke to an exhausted skipper. While we slept soundly, the empty horizon had filled with fishing boats. He had a maze of obstacles to dodge, including some low water level areas to maneuver around.

He briefed me for my shift. There were a few buoys to avoid and one fishing boat just in front of us, but at a safe distance. I had a straight shot toward our target marina. We were on pace to arrive around 04:00, a good five hours before originally predicted. The skipper asked me to wake him when we were five miles from the port.

I had no major issues, but night watches continued to be stressful for me. I was more comfortable, but the lights through the binoculars still played tricks on my eyes, and my whole body tensed for almost the entire three hours. About an hour into the shift, I saw the red and yellow glow of our port begin to shine above the black horizon in front of us. As we slowly got closer, the city of Saint-Valéry-en-Caux came into focus.

I stared at it for the next two hours and was amazed that in the open ocean you can see something clearly in the distance while it is still miles and miles and miles away. It was another reminder of what a small speck we were compared with the huge world in which we live.

As instructed, I woke the skipper when we were five miles from port—around 04:00. We had to wait for high tide to enter the marina, which was three hours away. So close! It seemed a pity to arrive so early and then have to wait. We performed long tacks in the waiting area outside the marina for all of those three hours. It was a difficult and narrow pilotage into the harbor, but as the sun began to rise, we saw that the destination was gorgeous.

The water was that same never-before-seen greenish color, but now it was mixed with deeper and more brilliant shades of green all lined up—a light-to-dark ombré. A lighthouse with white cliffs was in front of us as we maneuvered our way in, fighting the jetties and groundswells into the harbor. We couldn't prepare the boat until we were safely inside the wind shadow of the high marina walls because the force of the waves and the rising tide were so severe.

We secured *Seefalke* and got settled. I gave the pups a long, well-deserved walk while the skipper checked in with the harbor master. Then I crashed. I didn't move a muscle for the next 4.5 hours. My body and my mind were whipped.

Exploring the French Village of Saint-Valéry-en-Caux

Around 12:30, as I slowly awakened from my exhaustion coma, the sun was shining brightly through the open hatches above us. A cool breeze flooded the cabin with fresh sea air. I forced myself out of bed and took the pups on another walk while I searched for postcards and a few supplies. For lunch, we treated ourselves to delicious French cuisine at a sweet little café in the city's center.

Although we didn't recall seeing many people when we entered the harbor the night before, apparently our mooring was quite the spectacle. I suppose it was hard to miss a big, bright orange vessel entering the small marina. *Seefalke* didn't look like any other ship. Generally, about 95% of the sailboats we saw in harbors were white. *Seefalke's* bright orange hull never got lost in the crowd.

Several people approached us and asked about *Seefalke*. The owner of the restaurant was among them and asked specifically about our jib boom, explaining that he had never seen one before. That was another unique feature of *Seefalke*. She sported three booms—one on the jib, the main boom, and the mizzen boom on the stern. A waitress brought Cap'n Jack and Scout water bowls and said she saw us coming in and remembered seeing the sweet puppies on the big orange sailboat.

After lunch, I unleashed the hounds for a couple hours on the gorgeous beach. It was interesting to see the marina entrance at low tide. Where the gorgeous hard-to-describe-green water once filled the channel, the absence of water left just the dirt and rocks that make up the ocean's floor. Rocks, coral, seaweed, crabs and other crustaceans peppered the surface.

The pups literally played on the bottom of the sea. It was now obvious why a low-tide entry was not possible.

We spent the next few days catching up on work, resting, and boat maintenance while the storm front passed through. We hoped to catch another good weather pocket for our final pass along the English Channel and then into the challenging Bay of Biscay—a horrifying passage that lurked in the shadows on the other side of the channel.

An Eventful Night in Port

FRIDAY, 7 SEPTEMBER 2018

I was awakened by an abnormal scraping sound, perhaps the floating piers rising with the tide, I guessed. The skipper heard it, too, and awoke from his deep sleep. He leaped to the cockpit in his underpants and yelled down to me, "Get up here!"

We were flanked on the starboard side by the bows of about four other ships. Two of the ships' captains were on their respective decks trying to push an 11-ton, drifting, orange steel ship away from their bows. Our lines were no longer secured to the pier, and the incoming tide had pushed us away from our mooring, sideways into the marina.

Springing into action, the skipper turned on the engine while I manually pushed against the other ships. We maneuvered our way back to our spot alongside the edge of the pier. The tangled mooring lines on the bow and the stern floated in the water.

The other two ship captains sprinted over to our pier to help. I tossed them the bowline and then the stern line. They tied us to the mooring cleats while we safely secured *Seefalke*. The skipper disembarked and joined the other captains on the pier, still in his underpants. They were all scratching their heads trying to figure out what had happened.

There was no possible way that all four of our securely tied lines had come untied without help. One of the French captains suggested that some teenagers were playing a joke. The other captain said that we could have been a target because of our German flag. We were in Normandy, after all.

Nothing was stolen or missing from the boat. And thankfully, no damage to any of the other boats. To further secure the boat, we decided to drop the anchor. There was no possible way *Seefalke* could now move without intention.

The next day we spoke with the harbor master, who had already contacted the local police. He told us that there was a football match in town the night before. He suspected it was the work of drunk hooligans in search of trouble. Cap'n Jack and I decided to sleep in the cockpit the next night. His very loud howl would come in handy if the hooligans returned.

Meanwhile, severe weather continued to threaten, and we were forced to strategically plan our passage through the remainder of the English Channel. But even with careful preparation, we didn't anticipate the battles with forceful tides, uncooperative currents, and challenges with learning to live on a 20-degree tilt—all while trying to avoid a face-to-face meeting with a hurricane named Helen, who was directly in our path.

CHAPTER 7

20-DEGREE TILT

ENGLISH CHANNEL PASSAGE (PART TWO)

A 20-degree angle may not seem like much at first glance. If you look at it on an axis it's barely even an incline. However, if you are on a sailboat flying through the water at a 20-degree tilt for four or five straight days and nights while trying to perform daily living activities . . . well, then it may as well be a 90-degree angle.

You are just sideways. All the time.

Everything you do—even just standing or sleeping—requires balancing your entire body and holding on with at least one hand. You train yourself to find balance. You learn to hold on. But finding mental balance became even more of a challenge on this passage.

Passage Planning

TUESDAY–MONDAY, 6–10 SEPTEMBER 2018

While in port, we worked, explored, and spent time strategically planning each leg of the voyage. The skipper took on the lion's share of the passage planning. He carefully studied weather sources, and pored through the *Reed's Nautical Almanac* and all the paper charts required for each voyage. He determined just the right time for departure and considered the weather, wind, currents, and conditions to plan the best route.

After several days in lovely French port, we were itching to continue our voyage through the English Channel. We planned a Saturday departure at 22:00. I prepared the boat, replenished our food supplies, and cleaned the cabins. Then I fed and walked the pups, letting them play on the beach for about an hour. When I returned to *Seefalke* around 20:30, the captain told me that he had changed his mind.

Due to the tides and the almost nonexistent wind, we would have to motor sail slowly through the channel for about a day and a half. Then the wind and currents would be against us, requiring us to fight uncomfortable battles. We decided to wait a few more days for more favorable conditions.

We were busy creating a video recap of our North Sea passage for our YouTube channel and decided to film interviews to help tell the story. I got extremely emotional reliving it. I had made two critical mistakes during that passage—critical enough that I considered giving up on the entire journey. Reliving it was brutal. I could barely talk about it without bursting into tears.

The skipper told me to quit crying, which upset me more. A man who never shows emotion of any kind, the skipper had no patience with me when I cried. Empathy is an emotion the skipper was incapable of feeling, as he had proven to me many times through the years.

Living inside this grand experience, I was grateful every single day for the opportunities to challenge myself. But it was impossible to pretend that it was all sailing and sunshine all the time. Most of the time, I enjoyed it and embraced the challenges and the adventure. But sometimes it was hard.

For seasoned sailors, it's innate. It's so much a part of their soul that it comes naturally. I could understand that, but I also tried to remember that it was the hard parts that made the experience special. If it was easy, anyone could do it.

That night, the skipper told me he didn't like the video and didn't think we had an interesting story to tell. That pissed me off. The challenges I faced may not be a big deal to him or to anyone else, but it was a big deal to me. I was determined to document all of it—the good, the bad, and the ugly. It was not for YouTube or for Facebook, or even for my family and friends. It was for me. I never want to forget or discount a single emotion or experience.

Everyone has an interesting story to tell.

Day 1

TUESDAY, 11 SEPTEMBER 2018

The next morning, I felt less emotional. I took a long walk with the pups and gathered fresh fruit and vegetables. When we returned to the boat, I slipped on the concrete stairs while walking down to the floating pier. They were slippery and slimy from the earlier high tide.

I fell mostly on my bum, which is the most padded part of my body, but I also twisted my right foot forward trying to catch my fall and stubbed my big toe badly, ripping the entire nail from the flesh. It was just a toe, but damn that hurt! *How can something so small hurt so much?*

My shoe filled with blood. It was throbbing, but of course, I tried not to cry because the skipper hated it when I cried. I contained my emotion and bit my lip. I washed the bleeding flesh, bandaged it, and said a few four-letter words that would embarrass a Navy SEAL.

We decided to set sail at high tide, so we frantically began preparations.

I was not feeling well. My toe was throbbing, and now I felt rushed. We generally had more time to prepare for departure. It was chaotic and tensions were high, but we got it done. We departed at 15:30, as planned. The high water produced huge waves as we ventured back into the channel. I marveled again at the gorgeous green water—a color I still couldn't describe, but I knew I would never forget.

We fought the groundswells and the currents. Once in the open sea, it was time to put up the sails. I hoisted the main sail, but not without some struggles as the forceful winds weighted it considerably. The skipper asked me if I wanted to go to the bow to hoist the jib or hold the wheel and keep us in the wind while he did it. The currents were forceful and so was the wind, so I decided the best option was for the experienced captain to keep *Seefalke* steady while I lifted the smaller sail.

Onboard *Seefalke,* only the genoa can be manipulated from the cockpit. To maneuver any of the other sails, you had to go on deck—no matter the conditions.

I crawled onto the bow, maintaining a low center of gravity. The wind howled, and the boat rocked in all directions. We were already on at least a 20-degree tilt, so I had to position my body just right to stabilize myself with my legs while working with both hands to untie the jib ties.

I got the first two loose, but there was a huge knot in the tie that secured the jib boom. It took several minutes to untangle the knot. I finally loosened it and hoisted the jib as the boom swiftly flew over to the starboard side to join the main boom. I had to hang on with both arms and legs to keep from flying across the boat along with the sails.

I crawled back to the cockpit, feeling proud of my accomplishment. I had hoisted the main and the jib a million times, but those were extremely rough conditions. The skipper told me I did a good job, which he rarely did. That was enough to make me happy.

I felt queasy and uneasy from the extreme motion. But there was no time to catch my breath. I was instructed to hoist the mizzen—the sail located on the stern mast. That wasn't as difficult because the two other sails were cushioning the effects of the waves.

I was fighting the good fight. The skipper noticed the color was leaving my skin. He handed me Yvi's potato, which made me laugh and relieved some of my tension and uneasiness. Sometimes mind over matter is the best cure. Since it was still daylight, I took the helm at 16:00 just before sunset.

It was a beautiful afternoon, but the wind was strong. We were already on that 20-degree tilt. I battled the queasiness as the ever-challenging balancing act had already begun.

I tried to focus on the beauty that surrounded me. As the sun set, it reflected onto the gorgeous green water. It looked like the sea was filled with sparkling diamonds. As my shift ended, I wondered if I would ever see that green color again.

Day 2

WEDNESDAY, 12 SEPTEMBER 2018

I awakened at 02:00 to discover a fight against the currents. The wind was coming from one direction, but the currents were moving in a different direction—against us. That caused the waves to be confused and rocky, and the currents pushed us backward.

It was a frustrating watch because I had to tack off course to wait on the wind to shift. Per the skipper's instruction, I basically backtracked right over the course he had taken earlier in the night. It was kind of a north-to-south reverse move. It was frustrating to feel like we were working so hard but not getting anywhere.

The night was black and foggy. There was not much traffic, which helped my nerves, but it was difficult to see anything. Following my shift, I was restless, queasy, and uneasy. I cuddled with Cap'n Jack and Scout for a couple hours and tried to find the mental and physical strength to keep going.

I returned to the cockpit around noon, but I felt horrible. I tried to balance my body and mind, but it wasn't working. Around 12:30, I could feel the contents of my belly rising to my throat. I reached for the potato, but it was too late. I was pissed at myself for getting seasick, even though I knew it wasn't my fault.

I found some courage and decided that this time I was not going to let seasickness control me for the next however many days we would be at sea in those rocky conditions. Still a bit unsteady, I reached for a banana. I wanted to put something on my tummy that didn't taste like acid. I told myself, *If I'm going to be puking all day, I'm at least going to have something besides vile stomach lining coming back out.*

Then I drank some water and ate a few saltines. I tried to get my shit together—mentally and physically. Mind over matter was working, and I began to feel better. I took the next shift and convinced my mind and my body that I was fine. And unbelievably, I was.

At least, for now.

Day 3

THURSDAY, 13 SEPTEMBER 2018

It was an extremely black night but tons of stars sparkled in the sky, lighting the way. Low traffic enabled me to relax enough to listen to an audiobook. But by 06:00 I was exhausted. It was a long shift, but I wanted to let the captain sleep.

The next morning I was starving after a steady diet of gummy bears and saltines for the past couple days. It was always a challenge to cook and balance, but my galley skills were improving. I was motivated to put some real food in our bellies.

At that time, it was the farthest offshore we had been without seeing land—and the longest time. We could faintly see England to our starboard side, but only through the binoculars.

It was odd to think about the geography of the waterway. On a map, the English Channel appears very narrow compared with other bodies of water. But it is 100 nm at its widest point. When in the middle of it, all we saw was water and the horizon in our 360-degree view. The English Channel is part of the Atlantic Ocean and separates the island of Britain from northern France, joining the North Sea to the Atlantic. It is approximately 350 miles long and is one of the busiest shipping lanes on the planet.

On that day, everything was gray—the sky, the water, everything. The only color we saw that wasn't a shade of gray was *Seefalke's* bright orange body cutting through the waves at a steady 20-degree tilt. I had no idea the date on the calendar or even the day of the week. Day turned into night and night turned into day as sailed along through the magnificent and sometimes eerie English Channel.

Hurricane Helen threatened but lost momentum coming in from the Atlantic and spared us any drama.

Other than the colorless landscape, it was a beautiful day. I had a little headache, though, and squinting at the sun made it worse. My nailless toe throbbed, and my head pounded in sync with my toe. I felt feverish and congested—achy all over, like I was getting the flu.

I took another two-hour nap, but we were on such a heavy tilt I felt like I was battling to hold on the entire time. It was not restful at all. I reluctantly returned to the cockpit for my 14:00 shift. Usually, I don't mind the tilt. It means that the winds are cooperating and that we are making good speed. But at that point, I was having a really bad day. I was just pissed at the tilt.

I also wrestled with feelings about being at sea for so long. I truly did love it most of the time, but I would be lying if I said I loved it all of the time. I started to feel guilty for feeling that way. I know I just wasn't feeling well. Mentally and physically, that particular passage was taking a toll on me.

My head kept throbbing. I was frustrated with trying to stay balanced. My sore toe pressed against the end of my boot causing pain that couldn't even compete with the headache and feverish aching. My ankles hurt from the awkwardness of the balancing act. I was wrapped up in a full-on pity party and wondered what the hell I was doing out there.

I don't think the skipper ever felt like that. It was obvious that he loved it all the time; at least that's what he said and how he acted. He ignored the discomfort and the pain and seemed to enjoy the challenge and the experience. I guess I was just not there yet. I had to be honest with myself that sometimes sailing was neither comfortable nor fun for me.

I also missed companionship. I know that sounds crazy since we were together 24/7. But when sailing in shifts, I slept when he was awake and he slept when I was awake. We were like two ships that passed in the night.

While I focused on all my frustrations and discomfort, I started to think about Cheryl Strayed. I had read her book *Wild* about four years previously and had also seen the movie. She was dealing with the death of her mother, a divorce, and fighting drug addiction when she decided to punt her life and just start walking, all by herself.

She hiked 1,100 miles alone along the Pacific Crest Trail on a quest to re-start her life and find peace and contentment. It was her book that inspired me to abandon the life I was living at the time in Birmingham. I decided to sell the house I had lived in for 23 years and move to Gulf Shores. I wanted to be near the water.

The things I remember the most about her book were her struggles, not her accomplishments. She fought the demons inside herself and came out cleaner and happier on the other side. She didn't love every day of her journey. But she didn't stop. She didn't give up. She kept going.

And so would I.

Day 4

FRIDAY, 14 SEPTEMBER 2018

I decided to be strong. On my next shift, the skipper told me to wake him in two hours. I challenged myself to make it at least four.

The night was black. There were no stars. Just black—kind of like my mood. I wondered if other sailors ever felt that way—burned out on passion. Even too much of a good thing can sometimes be too much. *Right?*

I was still feverish. My face was hot, but the rest of my body had chills. I had a scratchy throat and was achy all over. But soon the stars came out and filled the clearing sky. Some were as bright as the ships on the horizon. I relaxed and breathed in the fresh salt air as the wind cooled my hot face. I was completely soothed by the sound of the waves.

I had taken my shift even though I didn't feel like it, and I was glad that I did. Just like that, I felt free and happy again.

And I remembered why I do this.

The captain took over at 04:00, and I finally got a few hours of sound sleep. I had stopped moping and whining about the bad stuff and began to embrace the good things.

We approached the end of the English Channel where the opening of the North Atlantic begins. All of a sudden, the gray water turned a vibrant, deep, navy blue. It was amazing as brilliant shades of color began to burst onto the horizon—like in *The Wizard of Oz* when everything transforms from black and white to color. Swarms of birds flew all around us, and we clearly saw the gorgeous French coastline.

The heavy waves were no longer choppy and uncomfortable. They were still about 3 m high, but they were longer, smoother, and softer. They looked like a warm blanket rolling toward us.

We cruised along relatively evenly, no longer on a 20-degree tilt. The waves were no longer lifting us out of the air and slamming us back down onto the water. Instead, they raised us ever-so-calmly and then gently set us down as if we were made of glass.

All four of us sat on the deck and rode the waves for what seemed like hours.

A school of dolphins greeted us just as we crossed the line where the English Channel ends and the open Northern Atlantic begins. They intentionally swam right toward us and then played in the wake of *Seefalke's* bow for about five minutes. The beagles howled with glee and twitched their noses in the air to enjoy all the new smells.

The dolphins were huge—at least twice the size of our hometown dolphins—and so playful. The water was deep—more than

90 m—but I could see the dolphins clearly as they swam and played underneath *Seefalke* and all around us.

Then, in an instant, as quickly as they had appeared, they swam away and disappeared into the deep blue sea. Those kinds of moments stay with you forever.

And again, I remembered why I do this.

Preparing for the Dreaded Bay of Biscay

SATURDAY, 15 SEPTEMBER 2018

We anchored outside the marina at Camaret-sur-Mer around 01:00 and crashed until about 09:30. We awoke to gorgeous scenery and another exciting new place to explore while we awaited positive weather for the Bay of Biscay crossing—easily our greatest challenge to date.

The Bay of Biscay is an extension of the Atlantic Ocean, positioned off the western coast of Europe, and it is bordered by France and Spain. The bay is known for rough seas, particularly in the winter months. During World War II, it was called the "Valley of Death" among German U-boat sailors as the Royal Air Force sank more than 70 German submarines in its waters.

When planning this voyage, I never feared crossing the Atlantic. My biggest fear was tackling the Bay of Biscay.

I dreaded it.

I agonized over the very thought of it.

Visions of what it would take to cross it haunted me. But nothing could have prepared me for the reality. I was about to find out exactly why the Bay of Biscay is the body of water that is the most feared among sailors.

CHAPTER 8

THE BAY OF BISCAY CHALLENGE

"It is good to have an end to journey toward; but it is the journey that matters in the end."—Ernest Hemingway

L ife is supposed to be about the journey, not the destination. Right? As I prepared for our passage across the infamous Bay of Biscay, I began to question that theory for the first time in five decades.

I decided to focus on the destination—Spain. I had never been there, and I had always wanted to go. Now I had the opportunity! It's the power of positive thinking. Right? I brushed up on my Spanish and imagined the pintxos and the paella, the historic sights, and the sunny beaches.

It was important to stop thinking about what it would take to get there in a tiny sailboat.

Okay, I couldn't help but think about it a little. I was terrified.

Crossing the Bay of Biscay was the only part of our worldwide sailing voyage that had me shaking in my skin. It's been called "The Valley of Death," "The Vomiting Venus," and "The Trunk of the Atlantic U-Boat Menace." Jane Russell, author of *The Atlantic*

Crossing Guide, was seasick for eight days while crossing the Bay of Biscay. That was the first thing I read when I began studying her book about a year before my own voyage.

The Bay of Biscay is a gulf located in the Celtic Sea of the northwest Atlantic Ocean between the northern coast of Spain and the western coast of France. The average depth is 1,745 m with a maximum depth of 4,890 m. In addition, there are many dangerous shallow areas. It is home to large, fierce storms during the winter months and the gruesome weather has resulted in countless shipwrecks.

Depressions enter the bay from the west. They dry out and then are born again as thunderstorms that look like hurricanes and crash into the bay. When the wind and waves come in from different directions, they collide and create confused water inside the bay. Many sailors compare the movement to a washing machine.

Huge Atlantic swells can form near the coast, making many ports inaccessible. Because of the extreme weather in winter, there are abnormally high waves at times.

Camaret-sur-Mer, Brittany, France

We sat in Brittany, France, at Camaret-sur-Mer for nine days awaiting the perfect weather window. The first few days, we enjoyed warm, sunny weather, and had a great time exploring the area.

The sweet fishing town is situated in the far northwest of France. The exposed location at the end of Crozon Peninsula has been of great military relevance for many centuries as armed guards defended the Goulet de Brest—the entrance to France's largest naval base. Remains of fortifications, batteries, and bomb craters from a range of eras can be found there.

The best view is from high atop Pointe de Pen-Hir on the mountain's edge, one of the tallest cliffs on the Brittany coast. The old French province features some of the Atlantic's most fantastic beaches that can be seen from the high leather-clad sea cliffs that plunge toward secret coves. Blue hydrangeas line a spectacular walk along the cliff's edge.

From Camaret-sur-Mer's sea wall, the Atlantic looks heavenly. In the early evening sun, the walls of the Chapelle Notre-Dame-de-Rocamadour at the end of the jetty sparkle and glow. Inside, wooden boats and life belts hang from the ceiling beams, tokens of thanks from mariners who survived perilous Atlantic crossings. In front of the church, a fishing vessel graveyard reminded me of a time when sardine fishing rather than tourism was the main source of income in the small village.

It was stormy, rainy and very windy for several days, but we hunkered down inside *Seefalke's* belly—warm, cozy and safe. I wondered if it was similar to life inside a submarine. We heard water echoing as the waves lapped against our floating home's steel hull.

We didn't go outside much during those pre-departure storms, opting instead for the dry shelter of our bright orange cocoon. Securely tied to the pier, we still rocked and swayed as if we were at sea. The angry wind howled outside.

But there was some good news...

- We had a favorable weather window, a solid passage plan that took nine days to develop, put us on a straight course to Spain, and a patient skipper who would never take any unnecessary chances.

- Our 43-foot ketch was built for this type of bluewater sailing. With its deep center cockpit, we were protected completely on all sides. Its two masts with adjustable sails in many sizes could be manipulated to cushion the blows of heavy gusts and gale-force winds.

- There was an opportunity to see cool sea wildlife since many different species of whales and dolphins live in the bay's deep waters.

I reviewed all the pros and decided maybe it wasn't wise to totally discount the journey. With exciting Spanish lands to explore on the other side, I had the opportunity to face another fear and challenge myself in ways I never thought possible. Perhaps there is joy in the journey, after all.

Preparing Mentally

The Bay of Biscay is located somewhere at the corner of your wildest dream come true and your worst possible nightmare. You dread it, and you look forward to it—all at the same time.

My excitement competed heavily with my fear—a fear I couldn't quite convince myself was not there no matter how hard I tried. The battle of conflicting emotions was like a rivalry football game that went into five overtimes.

I knew the experience would tap into every possible emotion. The physical and mental challenges were destined to deliver the ultimate sense of accomplishment. It was kind of like having a baby. Women experience brutal pain and discomfort during pregnancy and especially during childbirth. We put our bodies through extreme torture to create this tiny human who gives us so much joy.

The experience didn't even come close to the joy of motherhood. But I can tell you that it was something like that—the personal reward of making it to the end of the Bay of Biscay greatly outweighed the struggle.

Day 1

MONDAY, 24 SEPTEMBER 2018
   Departure 11:15
   Our original plan was to get through the Bay of Biscay by the end of August. Delays preparing *Seefalke* for her bluewater voyage forced us to miss that mark by a long shot. It is not recommended for small leisure craft like *Seefalke* to cross the bay in the winter months. It's not a fun time for huge heavy freighters, either. There are ships much larger and heavier than *Seefalke* sitting at the bot-

tom of the Bay of Biscay's 4,860 m deep waters. Don't think for a second that wasn't on my mind.

We were lucky. We waited patiently for nine days in the Camaret sur-Mer port in Brittany and finally found an opening—a pocket that provided northeasterly winds for four straight days pushing us on a direct course with minimal wind changes all the way down to A Coruña.

It was our best chance, and we took it.

It was magnificently beautiful as we sailed into the Celtic Sea. The sun was bright and the French coastline scenery was stunning! Waves crashed against the gorgeous rock formations along the cliffs and provided us a strong wind shadow that protected us for a short time from the open sea—a very short time.

I asked the skipper when we would officially be inside the Bay of Biscay. His response was matter-of-fact:

"You'll know it when we get there."

A school of common dolphins swam toward *Seefalke* and played with us for a long time. The waters were so calm I relaxed on the deck with the pups and took a short nap as the hot sun kissed my skin. I was completely calm. But something deep inside warned me not to expect that for long.

About an hour before sunset, the waves began to swell and the wind grew stronger. At that point, the waves rolled in from the Atlantic at only about 2 m high. But I knew it—it was obvious we were now in the Bay of Biscay. The waves rocked our 11-ton battleship forcefully from side to side, and it became immediately uncomfortable.

There was no land in sight—only the deep blue sea. We were committed—no turning back. The only option was to push forward all the way to Spain.

There was traffic, but thankfully not much. The wind was strong, steady, and blew from a favorable direction. The waves were getting larger—some were 3 m to 4 m, but they pushed us mostly from behind. The conditions were as perfect as we could possibly hope for in the Bay of Biscay in winter.

The skipper took the first watch from 20:00 to midnight. I went down into the cabin with Cap'n Jack and Scout and tried to sleep. We were on a heavy heel to the starboard side. The dogs were secure in their barricaded bunk and didn't seem interested in joining me in mine. I could tell they were a little afraid.

My regular bunk was on the port side, so there was a feeling of constant sliding down to the right. It was like trying to sleep on a very slippery, slanted block of ice. I tried to get up at one point to reposition myself at the exact moment that a huge wave rocked *Seefalke* and threw me to the other side of the cabin. I banged the back of my head on one of the wooden lockers while my shoulder blades crashed against the corner of the cabinet.

I struggled to find a comfortable position, but it wasn't easy. I buried my arm underneath the mattress to support myself from sliding and leveraged my right leg against the bunk on the opposite side of the cabin.

Nothing was flying across the cabin. But I was annoyed by the many things moving around inside the cabinets—pots and pans banging against each other, metal cans rolling, forks and spoons shuffling inside a drawer, cups and dishes clanking inside a locker.

The bay shook *Seefalke* like a martini.

Day 2

TUESDAY, 25 SEPTEMBER 2018

During my midnight shift, the sweet dream collided with a nightmare. On the one hand, it was a gorgeous evening—clear, black sky with millions of bright, sparkling stars while a full moon casted a brilliant spotlight onto the gigantic waves. I looked behind me and saw a huge wave rolling in with a couple dolphins surfing it. It was so cool!

On the other hand, it was terrifying!

I huge swell rolled toward us. My first reaction was, "Wow! That is so beautiful!" But before I could get the words out, that same wave slammed against the side of the ship's beam. Freezing saltwater drenched me, throwing me violently to the other side of the cockpit with so much force I could barely catch myself.

At least the bright moon provided enough light to warn me. I could brace myself before contact. We always wore life vests, but in those conditions, we strapped ourselves into the cockpit. For 240 straight minutes, I stood in the middle of the cockpit with my legs spread a little more than shoulder width to balance myself, and just held on as tightly as I could. It was all I could do.

Meanwhile, the skipper and the pups slept comfortably below. It was interesting how the skipper could turn off his ears to the annoying sounds. He could hear the slightest flap in the sail from a deep sound sleep, but the clankety-clanking pots and pans and silverware tossing around in the cabinets didn't bother him at all.

When I went back down at 04:00 I was exhausted. I couldn't do anything about the heavy waves and the rocking sailboat, but I decided to do something about the clankety-clanking in the cabinets. I grabbed six huge fluffy beach towels and stuffed them into the cabinets—an effort to cushion the noises that annoyed me.

I couldn't sleep comfortably on the bunk with the heavy tilt and rocking boat. So I got creative.

I threw a sleeping bag onto the floor of the narrow walkway between the two bunks and crawled onto the floor. I had both bunks to cushion the motion and to protect me from sliding in either direction. It felt like I was in a baby cradle. I could sleep without having to hold on to something, and for me, that was perfect. At some point during that shift, the pups joined me. I awoke with four velvety beagle ears tickling my face. With a little sleep, I returned to the cockpit at 08:00 for my next shift.

The waves were HUGE—some of them were 5 m high. And they were constant. Sometimes while sailing there is a period of heavy waves and then there are breaks with calm waters. We had zero breaks from the waves. They just kept coming. They varied in size, but they were always there. The wind blew at a steady 20 to 28 knots the entire time with occasional gusts of more than 30 knots.

About 30 minutes into the shift, I was amused and entertained when a few dolphins flipped around in *Seefalke's* wake. Scout came up to the cockpit for a quick potty and decided to stay with me. It was nice having her there. The pups were always such good company on those long lonely nights. Cap'n Jack and Scout are not good conversationalists, but they are great listeners!

At around 09:30, I my belly contracted. All of a sudden, I felt weak and dizzy—and nauseous. *Oh, no. Please don't let me be seasick!*

I reached for my potato with my left hand and began reciting the Greek alphabet. It's a great trick—to concentrate on something and distract the brain from the uneasiness. But it was too late. I leaned over the port side sea rail while everything inside my belly spewed forcefully. It always amazed me how the seasickness was so violent.

While leaning over the sea rail completely helpless and in misery, the massive waves continued to roll in. The wind blew forcefully at around 25 knots. I held on to the winch drum for support between heaves. I knew I had to fight. There was no way that one sailor could effectively handle the Bay of Biscay alone in those heavy conditions for two more days and two more nights. I had to keep going.

At noon, the captain awakened and was feeling as bad as me. Maybe worse. I wanted to stay in the fresh air, so I told him if he wanted to sleep some more, it was okay. I wasn't going anywhere. It was imposslible for me to leave my corner of the cockpit, or my grip on the winch drum.

He slept another hour then joined me. The fresh, cool air helped, so I tried to lie on the hard, wooden cockpit bench. But the heavy tilt made it too difficult to hang on. After two more hours, I gave up and went down to sleep in the cradle on the floor.

Each shift was more difficult.

I was green, weak, and feverish. My face was broiling hot. A whole sack of potatoes couldn't help me now. And even if they could, I couldn't let go of my grip. My arms and shoulders ached from constantly holding on as I struggled to maintain balance.

The skipper suffered, and the dogs were uncomfortable. We decided to make an adjustment and take two-hour shifts through the night because four hours was just too much for either of us in those conditions. That meant shorter spurts of sleep, but a bit less brutal for the helmsman.

For me, though, each night shift was like déjà vu all over again.

Sail, puke, sleep, repeat.

Sail, puke, sleep, repeat.

But the bright full moon continued to light our way.

Day 3

WEDNESDAY, 26 SEPTEMBER 2018

My stomach was empty. In the past 24 hours I had eaten only half a gummy bear, which I threw up before I could make an effort to eat the other half. On my next morning shift, I awoke to knotty charley horses in my calves, back spasms, and a pounding headache. I felt weak. My legs could barely support my own body weight. I knew that dehydration had set in.

I needed to eat and drink something. I slowly nibbled half a banana, half a cracker, and a few sips of water. It helped. It gave me just enough strength to throw it back up shortly after consuming it. I felt dreadful, but I knew I needed to push on.

I challenged myself and declared that no matter how bad I felt, I would not miss a shift. That became my goal and my quest. At that point, we only had one day and one night to go. We were on the home stretch.

Even while feeling so icky, I couldn't help but notice that it was such a beautiful day. Bright, clear, blue skies and an ocean as deep and vibrant blue as anything I could ever imagine. I felt miserable, but the scenery was glorious!

We continued the four-hour shifts during the day and at around 17:30, something amazing happened.

I heard a loud blowing sound that I first thought was a distant foghorn. I looked to the port side and through the gigantic waves saw a huge gray form on the surface of the water. It was at least three times the size of *Seefalke* and only about 30 m away. I only saw it for a couple of seconds and then saw a huge gray tail splash in the air. A whale!

It was magnificent, and something told me we were going to make it. The whale was a positive sign that gave me renewed energy. I didn't care that I was sick, tired, hungry, and hurting. I searched the water to steal another glimpse of the remarkable creature. But he had vanished into the depths of the deep blue sea.

I ate a whole banana, an apple, and three crackers. I drank a few sips of water. I wanted to get my strength back. I needed to find a way to embrace the challenge and make it to the other side.

Day 4

THURSDAY, 27 SEPTEMBER 2018

After another night of familiar four-hour shifts—sail, puke, sleep, repeat—I was awakened around 08:30 by an exhilarated skipper. "Get up here! I SEE LAND!"

I charged to the cockpit and almost burst into tears! It was way, way, way off in the distance. But we could see Spain! We raised the Spanish courtesy flag, and it was glorious to see it flying high on our mast. We were still about 7 hours away, but the end was in sight.

We saw beautiful birds gracefully flying overhead and grazing along the surface of the water. I thought about the old sailors who were at sea for months and even years at a time. They didn't have weather-predicting technology, GPS or other instrumentation to guide them—only a compass.

Some of them traveled with a cage of ravens. They would release one and if it circled overhead, they knew that they were not close to land. But if the raven flew in a certain direction, the sailors would follow the flying bird toward land.

More dolphins greeted us and played in *Seefalke's* wake. Within a couple of hours, after three straight days with no break from the nonstop heavy waves, the waters finally began to calm. All of a sudden, we were floating on a sea of glass. It was so clear and smooth I could see my reflection in the water.

We avoided any celebration. Sailors are very superstitious, after all. I thought about the challenge and about the adventure. As bad as it was, we had the best possible conditions we could have ever asked for during that time of year. The wind always blew from a favorable direction. We didn't have to tack or change course. The waves were behind us or beside us and never against us. The sun was always shining. We had a full moon to light our way every night. There were no storms or squalls.

I was beginning to see the positive side of things.

The captain told me he was proud of me. He doesn't hand out compliments very often. It's just not his style. That made me proud. I was proud of myself. As bad as I felt almost the entire time, I had never missed a shift.

With the calm waters, my appetite returned. We still had about four hours to go, so I cooked some pasta and veggies to fill our bellies and warm our souls. But our challenges weren't over yet.

A heavy fog rolled in. We saw a huge freighter in front of us. The top half of the gigantic ship was hidden completely by the fog. Soon, the ship disappeared from the surface of the sea completely. It just wasn't there anymore. Once again, the wonderful dream was interrupted briefly by a nightmare.

Soon the fog was all around us. We could not see the bow from the stern. Zero visibility. And worse, other ships could not see us.

We received AIS signals on the plotter that there were three ships close to us. We could hear their loud, long foghorns blowing in the distance. We could tell one was in front of us and two were off to the starboard side. But we couldn't see them at all. We had no idea the distance between us. They blasted long horn signals, and we responded with our own blasts.

If there is restricted visibility, ships are required to blast their horn every two minutes. While using the motor, the signal required is a long, eight-second blast. While under sail, the signal is one long blast followed by two short blasts.

Soon the fog lifted, and we could see clearly again. The Spanish coastline came into focus, bursting with vibrant color.

That's the thing about nightmares. You eventually wake up from them. The nightmare was now over and the dream of making it through the Bay of Biscay was a reality.

I'm glad we did it. I felt and still feel an incredible sense of accomplishment. But I'm not sure I ever want to birth a Bay of Biscay baby ever again!

At least that's how I feel today. Ask me again tomorrow, and the answer may be different.

We settled into the sweet little village of A Coruña, replenished supplies, and anticipated some beachside cruising around the Spanish Atlantic coast on our way to Morocco. Finally, maybe I would get a taste of the bikini and martini sailing life for a change.

CHAPTER 9

ANCHORAGE HOPPING THE SPANISH ATLANTIC COAST

A dventure comes in all shapes and sizes. It can be dramatic or poetic, heart pounding or profound. It can be all of the above or something totally and completely unexpected.

And sometimes, it's the simple things.

I felt worn out—mentally and physically—after the grueling passage across the Bay of Biscay. I needed to take a breath.

We decided to take one week to rest and explore A Coruña and then set sail for some light anchorage hopping along the unbelievably picturesque Spanish Atlantic coast. I craved some peaceful, easy-feeling vibes to help me recover from the heavy offshore sailing.

Cap'n Jack and Scout also looked a bit ragged, and even though he would never admit it, the skipper also showed signs of wear and tear.

I looked forward to finding adventure in just sitting at anchorage . . . rowing to private beaches . . . watching the dogs play as the sun set over the brilliant blue Atlantic Ocean . . . listening to the sound of nothing—nothing but the hypnotic waves and the wind.

We had outrun the northern European winter and were now in warm, sunny Spain. It was time to enjoy the reward of all that heavy offshore sailing—a few days of gentle weather with drama-free day sailing to magnificent anchorages and private beaches along the unbelievably gorgeous coast of Spain.

A Coruña, Spain

27 SEPTEMBER–3 OCTOBER 2018

A Coruña is known for its Roman lighthouse—the Tower of Hercules, which has been in operation since possibly the 2nd century AD. A statue of Maria Pita, the local heroine, is the centerpiece of the city center plaza. She led the defense of Coruña during an invasion by Sir Frances Drake and the English Armada in the 16th century. In the heat of battle, she wielded her dead husband's spear and cried, "Those with honor, follow me!"

Unlike many of the other ports we had visited, A Coruña is a large, industrial city with a huge artist community and tons of touristy restaurants, shops, cafes, and bars in the city's center. There was a private beach near our marina that was perfect for unleashing the hounds.

The former captain of *Seefalke*, Helmut Hombergs, was traveling alone in his RV through Spain and decided to meet us in A Coruña. He is a salty sailor who spent many years as *Seefalke's* skipper while it was the crown jewel of the VBS sailing club in Bremen, Germany.

Helmut joined us for dinner almost every night that week and one evening treated us to delicious homemade Finnish fish soup in his tiny RV. I found his company delightful. For the longest time, the skipper tried to convince me that all Germans are stoic and unsympathetic. But the more Germans I spent time with, the more I realized that those adjectives are reserved for individual personalities, no matter their homeland or culture.

Helmut was the antithesis of the skipper. He was kind and complimentary, empathetic and compassionate. He told me I should be proud of my accomplishments and shared tales of many experienced, skilled sailors he knew who refused to sail at night because of the danger.

He talked about his sailing comrades who would do anything to avoid a passage through the Bay of Biscay. He admitted that he often fought seasickness in heavy offshore conditions. He reassured me that it was nothing for which I should be ashamed and rather a rite of passage for sailors.

Most evenings I was on a quest for authentic Spanish paella. I had craved it since we landed in Spain, but we couldn't find any restaurants that served it. We did, however, enjoy an amazing baked fish one evening. I can't remember the name of it, but it was native to Galician waters and was outstanding. The freshest fish I had ever tasted, I believe it came out of the Atlantic just hours before we ate it.

We spent time working, resting, and as usual, performing boat maintenance on *Seefalke*. She was in surprisingly great shape—even after the torturous passage through Biscay. I patched her wound from the North Sea offshore buoy by using liquid steel and lots of bright orange paint.

We enjoyed the time off, but by week's end, we were ready to set sail again.

Private Beach Praia do Osmo

WEDNESDAY, 3 OCTOBER 2018
We departed for an island-hopping adventure and spent most of the first day under sail. However, because of very light wind, we also had to motor sail at times. It was refreshing and fantastic to be back on the water—especially in the light, relaxing conditions.

It was my kind of sailing. The skipper loved the challenges of heavy offshore sailing, but I needed a break.

We enjoyed the gorgeous Spanish coastline, which was filled with splashes of vibrant color and interesting architecture. We sailed 37.9 nautical miles in just less than eight hours and found a private anchorage with a secluded beach at Praia do Osmo. We secured *Seefalke* and then pumped up our little red dinghy, *Nela*.

There was barely enough room for one person, much less two people and two dogs. But we engineered the puppy crane to lower the dogs into the tiny dinghy. Scout appeared to love the adventure—her tail wagged the entire time. However, Cap'n Jack was not too happy about it. He moaned and groaned like a grumpy old man.

Once the other three were secure on *Nela*, then I climbed in. That presented a completely new challenge as we tried to keep the dinghy balanced. Somehow, I got onboard without tipping everyone else over. It was crowded—we were all on top of each other.

Then the skipper tried rowing the heavily over-weighted *Nela* to shore. He had to row backward—the opposite direction of how the raft was designed. It was hysterical. We belly laughed all the way to the beach, and I realized it was the first time I had laughed like that since we left Stralsund.

The dogs were in heaven. They chased each other and played on the beach as the sun set over the water. It was exactly the simple adventure I needed. I played with the dogs for a while, but then I stopped for a minute and glanced at the smooth sea. I smelled the salt in the air and heard the faint sound of the light waves washing ashore onto the golden sand.

The sun kissed the water and painted the sky with bright magenta and purple hues. The beauty overwhelmed me. I took a deep breath and felt completely relaxed for the first time since we had set sail in August.

It was a romantic setting, one that I had spent months dreaming about.

We were all alone on the secluded beach. From where I was standing, I could only see the black silhouette of the skipper against the backdrop of the glorious sunset. He was standing about 50 yards away from me near the dinghy.

I slowly walked toward him, feeling amorous and hoping to steal a romantic moment. In our furious and stressful efforts to make it across the brutal northern European coastline, there had been no time or opportunity for romance.

I wanted to sit on the beach and cuddle and kiss and enjoy the sunset together while the dogs played around us. I desperately needed to find comfort in the arms of the man I loved.

He turned toward me, but didn't see me.

As I approached, he was no longer just a black silhouette. The details of his face became illuminated by the dim, blue light from his phone. He was completely engaged with his screen—texting and smiling. It was the kind of smile that happens unconsciously when something makes you truly feel special and happy inside.

I had seen that smile before. But this time, I knew it had nothing to do with me, or the dogs, or this voyage.

I asked him who he was texting. Without looking at me or removing the sly grin from his face, he flippantly told me it was work emails.

Deep down, I knew better. I had been the skipper's victim of betrayal before. I felt my heart drop as my eyes filled with water.

Was it possible that he would share such a romantic moment with someone else? Would he let me go through the seasickness, exhaustion, hard labor, dehydration, and fear on all those dangerous sailing passages and still be thinking of other women?

I knew it was possible, but I convinced myself I was overreacting. He was a master of manipulation. He had a special skill for gaslighting and for convincing me that what I could clearly see with my own eyes was just my imagination.

And this time, convincing myself was easy because I didn't want to believe it.

He was on the voyage with me. He was sharing with me the thing he loves the most—his passion for sailing. He was bringing his precious boat to Alabama to live with me and build a life there together. He couldn't possibly be thinking of someone else. Right?

I knew that to press him for details would only end in a fight. Or worse, he would inflict the silent treatment on me—a torture I could not bear after such a happy day.

I convinced myself it was nothing—just work emails, as he said. Work emails that put a smile on his face that I had not seen in months. Rather than force a romantic interlude that clearly did not interest him, I loaded the dogs onto *Nela* and waited for him.

He took his time.

He finally finished his text conversation and then without saying a word, he climbed onboard the tiny raft and rowed us all back to *Seefalke.*

Even though he was lying next to me in the bunk that evening, I felt all alone.

Ria de Corcubion at Praia de Quenxe

THURSDAY, 4 OCTOBER 2018

We slept in, had coffee and a light breakfast, and then prepared *Seefalke* for departure. It was another day of light sailing with some motor sailing and even more tremendous appreciation for the gorgeous scenery that surrounded us.

On our way to a semi-private anchorage in Ria de Corcubion at Praia de Quenxe, a wide inlet which opens to the south from Finisterre, we passed a famous lighthouse. The Romans believed Cabo Finisterre was the end of the world (finis = end, terrae = of the earth). It is believed by many to be the westernmost point of the Iberian Peninsula.

Cabo da Roca in Portugal is about 10.3 miles farther west. Monte do Facho is the mountain on Cape Finisterre, which has a peak of 781 ft above sea level. Most of the beaches in that area are framed by steep cliffs. Several rocks are associated with religious legends, such as the "holy stones," the "stained wine stones," the "stone chair," and the tomb of the Celtic crone-goddess, Orcabella.

After sailing 21.5 nautical miles in 9.5 hours with hardly any wind, we arrived at our anchorage after sunset. We secured *Seefalke*, had a light dinner, and went to sleep.

Ria de Muros at Praia de Aguieira

FRIDAY, 5 OCTOBER 2018

The next morning, the skipper wanted to work. With a European phone, he generally had internet wherever we were. With my U.S. -based phone, I rarely had internet connection and felt completely isolated from family and friends and was unable to do much work.

But I didn't want to sit on the boat and watch him work when there was another spectacular, semi-private beach about 100 yards away from the anchorage. I rigged the puppy crane, loaded up *Nela*, and rowed toward the beach—this time with one less human on board. It wasn't easy to row to shore. I needed a kayak paddle to handle the dinghy. Or better yet, a small outboard motor.

It was hard work, but worth the effort when we got to the beach. The dogs ran and played and dug deep holes in the sand for about an hour. I looked out at the boat and saw the skipper waving for us to return. We boarded *Nela* and rowed back to *Seefalke*.

We hoisted the anchor and set sail again toward Ria de Muros at Praia de Aguieira. This time we had some wind and were able to make our way under sail most of the day—traveling 21.5 nautical miles in 4.5 hours.

During the day, we talked about the difference between this type of sailing and the kind of sailing we had experienced since we left Stralsund. We agreed that this was about as close to bikini and martini sailing as we would get.

We made it to our anchorage around 18:30 and once again lowered the puppies onto *Nela*. We rowed to shore and let them frolic on another gorgeous semi-private beach with fantastic views. I loved the slower lifestyle. I wanted more of that casual, relaxed anchorage hopping.

But the skipper booked a flight to Germany. He said it was for work, and I believed him.

Sailing Passage to Vigo, Spain

SATURDAY, 6 OCTOBER 2018
Departure 07:45
Because of the skipper's flight, we set sail at 07:45. We needed to make it to Vigo by nightfall. He was scheduled to travel to Madrid and then to Germany early the next day. That was the first day in a week that we were on a time schedule of any kind.

I did not look forward to spending a week all alone on the boat. But my adventurous spirit took over, and I reminded myself that I love to explore new places. Perhaps the newness of Vigo would provide a much-needed distraction. We were treated to more good weather and favorable winds—sailing 47.3 nautical miles in about 10 hours to our destination—Marina Davila in Vigo, Spain.

As we settled in at the marina in Vigo, the skipper packed for his flight. I asked him about the work schedule for the trip. He was aloof. I knew I would not hear from him much while he was gone. I wanted to ask him who he was planning to spend time with, but I didn't. I knew whatever he said would probably be a lie anyway. He would never reveal his secrets.

A part of me didn't want to know. I tried to bury my suspicions and focus on work while spending the next week all alone in Vigo. But I had no ideaI that an unexpected visitor was on the way—a hurricane named Leslie.

CHAPTER 10

A NAUTICAL SPIDERWEB

It seemed strange to be on the boat all alone. Cap'n Jack and Scout were great company, but I missed human companionship. It was especially lonely because we moored the boat at the front entrance of the marina, and there were no other boats anywhere near our berth. It was about a half mile walk to the marina facilities.

I focused on work and performed my in-port chores. At one point I caught a little bit of internet signal and decided to FaceTime my best friend, Trisha. We had been friends for almost 30 years. She took care of my condo in my absence and managed the Airbnb rentals that subsidized my income. But I didn't want to talk business. I needed a friend.

I put on a happy face and told her about the anchorage hopping and about how much fun we were having on the voyage. I told her the dogs were happy and mentioned that the skipper was away on business. I tried to hide my disappointment, but best friends always see through the bullshit.

Concerned, she asked me if I was okay. I told her I was homesick and missed my friends and family, especially my kids. But I maintained that I was happy and tried to convince her while simultaneously trying to convince myself. Always supportive, she told me to call anytime. She meant it.

Meanwhile, there was an unexpected repair for *Seefalke*. Cap'n Jack had chewed up one of the cables of an on-deck solar panel. I had always been handy but generally avoided anything electric. I needed an electrician to help with this repair. As I walked toward the marina office to see if they had any recommendations, a white van with the word "electricista" emblazoned on the side just happened to pass by. I couldn't believe my luck.

I flagged the guy down and told him in very broken, very rusty Spanish about my problem. People often make fun of me when I try to "speak Europe" with my heavy Southern accent. But sometimes I was able to get the message across.

My high school and college Spanish was slowly coming back to me as I tried to communicate with the locals. David, the electricista, said he would return mañana (tomorrow) to take a look at the chewed-up cables. Of course, he never returned. So much for my southern-charm-mixed-with-a-little-rusty-Spanish approach. The next day I was able to find the marina electrician, Rafa, and he repaired the cable in about 20 minutes.

Meanwhile, the pups and I ventured out to explore. Vigo sits on Spain's northwest coast. The mouth of the nearby Vigo Estuary is sheltered by the Cíes Islands, which form part of the Atlantic islands national park. The Cíes are known for their rich birdlife and the crescent-shaped Playa de Rodas. The city's old quarter is home to the neoclassical Church of Santa María.

I was still on the so-far-unsuccessful hunt for paella. I walked to the fresh fruit and vegetable market every day and enjoyed the gigantic eggplants, papaya, bananas, and huge portobella mushrooms.

On Monday it was Columbus Day—which made me think about Christopher Columbus and how we were on the exact same route that he took to America. Columbus led his three ships out of the Spanish port of Palos on August 3, 1492. His objective was to sail west until he reached Asia (the Indies), where the riches of gold, pearls, and spice awaited. His first stop was the Canary Islands, where the lack of wind left his expedition becalmed until September 6.

Once underway, Columbus benefited from calm seas and steady winds that pushed him steadily westward. Columbus had discovered the southern "trade winds" that would later fuel the sailing ships carrying goods to the New World. However, the trip was long—much longer than anticipated by either Columbus or his crew. To mollify his crew's apprehensions, Columbus kept two sets of logs—one showing the true distance traveled each day and one showing a lesser distance. The first log was kept secret. The latter log quieted the crew's anxiety by under-reporting the true distance they had traveled from their homeland.

This deception only worked temporarily. By October 10, the crew's apprehension had increased to the point of near mutiny. Columbus headed off disaster by promising his crew that if land was not sighted in two days, they would return home. They found land the next day.

We had timed our route so that we could hopefully benefit from the same trade winds that Columbus had used to his advantage. Ideally, the trade winds would push us from the Canaries all the way to the Caribbean. We were on schedule to make that 20-to-40-day crossing beginning in December.

The rest of the week I stayed busy with work for my clients. I wrote about a dozen articles. I tried to find distractions from thoughts of what the skipper was doing in Madrid or Germany or wherever he was. He checked in a few times, but not every day.

I never understood that about him. We were in a long-distance relationship for many years—separated by 5,000 miles and 7 hours—and he refused to contact me every day. I had a simple request—tell me "good morning" and "good night" every day. It was okay with me if that communication came in the form of a text message. It couldn't possibly take more than five seconds to text someone you love once in the morning and once in the evening, but he always refused.

I questioned him about why he wouldn't do it. His answer: "Because you asked me to."

I was in communication with American sailing friends Molly and Baxter, who were on our same route. We had met them in A Coruña, and I often asked Molly for advice because she was a much more experienced sailor than me. They happened to be in Vigo at that time, but they were in a marina on the other side of the city—about 20 miles away.

Neither of us had cars, of course, so getting to them was no easy task. We tried to connect a few times while we were all out exploring the city, but it never worked out. I was disappointed. I was lonely.

Toward the end of the week, the sky became black and huge gusts of wind attacked the marina. Our berth was exposed to the open Atlantic—sending gigantic swells and heavy wind right onto *Seefalke*. I heard on the radio that we were expecting company—Hurricane Leslie.

Single-Handed Hurricane Prep

THURSDAY, 11 OCTOBER 2018

Molly and Baxter asked if I wanted to move *Seefalke* to their marina, which was better protected from the oncoming storm. They offered to help me move the ship. I wanted to accept their assistance, so I contacted the skipper. He said no. He didn't want anyone else operating his boat.

I was afraid. But I didn't feel comfortable moving the ship by myself in the heavy conditions. Instead, I worked hard to try and safely secure the boat. I pulled out every line I could find and created a rope barrier around *Seefalke*, attaching her to every available cleat on the piers on either side of us.

It was a long night. Heavy wind and rain had already made an appearance on the western Spanish coastline. Even though the dogs and I were in port, the boat rocked and rolled as if we were at sea. I probably checked on the lines and the fenders about 15 times during the night—each time getting drenched from the soaking rain.

The little sleep I did get was tainted with nightmares about the boat coming untied, or a line snapping. I worried that if *Seefalke* came loose, I would not be able to maneuver her back into the slip by myself. I kept tying more lines until *Seefalke* looked like she had been captured in some sort of nautical spiderweb.

I was afraid, lonely, and homesick. It had been almost two months since we departed from Stralsund and almost three months since I had set foot on U.S. soil.

I felt so alone.

FRIDAY–SATURDAY, 12–13 OCTOBER 2018

Friday was more of the same as Hurricane Leslie was fast approaching the coast of Spain and Portugal from the Atlantic. Our safe harbor was exposed to the Atlantic, and harsh winds rocked *Seefalke* all day and all night. The pups and I stayed hunkered down in the safety of our orange, steel cocoon. Before sundown, I double checked all the sails to make sure they were secured and could not be hoisted by the heavy wind.

I also provided extra protection for the booms to be sure they were secure and stable. The main sail was full of gallons of rainwater, so I assumed the extra weight would prevent even forceful winds from blowing it open. The spiderweb protecting *Seefalke* expanded when I found more lines inside the ship's many compartments.

After another sleepless night, I begged the skipper to return to Vigo on Saturday rather than waiting until Monday. He agreed but pointed out that it was only to protect the ship. I was an adult, he reminded me, and capable of taking care of myself.

His flight landed in Porto around 18:00, but it was slightly delayed so he missed the connecting train to Vigo. He booked a rental car and drove the 1.5 hours to Vigo and arrived around 22:00. Rather than greeting me with a hug and asking how I was, he immediately reorganized the spiderweb I had created around

Seefalke, and made sure I knew that the work I had done to secure the boat was not good enough.

On Saturday night we experienced much less motion than the previous two nights. The spiderweb kept us protected. And while there was not much companionship or compassion from the skipper, I was glad he was there.

We awoke Sunday morning to news about Leslie's landfall. It was the strongest storm to strike the Iberian Peninsula since 1842. She swept across the coastal areas packing winds of more than 170 km per hour. The strong winds brought down trees, cutting power to more than 15,000 homes, and more than 30 flights were canceled. It could have been much worse, and we were certainly lucky to miss all the more serious action. Still, our immediate aftermath left plenty to clean, reorganize, and repair.

Monday, we awoke early. Since we still had the rental car, we decided to do some provisioning. We drove into Vigo's city center and loaded the car with groceries and supplies. Later that afternoon, we took a little road trip to return the rental car back to the airport.

We drove along the coast of Spain into Porto. It was bizarre to be traveling by car rather than by boat. It had been a long time since I had been in a car. We enjoyed the scenery with miles and miles of vineyards lining the back road along the coast of Portugal.

The dogs were in the back of the car, and at one point they tried to frantically climb into the front with us. We stopped on the side of the road and pushed them back into the rear. Cap'n Jack reeked of nasty-smelling shellfish. It didn't surprise me because I had been fighting to keep the pups away from all the clams and mussel shells along Vigo's pier all week. More than a few of those shells made it into the beagles' bellies. Those crazy pups would eat anything.

About five minutes later, we stopped again to fill the rental car with gas. The pups escaped into the front again, and that is when we discovered the vomit all over the back that was mostly a mixture of stinky broken shells.

I went into the gas station in search of cleaning supplies. I found paper towels in the washroom, baby wipes, and one of those pine tree-shaped car fresheners. I did the best I could to clean up the mess, but I couldn't do much about the smell.

We believe the puppies were car sick, which we also found to be bizarre. They survived all those dangerous sailing passages without getting seasick. How was it possible that they would puke their guts out in a regular car?

We arrived at the rental car place, where the smell did not go unnoticed. Fortunately, the ladies there responded to the skipper's charm combined with the two sweet beagle faces and gave us a break on the cleaning fee. We took the shuttle to the airport where we caught the train to the main station and then boarded a train back to Vigo. On the train, the motion sickness continued for poor Cap'n Jack and Scout.

We made it back to Vigo around 22:00 and prepared for departure to Porto the next morning. That was when the skipper told me he had booked another flight—from Lisbon, our next destination after Porto.

This time I resisted. I asked him not to go.

"I have to work," he stated. He was going to Alabama for a project installation. Even though he had a colleague who would be there, he felt a need to go.

"I can understand that, but I need to work, too," I told him. "And I would like to see my children."

"So, go," he said unsympathetically, without even looking at me.

There were two problems. First, I had dumped my entire life's savings into the sailing voyage and every dime I made working was spent on mortgage and expenses for the condo in Gulf Shores, along with college tuition and other fees for my son. I had no money for a flight. Secondly, if the skipper went away and I went home, who would take care of the dogs and the boat?

I felt trapped. The skipper would leave me alone again just as soon as we made it to another port. I complained, but his only response was, "Toughen up. You are a sailor. This is not for sissies."

I found that ironic since I had been roughing it on the boat while he was staying in five-star hotels with a comfy bed, hot shower, high-speed WiFi, television, nice restaurants, and all the other modern conveniences that I was sacrificing—including human companionship.

But I had no options. His flight was booked, and as soon as we made it to Lisbon, he would leave me alone again.

CHAPTER 11

UNDERWATER FIREWORKS

PASSAGES TO PORTO & LISBON

After a week alone at port in Vigo, I was ready to get back to sea. I think even Cap'n Jack and Scout got excited when they saw us preparing *Seefalke* for departure. But first, after I struggled to row the dinghy to shore, the skipper purchased a small outboard motor for *Nela*. I was ecstatic! At midmorning, we loaded the new motor onboard and secured it on *Seefalke*.

TUESDAY, 16 OCTOBER 2018

We set sail for Porto—a 20-hour passage. The plan was to arrive during high water the next morning. It was a beautiful, sunny, warm afternoon, so on our way we decided to take a little detour and check out Playa de Rodas, one of the most beautiful beaches in the world. It did not disappoint.

We anchored about 50 m from the shore. The beaches were sugary white, which reminded me of home on Alabama's Gulf Coast. The water was crystal clear with a brilliant turquoise hue. We didn't have time to get out the dinghy and test the new motor. I think the pups were disappointed because they could see the beach but couldn't get off the boat.

But unfortunately, we had a deadline. The skipper was scheduled to travel to the U.S. from Lisbon five days later. After about an hour of enjoying the incredible beach scenery and serenity, we pulled in the hook and got back on course toward Porto.

I took the 18:00 shift that evening and was immediately greeted by a large school of common dolphins. This time, there were so many I could barely see them all. I hopped from port to starboard to watch them play and frolic alongside *Seefalke*. The pups ran from side to side of the cockpit with me as the playful mammals showed off their incredible athleticism.

At sunset, I enjoyed the most brilliant colors. To the starboard side, a deep, blood red on the horizon faded into an orange as bright as *Seefalke*. The colors kissed the electric blue water as dolphins swam alongside us. To the port side, the sky above the mountains on the coastline was pink with baby blue highlights. The water was silvery gray.

It was spectacular, but I wished I was not alone and had someone to share it with me.

As the night faded to black, there was an amazingly bright crescent-shaped moon lighting the way. The light danced off the water, and the dolphins joined us as we skimmed along in the peaceful night. Then the skipper took over, and I slept. We continued to be two ships that passed in the night.

Bioluminescent Dolphins

WEDNESDAY, 17 OCTOBER 2018

Humorist James Thurber once wrote: "There are two kinds of light—the glow that illuminates and the glare that obscures."

I thought of that as I looked into the water and discovered something I had heard about and read about but had never seen with my own eyes—the quiet glow of bioluminescence.

Bioluminescent tides exist in many locations throughout the world—generally caused by algae suspended in the water. The algae, or plankton, emits a glow whenever it is jostled. The jostling can be caused by tides rolling in, the breaking of waves, the motion of a boat, or fish moving through the water. In this case, it was the water skimming alongside *Seefalke's* hull and our unbelievably playful dolphin friends who were determined to keep us company throughout that entire passage.

In daylight, we could see the dolphins swimming in the clear Atlantic water. But something magical was happening that evening. With the bioluminescence in action, it looked as if we were in a 1970s discotheque with a black light shining directly on the dolphins.

They took deep dives and made magnificent jumps. They rolled and spinned through the water like Olympic divers. It was like watching underwater shooting stars bursting through the sea.

I hung over the side of *Seefalke* and watched them for at least two solid hours. I completely lost track of time and was mesmerized by the underwater fireworks show. The glowing dolphins kept me company the entire shift. Soon, the sun began to rise, and the flashes of bursting neon light faded away.

It was a dull, foggy morning, and as we approached Leixoes marina, a small fisherman's port, swarms of birds hovered over every fishing boat. It was eerie, like a scene from an Alfred Hitchcock movie.

We slowly motored into the marina, but there were no spots available. I could feel the ghosts of fishermen past all around me, but they were not inviting us in. There was no room for us there.

We sailed another 7 nm to the next port, Douro Marina, where we easily found a spot and settled in. It was a nice marina, and the staff showed us all kinds of fun things to do in Porto. But we were on a deadline.

We continued to check the weather. If we stayed, it was possible we wouldn't make it to Lisbon in time for the skipper's flight. We began to consider the possibility of skipping Porto and heading on toward Lisbon the next morning.

Sailing to Lisbon

THURSDAY–FRIDAY, 18–19 OCTOBER 2018

I awoke Thursday morning with a bad headache. Because I didn't feel well and the weather was sketchy, we continuously changed our minds about whether to set sail for Lisbon that day as planned. I took a long nap to hopefully sleep off the headache while the skipper prepared *Seefalke*, just in case.

We finally made a decision to leave around 15:00, but heavy winds in the marina made our departure maneuver tricky. A couple of salty Danish sailors sensed our dilemma and offered to help us back out of our slip. They also told us that the harbor master could give us a tow. We decided to accept the latter so that we could make our way toward Lisbon, which we knew would take about two days and two nights from Porto. The harbor master showed up in a souped-up dinghy with a powerful motor. He pulled us out of our narrow mooring slip, then slung us out into the open water.

The sailing was good that day—there was heavy wind behind us and large swelling waves pushed us forward. It was uneventful except for when we accidentally dumped the mizzen stay sail into the sea when the halyard popped loose. We were able to pull in the sail, but we couldn't use it anymore until we re-rigged the halyard. Even without the mizzen stay sail, *Seefalke* had many sails, and we had strong wind with huge rolling waves to propel us on our passage.

A Different Perspective

My struggles with the heavy, high offshore waves continued. On Friday morning, I paid the price again. After a short but memorable seasickness session, I grabbed my potato and willed myself to get better quickly. I forced myself to eat something. I had decided that apples taste about the same coming up as they do going down, so I nibbled away at a big red one and tried to quickly replenish and rehydrate. Fortunately, I fought it off.

By midday, we cruised over Nazaré Canyon and hoped to see some whales in that area. No luck, but it was kind of crazy to think that we were sailing over the top of a hole as deep as the Grand Canyon. My perspective of space widened and deepened intensely.

By 21:00, the full moon was illuminated with a bright orange/red halo around it. I had never seen anything like it. I later learned that halos around the sun or moon are caused by high, thin cirrus clouds drifting high above your head. Tiny ice crystals in the Earth's atmosphere create the halos by refracting and reflecting the light. The crystals have to be oriented and positioned "just so" with respect to your own eye in order for the halo to appear.

I learned that this is why, like rainbows, halos around the sun or moon are personal. Everyone sees their own particular halo, made by their own particular ice crystals, which are different from the ice crystals making the halo of the person standing next to you. I like the idea that these phenomena that we see at sea are *personal*—just as the sailing experience is personal. How remarkable to know that what I saw at night while at sea was intimately special—and just for me.

Whether your passion is sailing, or something else, perhaps you have experienced that personal nirvana that makes you continue to want and need the next special experience. I believe that is what makes your passion a part of your heart and soul and not just a hobby.

Arrival in Lisbon

SATURDAY–SUNDAY, 20–21 OCTOBER 2018

We awoke in Cascais, a city in the greater Lisbon region of Portugal on the Portuguese Riviera. We dropped the anchor to wait on high water. A couple hours later we cruised into the heart of

Lisbon and moored at the Parque das Nações (park of the nations) Marina, which was a five-minute drive to the airport.

We spent all day Sunday doing boat chores and laundry, and then we walked along the promenade and found some delicious Portuguese food. We took a quick ride on the gondola (Telecabine Lisboa) which was built in 1998 for the World Expo. Cap'n Jack and Scout loved it—especially Scout, who always wants to see everything! It was amazing how they had become such world travelers and were not afraid of any form of transportation.

The next day, the skipper boarded another plane, and I found myself all alone in Lisbon, Portugal. But I wasn't alone for long. Soon, I was surrounded by the ghosts that had been haunting me for years.

CHAPTER 12

SURROUNDED BY GHOSTS IN LISBON

22–28 OCTOBER 2018

Before sunrise, the skipper took a cab to the airport. I was disappointed to be alone again, but it was crucial that I focused on work. I had seven articles to complete, one with a critical deadline by week's end.

When the pups and I awoke, my laptop would not turn on. I called the Apple technical support line, and they walked me through several options, but no luck. It was dead. I quickly researched Apple repair shops in Lisbon. Fortunately, we were in a large city. The pups and I took a cab into the city center and found a place to inspect my laptop. One of the technicians spoke English and delivered the bad news.

The motherboard needed to be replaced. It would cost 700 Euros and five working days to repair it. The laptop was old, and I could get a brand-new one for just a little more than that in the U.S. By that time, the skipper had arrived in Alabama, and since electronics in the U.S. are significantly cheaper than in Europe, we agreed that he would purchase a new computer and bring it back to me in a week. Meanwhile, he had an old laptop onboard that I would use temporarily.

But when I returned to *Seefalke* and logged on, I uncovered mysteries that had haunted me for years. As photos, letters, and emails flashed onto the screen, my stomach felt as uneasy as it did while sailing the Bay of Biscay.

In fact, it was worse.

My mind drifted back to the fall of 2015.

The skipper and I had been together for two years. And while the relationship wasn't perfect, I was happy and in love. I trusted him completely and was excited about what the future held for us as we dreamed of sailing together forever.

There was a time back then when he was acting distant and disengaged. I wasn't sure why. He was not one to reveal much emotion. One day, he announced that he was going to Kaliningrad, Russia for the weekend for business. I was suspicious. *Why so urgent? Business on the weekend? Kaliningrad?*

Something didn't feel right. He went on the trip as planned, and I didn't hear from him at all for four days. Not one message. That was not completely unusual, but this time I could tell he was avoiding me and not just in one of his moods.

I tried to wipe any upsetting thoughts from my mind.

The next week he traveled to the U.S. to join me for a trade show in Chicago. He stayed with me in Birmingham for a few days before the conference. During that trip, he spent every waking moment on his phone and on his computer. Even though we had intimate, passionate evenings as usual, he was completely distracted during the day. We traveled to Chicago, where he spent most of the time in the hotel. He said he didn't feel well. I worked the trade show and was extremely busy during the three-day conference.

When we returned to Alabama, I could no longer keep my suspicions inside. I directly asked him what happened in Kaliningrad. He refused to respond and tortured me with his cruel silent treatment. While he sat in silence, I grabbed his phone and opened it while he stared catatonically at nothing.

I opened his messages and found the name of a Russian girl—Julia. I began to scroll. The messages were in Russian, but I could tell from the kissy-face emojis that this was not a business conversation. As I got deeper into the messages, photos began to appear—selfies of a beautiful young woman in her mid-20s with dark eyes and dark hair. There were also selfies of her posing cheek-to-cheek with the skipper.

He grabbed the phone and threatened to leave.

I stood my ground. I asked him again directly. "Did you have an affair? Did you have sex with this woman? Did you go to Kaliningrad specifically to see her?"

He emphatically denied every question, insisting it was all business.

Manipulation is an art that requires masterful gaslighting. The skipper is the gaslighting equivalent of Picasso. He brushed the strokes carefully, calling me a stupid and uncultured American who couldn't possibly understand the European way. It's perfectly natural to flirt with business colleagues, he told me. He insisted it was a common European sales technique.

He was convincing. I bought it.

But the feeling in my gut didn't go away.

A few weeks later, I traveled to Gulf Shores to visit Trisha. We relaxed on the beach, and I told her how happy I was in my relationship. I told her of our many adventures and exotic romantic rendezvous all over the world. But, as I mentioned before, best friends can see through the bullshit.

I confessed that I had suspicions about the young, beautiful Russian girl. I wanted to believe the man I loved. I wanted to believe that he would never cheat on me. Even more important,

I wanted to believe he wouldn't lie to me. But deep down, I didn't trust him.

A couple days later, Trisha and I joined my sister-in-law, Pam, who was vacationing on the Gulf with friends. I tried to distract myself with fun girlfriend time. But I was too upset. I didn't join them on their night out, and instead remained alone at the hotel all night trying to reach the skipper. He was in Berlin with friends and refused to take my calls or answer my texts. The next morning, he told me he had lost his phone.

Then the skipper did something that has become his modus operandi. Knowing that I was suspicious and upset, he distracted me with an invitation to join him in Toronto the next week for a business trip. He said we could take a romantic side trip to Niagara Falls. That excited me and quelled my suspicions of infidelity. His son joined us, and I spent the entire weekend babysitting the teenager while the skipper was glued to his phone and alone in the hotel.

It was a few months later when I discovered evidence of the truth. We had been fighting for weeks as I felt more and more uncomfortable about my suspicions. He agreed to travel to Alabama to join my family for Thanksgiving in Guntersville.

He was distracted by his phone, even while having coffee with my mom on the deck, which annoyed and angered me. I asked him to at least put the phone away when my parents were in the room. After dinner, we all watched *Christmas Vacation* together in the living room. He escaped into the bedroom, and I saw his phone sitting on the side table next to the sofa.

I couldn't help myself. I grabbed the phone and locked myself in the bathroom.

I am not proud of this. I know it was wrong. I know it was an invasion of privacy. But I had to know. I am only human, after all.

I easily unlocked the phone and went straight to the text conversation with Julia. That's when I discovered the truth that I already knew. I saw the photos. They were intimate. It was not business. Of course, deep down I knew that all along. I guess the reporter in me kicked in. I needed evidence to prove my instincts were correct. I now had it. I opened Google Translate and began to read the interpretations of the Russian messages.

With each revelation, my stomach turned.

My heart was breaking one message and one photo at a time.

I left the bathroom and entered the bedroom where the skipper was lying on the bed. I forcefully threw the phone at him.

"I looked," I told him. "I know."

He looked at the phone and saw the exposed photos and messages. This time he didn't deny it. How could he? He knew he was caught. He fell to his knees and begged my forgiveness. For the first time, I could see desperation in his eyes. I saw some level of compassion—a little emotion.

I asked him why he would put me through that torture all those months. "Why continue to deny it and lie right to my face? Why make me feel like I was going crazy? Why let me question my own gut?"

His only answer: "I was afraid of losing you."

I asked him if there were others. He said there were not. I asked him if he loved her. He said he didn't. I asked him if he would end it. He said he already had.

All were lies, but I didn't know it at the time.

The next day we took a road trip to Chicago to see one of my clients. We talked the entire 660 miles and tried to work it out. I wanted to believe I was the kind of person who had the capacity to forgive. He swore it would never happen again. I believed him and forgave him. But it was impossible to forget.

We continued to have challenges as I continued to invade his privacy and search his phone for answers when my instinct told me I shouldn't trust him. My gut was always spot on. I always felt guilty for looking at his private messages. He convinced me that my crime of invading his privacy was worse than his infidelities.

That's how gaslighting works.

I was a naïve and easy target for him.

When I was back in Guntersville to spend Christmas with my family, I confessed to my brother, Tim, about my heartache. I told him everything. A pastor and marriage counselor, my baby brother explained to me that if I chose to stay with the skipper, I had to forgive him and never again bring it up. I had to push a reset button on the relationship. Trisha had given me the same advice. It seemed an impossible task, but I felt like the relationship was worth it.

My brother also told me something I have never forgotten. In a trusting relationship, he explained, neither party can have any secrets. He reminded me that people keep their most intimate secrets on their phone and carry them with them in their pocket everywhere they go. Anyone who would not let me see their phone could not be trusted and most certainly had something to hide. I never forgot that.

But I did move forward with the relationship.

Manipulation is a deadly drug. Apparently, I was an addict.

As I sat in *Seefalke's* cockpit in Lisbon, I tried to shake the memories of that heartbreaking period of our relationship. But as more evidence surfaced on the skipper's laptop, I was haunted by the ghost of the beautiful Russian girl. And there were others.

The ghosts were all around me and continued to flash on the screen in front of me.

I found more photos. Hundreds of them.

I had uncovered his picture-hunting collection.

I first learned of his picture-hunting game shortly after the conversation with my brother when he warned me of secrets hidden on phones. The skipper had convinced me to travel with him to Italy. He was at a business meeting, and I was working in the hotel room. My hard drive was full, and I needed to save some work, so

I looked in his backpack because I knew he had a few flash drives. I grabbed one randomly and loaded it onto my computer.

I opened it to discover several dozen folders. Each was labeled with a different girl's name. None of them were labeled "Michelle." I opened a few of them. All were nude and revealing photos that these women obviously had willingly sent to him. I was frustrated and furious. I didn't open them all, but I didn't have to.

About an hour later, the skipper called and invited me to join him and his colleague for dinner. I refused. He asked me why not, and I said, "Because I can't stand to see the sight of your face right now."

He immediately returned to the hotel room, and I showed him what I found. He was unfazed. He laughed at me—told me it was no big deal and insisted he had done nothing wrong. They were just photos, he said, unapologetically.

Then he proudly described to me his "picture hunting" game.

He would seduce women through text messages and phone calls—convince them they were beautiful and then prey on their insecurities. Once he had convinced a woman to send a few revealing photos, he added the trophies to his collection and then ghosted her. He never spoke to her again. It was deplorable.

How could I love a man who would treat women this way?

I asked him if this was just his form of porn. I was trying really hard to understand. He quickly informed me that it wasn't the photos that turned him on. It was the manipulation.

I asked him why he never tried to seduce me into sending him that kind of photo. His answer was simple: "Because I love you."

His gaslighting was not working on me this time. I told him I would try to get an earlier flight home and leave Milan. He didn't try to stop me. But that evening, I threw out my back. With a bulging disc, it was something that happened often. This time, I could not bear the pain, and in the middle of the night I asked him to call an ambulance. He refused, not believing I was really in pain.

Disgusted by his lack of empathy, I called his business colleague who was staying in the same hotel and asked if he would take me to the hospital. He agreed without any need for explanation. But he was unable to help me into his car, so we called an ambulance. Fortunately, he was Italian and could tell the non-English-speaking technicians what was wrong with me, something I was unable to do. The skipper went with us to the hospital, but as I was being treated, he looked at his watch and announced that he needed to leave for his business meeting. Our friend, surprised by the skipper's lack of compassion, said, "No. You can't leave her. I'll go to the meeting. You stay here with Michelle."

He went anyway.

A couple hours later, I was released. I called the skipper and asked him to pick me up, but he refused. In severe pain, I walked a mile from the hospital to the pharmacy, then gingerly limped another two miles to the hotel. They wouldn't let me in the room because it wasn't registered in my name and I didn't have a key. I lay on the hotel lobby floor for four hours until the skipper showed up and reluctantly let me into the room.

The next morning, I boarded a train for Frankfurt to catch an early flight home and swore I would never speak to the skipper again. As usual, he manipulated me into staying with him—even after being abandoned at the hospital and after discovering the picture-hunting collection.

I am ashamed that I let him back in my life after that. I often wondered if the mental and psychological abuse and manipulation that continued for many years were my fault.

I wrestled with whether to share that story. I often feel like an idiot for continuing to go back to this man after uncovering such horrible flaws in his character. The only way I can explain it is that I was deeply manipulated into believing that he cared for me.

I wasn't part of the picture collection, so he must love me. These women mean nothing to him.

My confidence was stripped. I didn't feel like I was worthy of honorable love. I didn't feel I was good enough or attractive enough to be loved by a better man—a man of character.

Loyalty, to me, is the most important quality a person can have. I was loyal to him even though he was not loyal to me. When I questioned his character, I reminded myself of all the many good times—all the romantic and fun adventures. For reasons that are difficult to explain, my heart spoke louder than my brain. Even though I could see the damaging evidence clearly, I was blinded by love and loyalty.

But mostly, I was weak. Simple as that.

Back in Lisbon, I went straight to the folder labeled "Julia." Even though there were many women, I was laser focused on her. Most of her collection were photos obviously taken by him in a bed and breakfast in Kaliningrad—images of a young, beautiful girl with dark hair and dark eyes lying naked on a bed in front of an open window while the sun illuminated her body. There were dozens of them.

How many photos did he need of this girl?

Even more painful, I found emails and love letters. In one email, the Russian girl asked the skipper to send her a photo of what he saw outside his window. The photo was of my yard in Birmingham featuring the blooming flowers I had recently planted. He had obviously sent it to her while he was visiting me—an image snapped from my bedroom window. The level of deceit enraged me.

I found a love letter to her that was an exact copy-and-paste of one he had written to me, only it was translated from English to Russian. I also discovered photos from a trip he took with her to Berlin. I checked the dates. It was the same weekend I was vacationing with Trisha and Pam when he told me he had lost his phone.

I was furious. Disappointed. Heartbroken. Crushed.

I was prepared to pack my things and arrange a flight for the dogs and me to leave Lisbon, abandon the sailing journey, and return to Alabama. Then I found another correspondence—an interaction with one of the skipper's best friends in Birmingham. He was a mutual friend, one I admired and trusted.

The message exchange happened during a time I broke up with the skipper and demanded a few months of silence in the fall of 2017. I needed a break from the many infidelities that followed the affair with Julia. I loved him, but I could not trust him and could not continue with the inevitable heartbreaks.

I had decided to date other men. There was one man with whom I shared a deep attraction. He was much younger than me but much more mature than the skipper. He was engaging and empathetic and even listened to some of the horrible stories I told him about the rocky relationship.

He was a polite, generous man with honorable family values who enjoyed simple pleasures. We had fun together and one beautiful afternoon we went fishing. That evening, I was sending photos from the day to him, but I accidentally sent them to the skipper. At first, I panicked because of my mistake. The pictures included selfies of the two of us smiling and having a great time together.

But then I felt relief. I told myself, matter-of-factly: *Well, that did it. I'll never hear from him again.* I was mentally breaking away from the unhealthy relationship.

The skipper never mentioned receiving those pictures, but it became clear to me that he saw them. A few days later, he showed up unexpectedly at my doorstep and once again begged me to come back to him. He had traveled all the way from Germany and jumped the security gate to get inside the condo complex.

I reluctantly let him inside the front door, and we sat on the floor of the foyer all night long talking. Once again, he convinced me to come back to him. This time it was different. He told me he was there to stay. He was moving to Alabama to live with me full time. There would be no more distance between us.

That's when he revealed his plan to bring his boat across the Atlantic, which convinced me that he was serious. Nothing meant more to this man than *Seefalke*. To bring her to Alabama was a commitment to our future.

The message exchange with our Birmingham friend that I found on the skipper's laptop was that plan to show up on my doorstep and win me back. For some reason, while reading it I felt his love in his desperation to hatch the plan, and it overshadowed all the unsettling evidence I found on the laptop of secrets. I believed that people could change.

Nobody is perfect. It was all a long time ago, and I had promised to hit the reset button and leave the past behind.

This time, I gaslighted myself.

I never mentioned to the skipper what I found on the laptop, although I did tell him that I felt haunted by ghosts of the past. He never asked for an explanation. I never confided in anyone else about it, either. I buried the laptop at the bottom of the bow locker and kept the secrets locked inside my soul—hidden deep down in a place where I could hide from the shame that I felt for the way I discovered them and for the way I overlooked them.

I was ashamed about what continuing to stay with this man revealed about my own character. It would be impossible for anyone to understand why I stayed with him after all of that. I didn't understand myself.

Nevertheless, I stayed.

At about mid-week, the skipper let me know that he would be returning to Lisbon on Sunday, as planned, but then he would immediately travel to Germany the next morning to spend a week with his daughter.

I was furious at first. I couldn't bear another week without any human company. And then the skipper returned to his usual M.O. Whenever I was suspicious or felt uneasy, he would distract me with a fun adventure. This time he recommended that I try to find a place to board the dogs and travel with him to Germany.

The prospect of a week of creature comforts on land excited me. I also loved his children and looked forward to spending time with his daughter. I hunted for boarding options in Lisbon. Kennels and pet hotels are very common in the U.S. but not easy to find in Europe. After an exhaustive search, and a little help from the ladies in the marina reception office, I found a place in Cascais called SweetPet. I made all the necessary arrangements and was excited about a break from the sailing life.

28 OCTOBER–4 NOVEMBER 2018

The skipper returned to *Seefalke* just a couple hours before SweetPet came to the marina to pick up Cap'n Jack and Scout. Without the pups, we decided to eat out at a restaurant, which we rarely did. It was more economical to cook on the boat. We opted for sushi and had a nice evening out.

I never revealed to him what I found on the laptop, and I tried to block it from my mind.

We departed for the airport the next morning and settled into the skipper's small apartment in Halle, Germany. I spent the week focused on work. The skipper had returned with a new laptop for me, so I didn't have to use his old one that harbored so many secrets.

It was the first time in three months that I had not slept on *Seefalke*, and it seemed surreal. As I closed my eyes, I could still feel the slight swaying of the sea, even though the ground beneath me was still. It was also the first time in four months that I had been without Cap'n Jack and Scout 24/7. I missed them.

But I was happy to sleep in a real bed. I was happy to have freshly brewed coffee rather than the instant variety we drank onboard. I was extremely happy to take a hot shower with unlimited water and no time limit. I was also happy to have strong WiFi to get my work accomplished more efficiently.

I had grown accustomed to living without those amenities, and I had realized with time that I didn't need them. But to enjoy them occasionally was nice. Even as I enjoyed a few creature comforts, I missed my pups. I missed *Seefalke*. And I missed the sea.

Back to Sea Life

4–11 NOVEMBER 2018

After a week in Germany, we returned Portugal and were reunited with our dogs. We had been in Lisbon for two weeks, but we hadn't had the opportunity to see the city, so we took a day to explore.

We walked to Alfama, the oldest part of Lisbon. The colorful, quaint district contained many historical attractions, bars, cafes, and restaurants along its narrow streets and small squares. Superstar Madonna lived there and was often spotted in local shops.

We walked hand in hand and enjoyed the romantic surroundings. The skipper seemed fully engaged with me as we both embraced the adventure. I felt guilty about invading his privacy on the laptop. And while the ghosts still haunted me, I distracted myself with memories of all the times like this when he made me feel special.

We found a fantastic local café off the beaten path and enjoyed delicious coffee and key lime pie with a pistachio crust. The proprietor convinced me to take the coffee black instead of with my usual cream and sugar. After having mostly instant coffee at sea for many months, I could really appreciate the rich flavor.

We ventured to the Cristo Rei (Christ the King) statue, which is one of Lisbon's most iconic monuments. The statue stands high above the southern banks of the Tejo Estuary and depicts Christ with arms raised, blessing the city.

We walked a few miles to the Belem Tower, which is surrounded by dramatic crashing waves on all sides. Perhaps my favorite site was the Monument to the Discoveries. It was erected to honor the main characters of the Portuguese Discovery Age. Henry the Navigator, the Discoveries sponsor, is surrounded by kings and queens, explorers, navigators, artists, scientists, cartographers, and missionaries whose deeds granted them an important place in Portugal's history during the 15th and 16th centuries.

While I enjoyed the landmarks, my favorite way to explore any new city is to wander off the beaten path to see how the locals live.

We took the ferry across the river and landed in an old, remote district that felt like we had stepped back in time. We stopped at an outdoor family-owned restaurant. The proprietor took us straight to the "fish freezer" and recommended the fresh salmon, cod, and mackerel that were pulled directly from the sea just a few hours before.

He introduced us to his father who was stationed at an outdoor grill that was probably as old as he was—maybe older. That grill would never pass any American FDA inspection. The man had caught and cooked fish for the restaurant for 46 years.

We chose to ignore the rust on the broken, ancient grill and enjoyed one of the tastiest meals I can ever remember eating. Cap'n Jack and Scout devoured their shares of the freshly grilled fish.

We began planning our passage to Morocco—the destination I had been looking forward to the most. Before the skipper could book another trip, I announced that I had bought a ticket home to Alabama for Thanksgiving. It would be his turn to babysit the boat and the dogs.

I had no money but decided to put the cost of the flight on a credit card and worry about paying for it later. I desperately needed to be with my family. I contacted Shelby, Bo, and Trisha and asked them to help me plan a surprise visit for my parents.

Of course, when sailors make plans before reaching their destination, it can cause other inconveniences. All of a sudden, we were on a schedule. I wanted to explore the possibility of sailing to Gibraltar on the way to Morocco. The storms that pass through the

Strait of Gibraltar, which is the narrow opening into the Mediterranean, can sometimes last several days.

We couldn't take the chance. I needed to get to Morocco by the end of the next week. Nothing was going to keep me from boarding my flight—not even the allure of another grand adventure.

Meanwhile, the drone battery malfunctioned, making it impossible for us to charge the flying camera. The skipper purchased a new drone and had a great time the rest of the afternoon playing with his new toy. The money he unnecessarily spent was enough to purchase my flight home—something he would have never offered to do for me.

We waited on a good weather opening for the Morocco passage. I was so excited I was about to burst. I had never been to Africa, and since I was a little girl, Casablanca had been on my bucket list. But first, we needed to sail about 370 nm across the narrow strip of the Atlantic that separates Europe from Africa.

And I needed to find a way to deal with the ghosts of the past that continued to haunt me.

BLINDED BY
LOVE & LOYALTY

LIVING LIFE SIDEWAYS SERIES
BOOK 2

MICHELLE SEGREST

CHAPTER 13

FORGING AHEAD

PASSAGE TO MOROCCO

MONDAY, 12 NOVEMBER 2018

While planning our worldwide voyage, I had only one specific request—a long stop in Morocco.

I had dreamed of Africa since I was a little girl and was especially infatuated with the movie *Casablanca*—a romantic drama set this exotic location.

On the morning of our departure from Portugal to Morocco, I was ecstatic and ready to say goodbye to the haunting memories of my time in Lisbon and hopefully leave all the ghosts behind.

With the weather and wind conditions, we calculated that the passage would take about 90 hours. I had grown accustomed to those multiple-day, overnight passages, but I didn't always love them.

After three weeks in port, I knew it wouldn't be easy to get back my sea legs so I prepared myself mentally for another long and challenging passage.

It was chilly as we left the Parque dos Naçeōs marina. *Seefalke's* orange hull was eerily hidden behind a curtain of fog. We could not see anything. We forged our way out of the marina and blasted the foghorn signals as we cruised slowly and blindly along the Tagus River.

Light and no-wind periods were expected during the passage, which meant we would need to motor sail some of the way. The fuel station in our marina was out of order, so we motored a few miles over to one of the other Lisbon marinas to top off the fuel tanks. It was located next to my favorite landmark—the Monument to the Discoveries. I said goodbye to Henry the Navigator and to Lisbon.

At the same time, I was trying to say goodbye to the horrible secrets I had discovered on the skipper's laptop. I prayed I could keep them buried as I tried to move on from the truth that I did not want to face.

With full tanks, we ventured onto our course where we were immediately greeted by an amazing sight—the *USS Harry S. Truman,* an enormous United States aircraft carrier. Its call sign is "Lone Warrior," and its home port is the Naval Station Norfolk in Virginia.

The carrier dropped anchor in Portugal after a month of operations in the North Atlantic and became the first US carrier to operate in the Arctic Circle in 27 years. A pilot ship was making a delivery, and we could see several aircraft on board.

It happened to be Veterans Day, which made the sighting especially memorable. I made a post on social media about how thrilled I was to see the impressive freighter. A sailor aboard the vessel responded, telling me they would get just as excited when they saw cruising sailboats. He said he noticed the bright orange ship with the two barking beagles on the bow departing from Lisbon.

For the first few hours on board, I felt nauseous. I know it was part excitement, part nerves, and part anticipation. But the 3 m swells rolling in from the Atlantic that rocked *Seefalke* from all sides definitely had something to do with it.

I suspected the seasickness would not spare me after such a long break from the sea. I ate a few crackers and drank a couple sips of strong ginger tea, both of which helped.

Soon, the wind and waves began to increase, and so did the uncomfortable motion. The entire two-human and two-canine crew battled nausea, but I started to feel a little better just as the skipper was beginning to feel worse. We worked together to get all the sails hoisted and because I was feeling slightly better than he was, I took the first shift around 12:30.

I was extremely excited about seeing Africa for the first time, but I felt nervous about being at sea again. My emotions were always a battle for me. When the excitement and the nerves would meet the rocking waves at sea, it was never a good recipe.

I took my shift in the bunk around 16:00 but struggled to rest. The boat rocked significantly, and all the items in the lockers scattered. The familiar clanking and rattling sounds inside the lockers annoyed me and hindered my ability to relax. I tried to shift the items around in the lockers—stuffing them with towels and clothes. That helped to buffer the annoying sounds, but I could not get any rest.

I tried to sleep on the main bunk, but the boat tipped and turned heavily and unexpectedly, and before I could grab onto anything, I slid right out of the bed onto the floor in between the two bunks. I stayed there and tried to nest myself into a still position but was unable to get comfortable.

I took the helm again at 20:00. That's when it got especially rough for me. I knew from experience that when I didn't get sleep or rest when I was off watch, it greatly affected me when it was my turn at the helm.

By the end of my shift, at midnight, I had fed the fish three times and felt horrible. The seasickness had become so familiar to me that it was something I didn't even consider might not happen. I accepted the fact that I would probably get seasick at some point on every voyage. The difference was that I was building a tolerance for coping with it.

I developed techniques to manage the uneasiness and battle through the nausea. A few months before, the seasickness would wipe me out to the point that I couldn't move or function. It was impossible for me to do anything but lie still in pain and discomfort.

But after those first few months, I had learned to fight my way through it. I would get sick, then eat something. Then I would drink something. I would distract myself and try not to think about the discomfort. It wasn't easy, but I had learned that it was helpful to work my way through it rather than let it knock me out.

On this occasion, I was struggling a bit with diarrhea, too. I was forced to make frequent trips to the head. As gross as it was, I struggled to ensure that the sickness only came out of one end at a time. Throwing up was preferred because at least I could stay outside in the fresh air and not risk the additional queasiness that happened when I stumbled my way through the cabin to the head. I battled through the "throwing and going" and was incredibly grateful when my shift finally ended.

Day 2

TUESDAY, 13 NOVEMBER 2018

I had only eaten a couple of crackers during my last two shifts. When I took over again at 04:00, I nibbled a few bites of a pear, but my tummy quickly rejected them. I badly needed some fuel and energy. I hated feeling weak. I was able to hold down a few sips of water and a few sips of ginger ale, but the shift was long and difficult.

Four hours alone in the dark, cold night would feel like an eternity when my insides were upside down.

After that shift, the conditions calmed, and I was finally able to get some sleep. When I awakened, I was comforted by the smooth, steady motion as *Seefalke* worked hard to soften the blow of the large, breaking swells. We were not fully tilted anymore and only rocked slightly. I took advantage of the relatively calm waters and began boiling water for pasta. I had no idea the time of day.

When at sea, it was important to cook when the opportunity presented itself and not necessarily on a schedule. A regular routine of breakfast, lunch, and dinner was nonexistent when on long offshore passages. I saw the opportunity to get some warm food in our bellies, and I took advantage.

By the time we finished eating, I needed to lie down again. We were back on a heavy tilt to the starboard side, and I wanted to be in a regular bunk as opposed to the main cabin floor, so this time, I tried to rest in the stern cabin.

The stern cabin was shaped like a "V" with a twin bunk on each side of the V. If two people were sleeping in the cabin, both sets of feet were usually at the point of the V. The ideal situation was to sleep on whichever side was the low side of the tilt. That helped to stabilize the body, but only as long as the wind didn't shift and toss you to the other side.

I settled in with my full belly and managed a few hours of restful sleep. When I awoke for my 16:00 shift, I felt much better. The sun was shining. *Seefalke* was gliding along the waves and cushioning the bigger blows. I enjoyed a glorious sunset and continued to battle my way back to some measure of normalcy. When my watch ended at 20:00, I went back to the stern cabin and completely crashed.

Day 3 – Ghosts at Sea

WEDNESDAY, 14 NOVEMBER 2018

The midnight to 04:00 shift was rough. Wind had significantly increased, and the waves crashed from all sides. Even though I tried to fight it, I felt queasy again. This time, it was worse than before.

As I struggled through my shift, thoughts of Julia—the beautiful Russian girl with dark hair and dark eyes—drifted into my mind. I wondered how she would have handled those times when the sailing conditions were miserable. I wondered if the skipper had ever taken her sailing. I wondered if she would leave her family and friends and sacrifice her home and career to make his lifelong dream come true.

I wanted to hate her and to blame her for everything that was wrong with my relationship. But then I reminded myself that the affair wasn't her fault any more than it was my fault. In all likelihood, she didn't even know that I existed.

When thoughts of her creeped into my head, I could see the images that I found on the laptop. I would close my eyes, squeezing them shut, and physically shake my head many times—trying desperately to force the memories out of my mind forever.

It never worked.

After my miserable shift, I fumbled back to the stern cabin and felt grateful for another opportunity to lie flat. I awakened around 07:00 and still felt icky. I was queasy and still struggling with diarrhea. I took some more medicine and fought for a few hours then finally crashed again around 10:00.

After sleeping a few hours, I felt better. But I was as ornery as a hornet. I made frequent trips to the head and began cussing and fussing every time a wave would hit us from the side unexpectedly, throwing me across the cabin.

I continued to think of Julia sitting on land somewhere enjoying normal creature comforts and again wondered if any other woman on the planet would go through this for a man who probably didn't appreciate the sacrifice.

I became verbal with my complaints as I got more and more irritated with the situation. But I soon realized that it was not doing anyone any good—especially not me.

I looked out onto the horizon and then stared directly into the sun, feeling the full burn of the rays combined with the crisp chill of the wind on my face.

To make it to Africa, I needed to focus on all the things I loved about those long passages rather than all the things I hated about them. I sat in the cockpit and began listing them out loud.

I apologized to the skipper and told him I was sorry that I didn't love being out there all the time. He admitted that there were aspects about sailing that he didn't love all the time, either—a statement that surprised me. I needed to verbalize the things I did love about it.

I told him how much I loved the sound of the waves and the cool wind on my skin. I talked about how exciting it was to travel by sea to all these amazing places. I told him how grateful I was for the opportunity to see the world from that perspective and the personal pride I felt every time we make it to a new port.

The challenges enhanced the thrill of the adventure—something I realized for the first time when I said it out loud.

I looked at him directly in the face and asked him if he still loved me as much as he did that night when he jumped the fence at my condo complex and begged me to come back into his life. A year had passed since he had made that grandiose gesture.

"If it's possible," he said, "I love you even more."

I wanted to confront him about what I had found on the laptop, but I didn't want to spoil the moment. It was the first time he had told me he loved me since before we set sail from Stralsund. I needed to hear it.

We talked about what to do when the night watch hours would get long and lonely—the times when there was no traffic and the wind was steady—times when there was nothing to do but watch the time slowly tick away.

Sometimes I listened to audiobooks. Other times I listened to music. I wished that I could read one of the 20 books I had brought on board, but up to that point, the nausea would not allow me to focus on the pages.

Sometimes I would sing, but I often worried I would wake the skipper. Most of the time, I talked to Scout, who frequently joined me on my night watches. She was such great company on those long, black, lonely nights.

Then our conversation got deep.

I talked about the challenge of living on the boat and how even though it was uncomfortable and difficult at times, it was rewarding and fulfilling to make it to the other side of a long ocean passage. We talked about how most people viewed sailing as a rich man's hobby that was all about bikinis and martinis and relaxing on calm waters.

But in fact, the ocean is a very hostile environment. It was not meant to be a place for people to live. Without the steel construction we were floating on to protect us, we would most certainly be dead within a couple hours.

And yet, we continued to battle against the elements to make our way through an environment that was not meant for humans. The wind and the weather and the water did not care that we were living things trying to survive.

Sometimes in the middle of the night when I walked out onto the wobbly deck, I felt like how I imagined an astronaut must feel in outer space. I wondered if that was what walking without gravity on the moon was like. Just like the astronauts in space, we battled conditions that were not meant for human life.

I was feeling better. That's when I realized that we were only 24 hours away from Africa—a faraway land that I had dreamed about for most of my life.

I felt guilty for complaining and fussing so much. The opportunity was rare and precious. I realized that we needed to endure the bad things to better appreciate the challenging times. That's what made it such a grand experience.

That kind of journey was not meant to be easy. If it were easy, anyone could do it. If it were easy, it would be boring.

There was a time not so long ago when sailors were out at sea for months without GPS or nautical charts and had absolutely no idea if they were halfway to their destination or almost there or still many months away. They just drifted along knowing that one day they might get there.

I glanced to the horizon and could see no land, no life, and no other ships. This had happened to me many times at sea, but the experience was always surreal. When traveling by car, it's common to see many other vehicles. When traveling by airplane or train, hundreds of other people can be seen scattering in multiple directions.

There were hundreds, maybe even thousands of sailboats out there on those same waters with us. But the sea was so massive that we hardly ever saw any of them.

As the day turned to night, we settled back into our four-hour watch routine. I felt much better and embraced the passage in a more positive way.

And just as we settled into some measure of peace and contentment, the adventure continued.

The skipper was heading down to sleep around 18:00 when all of a sudden, the outhaul line on the main sail snapped apart from the boom. The large sail was flapping uncontrollably over the deep offshore water. I was able to grab the corner of the sail and secure it with a D-ring strap while the skipper created a temporary rig to tie it back to the boom.

A couple hours later, the jib boom traveler snapped, and the steel bar flapped in the wind with only one end secured. The skipper immediately went onto the foredeck and tried to repair it, but he couldn't get it secured enough, so he took down the jib completely.

Later that evening, the temporary rig on the main sail outhaul line snapped again and we were forced to creatively rig it again to keep it secure. To add to the excitement, the port side navigation light was blinking. I felt like we were falling apart with only 70 nm and about 12 hours left to Rabat.

I was reminded again that if it were easy, anyone would do it.

Day 4

THURSDAY, 15 NOVEMBER 2018

On my late-night shift, around 02:00, we coasted a bit too close to a fishing boat that was dragging a mile-long net. We were forced to take *Seefalke* on a large detour loop to avoid getting tangled in it.

A few hours later we crossed over into African waters and raised the Moroccan courtesy flag. It was a foggy morning, but the gorgeous coastline slowly came into focus through the blur. My heart began to flutter! We were finally in Africa!

The passage covered 369 nm in 75 hours, 32 minutes.

I had waited my entire life to see this beautiful place. My flight home for Thanksgiving was four days away, and I was ready to see as much of Morocco as possible.

It's difficult to describe how emotional it was to finally check off an item that had been on my bucket list for as long as I could remember. Still, I had no idea the depth of my connection to Casablanca.

I would soon find out.

CHAPTER 14

WALKING THE ARMADILLOS

MAGICAL MOROCCO

A frica has been on my bucket list since long before bucket lists were a thing.

I was first inspired when my father sent me a postcard from his African safari. It featured colorful images of an open savannah, a sandy terrain, wild animals running free, and rich wetlands.

I was about 12 years old and began dreaming of Africa—a place that seemed as far away from my home in Alabama as anywhere on the planet. As a young girl, a trip to Africa seemed about as unlikely as a journey to the moon or to Mars.

That was also the year I watched *Casablanca* for the first time. It wouldn't be the last. During the next four decades, I watched the Humphrey Bogart classic set in Morocco at least 20 times. So inspired, I named my dog Bogie, even though she was a girl. The movie was made in black and white, but with each viewing, my mind's eye began to see the colors of Morocco bursting through the shades of gray on the screen.

In the last scene, Bogart's character, Rick, stands on a foggy airport runway and chooses his love of country over the love of his life. I often wondered why that heartbreaking ending intrigued me, but even so, my dreams of seeing the faraway land intensified.

My daughter, Shelby, got the chance to explore Africa long before I did. She spent two summers in Kenya and one in Uganda. It was a different Africa than the one my father described. She went into remote villages to work with orphans and children with disabilities. It didn't take long for her to fall in love with the beautiful continent and its people.

Inspired by her grand experience, my desire to see if for myself was once again awakened. I watched *Casablanca* for the 21st time and continued to dream of Africa.

Knowing I would eventually get there, I honestly never imagined that I would enter Morocco under sail on a 43-foot, steel, bright orange magic carpet by way of Portugal—gliding in on the magnificent waves of the deep blue Atlantic.

The Africa I sailed into was the western coastal Africa—where only a narrow strip of sea separates the southern Spain/Portugal coast from the Moroccan shoreline. Where we set sail from and the final destination were only separated by 75 hours and about 370 nm, but these countries are uniquely different in culture and landscape.

A part of Africa that was once part of France, 99 percent of Morocco is Islamic. The Arabic and French languages are merged into a dialect as unique as the vibrant landscape, enriching culture, and delicious cuisine.

As we crossed over into African waters and raised the Moroccan courtesy flag, things immediately felt different. It didn't look different—I could still only see the sky kissing the sea on the distant horizon. It was just a feeling. I knew my Africa would be different than the ones my father and my daughter experienced.

The morning fog was so thick it was difficult to see where the sky stopped and the sea began. I thought about the fog on that airport runway in the last scene of the movie when Rick told Louis, "I think this is the beginning of a beautiful friendship."

When the coastline slowly came into focus through the blur, I heard myself saying those exact words out loud. It was, indeed, the beginning of a beautiful friendship with a place I had dreamed about for almost half a century.

As we approached Bouregreg Marina, we called the harbor master by radio. He greeted us in a small motor-powered wooden boat and guided us in, along with a gigantic catamaran that appeared from nowhere.

My heart was beating out of my chest with excitement as we made our approach. The Arabic and French architecture along the banks of the city of Rabat is as unique and spectacular as the ancient, bronze stone reflected in the emerald-green, glistening water. The entrance was made even more dramatic by the swarms of birds circling the dozens of brightly painted wooden fishing boats.

Many locals were taking our picture as we entered the marina. It's not a very busy port, so the locals didn't see many ships coming in—especially a bright orange one with two enthusiastic beagles on the bow. Cap'n Jack and Scout seemed as mesmerized as me. Their long ears flapped in the breeze while their sensitive noses twitched and sniffed the air to catch the fresh new smells of another unexplored land.

We moored at the customs dock and were greeted by friendly police officers and a sweet woman in traditional Muslim dress and head covering. She offered us Moroccan mint tea. The delicious treat was garnished with fresh mint leaves and tasted like hot honey.

We enjoyed the delicacy and spent about 90 minutes completing all the customs paperwork. They confiscated our drone cameras and the small amount of alcohol we had onboard. It was not a surprise since we knew those items are illegal in Morocco, but we were assured they would be returned upon our departure.

The harbor master then guided us into berth. There was one entire pier that was reserved for the king of Morocco's yacht fleet of six gorgeous luxury ships. It was carefully guarded by armed soldiers day and night, which gave us the security of marina protection by default.

The sailing passage was long and exhausting, but I was energized. I had a few days to explore this new place before my scheduled flight home, and I was more than ready to finally see Africa for the first time.

Where Are All the Dogs?

RABAT, MOROCCO

I immediately leashed Cap'n Jack and Scout and began to explore Rabat, the capital city of Morocco.

This was not my first time visiting an Islamic country. Having traveled to the Middle East many times, I was aware that women are treated differently in the Islamic culture, even though that was never fully depicted in my favorite movie.

I was prepared to embrace the culture by dressing respectfully. Even though it was hot, it's important for women to always stay covered. However, it's not necessary for Moroccan tourists to wear a burqa. In fact, most women in Morocco did not wear full burqas. Some women, mostly the younger ones, wore fashionable but modest clothes and covered their heads with a scarf. To be respectful, I always kept my arms and legs covered when venturing away from the marina.

We converted some money to dirham, the local currency, then began searching for a restaurant. Food in Rabat was inexpensive, and we didn't feel like cooking after our exhausting sailing passage.

We walked through the crowded downtown streets in search of local cuisine. Outdoor cafés were crowded with men. There were no women in sight. People were staring curiously at the pups and me. The locals seemed fascinated with my blonde hair. I realized later that I didn't see one other blonde-haired woman during our entire stay in Morocco.

But their main fascination was with the two beagles walking at the end of the leashes I gripped comfortably in one hand. The locals seemed frightened by my sweet pups, which surprised me. It's difficult to imagine how anyone could be afraid of Cap'n Jack and Scout with their floppy, velvety ears, expressive faces, friendly energy, and playful dispositions.

But in Morocco, I would learn that dogs are not generally kept as domestic pets. We saw many wild dogs roaming the streets and spotted dozens of stray cats. It quickly became apparent that there was not one other dog walking on a leash with a human.

Traveling the world on a sailboat, I had visited many ports with Cap'n Jack and Scout. They had all been dog friendly. The beagles were welcomed in restaurants, boutiques, museums, and markets. We were accustomed to seeing dogs being walked by their humans everywhere. In fact, in places like France, Spain, and Portugal, it was rare to see someone walking the streets without a dog.

We learned that Moroccans consider dogs to be wild animals—not domestic pets. I suppose it was strange for them to see us taking a couple of wild animals for a walk.

I could understand with some perspective. I considered how Alabamians feel about armadillos. We see the armored beasts everywhere and consider them to be wild animals. I've never known anyone who kept one as a pet. I can't imagine what my own reaction would be to see someone walking through the streets of Gulf Shores with an armadillo on a leash.

That must have been how the Moroccans felt seeing us walking the beagles. One local explained it to me in a simple way.

"Not all Moroccans can't or won't have dogs as pets, but most prefer not to . . . the reason being that our religion [Islam] says that dogs have very-difficult-to-wash saliva that doesn't go away with your typical one soap-filled sponge scrub. In fact, our prophet Mohamed says that if a dog licks a plate it should be washed six times with water and the seventh should be done with soil."

I have always found it to be so enriching to leave my Alabama bubble and learn more about different cultures, and I would do plenty of that during my time in Morocco.

Meanwhile, I was beginning to understand why other sailors told me that Morocco was a dirty place to visit. Garbage lined the streets, and it was difficult to find a trash can. Orange rinds, cigarette butts, paper food wrappers, and rotting banana peels were a common part of the local landscape. I saw at least three men peeing on the side of the street, and on one unfortunate occasion, I was shocked to catch a glimpse of a man pooing in full squat on the side of the road.

Cap'n Jack and Scout, however, didn't seem to mind wading through the trash-covered streets. With their ultra-sensitive noses, they loved all the stinky smells.

Somehow, we stumbled upon a special place—a very cool Moroccan restaurant called Ô Saveurs de la Médina—that welcomed women and dogs. We were treated to an exceptional meal and a beautiful Moroccan atmosphere that was exploding with color. Flamboyant pillows covered comfy sofas and chairs while lanterns illuminated the room with a warm glow. It felt more like sitting in the parlor of a close friend's luxurious home than the dining room of a public restaurant.

I ordered beef with grilled plums and apricots while the skipper had lemon chicken with grilled green olives—dishes bursting with unusual and intriguing flavors. We soon discovered that the restaurant was owned by a Frenchman, not a Moroccan, which is probably why they allowed us to bring the dogs inside. Cap'n Jack and Scout sat comfortably at my feet under the table, waiting patiently for any crumbs to fall.

We loved this restaurant so much that we returned the next night, which happened to be a Friday. We discovered that Moroccans eat couscous on Fridays, and despite our two leashed armadillos in tow, we wanted to blend in with the locals. We enjoyed the traditional couscous with fresh grilled vegetables as I continued my addiction to the delicious Moroccan mint tea.

Here's Lookin' at You, Kid

The next morning, I awakened with a foggy sunrise that once again reminded me of the movie that had inspired me for so many years—an appropriate start to the day we planned to spend in Casablanca. It was fortunate that we had a friend who was a native Moroccan. He offered to show us around Casablanca for the day, but first we had to get there.

We took the tram to the main train station, but when we approached the kiosk to purchase our tickets, we were told that we couldn't bring the dogs on the train unless they were in a bag. *A bag?*

It was confusing and frustrating. Where could we find a bag that we could use to carry our chunky, energetic, 35-pound beagles onto a train?

We tried to board a bus, but again, no dogs allowed.

About 20 taxis lined the street outside the station. We assumed it would cost a fortune to take a taxi 60 km into Casablanca, but it was worth exploring. We talked to a few of the drivers and learned from their broken English that their taxis were not allowed to leave the city. I started to panic. There was no way I could come this far and not see Casablanca!

One of the taxi drivers made a call on his cell—a 1990s flip phone. About 30 seconds later, a driver approached us and said he would drive us to Casablanca for 700 dirham. That's about 70 Euros or around $80 USD. More important, he was okay with having two four-legged, long-eared canines along for the ride.

A fair price and out of options, we agreed, even though we were confused as to why his taxi could leave the city, but the others could not.

When we got to the edge of the city limits, the driver pulled over to the shoulder of a very busy highway and made another call on his flip phone. I was in the back seat all squashed in between

145

two beagles with no clue what was happening. A few minutes later, another driver showed up in an unmarked car. He parked in front of us on the shoulder.

Our driver said matter of factly, "Get into the other car." As other cars on the busy street whizzed by us at warp speeds, we didn't have time to question the situation. We jumped out of the taxi and the four of us willingly got into the unmarked car with a driver we had never met while the first driver quickly sped away.

It felt like we were trapped inside an international spy operation, but we didn't have time to feel afraid or ask questions.

Our new driver was very kind, spoke a little English, and drove us into the heart of downtown Casablanca in about 90 minutes. We happily handed him the 700 dirham. The driver insisted, "Give me 1,000." We stood firm. "We agreed to 700." I quickly got myself and the dogs out of the car as the negotiation continued. Finally, we gave him the originally agreed upon amount with a small tip and waited for our local friend outside a nearby train station.

He offered to take us to his favorite restaurant, but of course, no dogs—or for that matter, armadillos—allowed. We opted for a street vendor gyro.

As we explored Casablanca, I stuck out like a sore thumb. The absence of other blondes remained obvious. With my golden hair, blue eyes, and Southern drawl, there was really no way for me to look or sound like anything but an American. It made sense to me, and I didn't mind the stares. I just smiled at the lovely locals and gave them all a friendly, "Hey y'all!"

Casablanca is densely populated. The streets were busy with thousands of people, constant activity, and tourist traps on every corner. Just like in Rabat, we only saw men sitting in the cafés, and we continued to get confused stares from locals who didn't seem to understand why we would walk through town with two wild animals on leashes.

The most notable tourist spots in Morocco are Agadir and Tangier. In Casablanca, we were the few tourists among mostly locals and quite the novelty for them. There were beggars everywhere,

146

and this American blonde was a hot target. I must have said "No, thank you" a million times.

Our first stop was the Hassan II Mosque, which was breathtakingly spectacular. It is the largest mosque in Africa and the fifth largest in the world. Its minaret is the world's tallest at 210 m. Completed in 1993, the minaret is 60 stories high topped by a laser, the light from which is directed toward Mecca. The mosque stands on a promontory looking out to the Atlantic Ocean. Worshippers can pray over the sea but there is no glass floor for them to actually look into the sea, as some mosques feature. The walls are hand-crafted marble, and the roof is retractable for a better view of the sky.

A maximum of 105,000 worshippers can gather together for prayer: 25,000 inside the mosque hall and another 80,000 on the mosque's outside grounds. The mosque is lavish and opulent. All Muslims are invited to pray there. They don't have to pay anything or be a member of anything. Our friend told us that the Moroccans believe that anyone should have access to God, which I found to be profound and lovely. The doors were always open for anyone and for Muslims during the standard prayer times, which are signaled by a series of bells ringing from the mosque tower that can be heard throughout most of the city.

We strolled along the shore, a popular place for tourists, as the sun began to melt into the sea and fill the sky with vibrant colors. We got more confusing stares from locals who continued to show a cautious, yet curious, fear of Cap'n Jack and Scout. I kept them on a close leash in an effort to soften the fears.

Some of the children wanted to pet Scout, who was always friendly and gentle with kids. The local children seemed to delight in touching her soft, velvety ears. The adults kept a safe distance.

Our friend took us to the one tourist spot I just had to see—Rick's Café, the famous gin joint from *Casablanca*. The upscale restaurant was expensive, and with the dogs by our side, we knew better than to even try to make a reservation. Nevertheless, I just had to catch a glimpse.

From the outside, it looked just like what I remembered, except that the soft black and white tones from the film came alive with vibrant pops of color. There were four guards outside the restaurant, diligent soldiers protecting the patrons from uninvited onlookers. I turned on my best sugary Southern drawl and politely asked them if I could take a quick peek inside. Their response... a very matter-of-fact, "This is not a museum."

I hung my head in disappointment and felt deflated. It was as if the air had been let out of my virtual tires. I had come so far, and I could not take no for an answer. I enlisted my local friend for assistance.

He approached the guards, and in the unique Moroccan French/Arabic blended dialect, he asked them if I could go inside for just a few minutes. He told them how I came all the way from Alabama in a sailboat just to see Rick's Café. On my behalf, he piled it on thick.

It was then that my efforts to feel like a local were replaced with the reality of my obvious disadvantage as a tourist. They could see the disappointment on my face but remained stoic and unsympathetic. My friend managed to convince them, but I was forced to leave my camera outside.

It was an upscale restaurant. While the style was similar to the film set, it was decorated to be much swankier than what we can see in the movie. In traditional Moroccan flair, vibrantly colored pillows with gold tassels were invitingly arranged on sofas and settees that were used as seating around intricately carved wooden tables.

The room was dimly lit with the warm glow of antique oil lamps. The spicy, fruity scent of incense filled the air. The waiters, all men, were dressed in classic black tuxedos and wore white gloves. You could see the chefs preparing food over steaming brick stoves through the open kitchen.

A spectacular black grand piano sat in the center of the main dining area. No one was playing it, but in my mind, I could hear the melody from the classic movie theme, "As Time Goes By," and I remembered the lyrics I memorized when I was a teenager.

It's still the same old story
A fight for love and glory
A case of do or die
The world will always welcome lovers
As time goes by.

It was a special moment—a simple experience that connected me with my childhood dream and my adult reality. Then I heard myself say aloud, "Play it again, Sam."

Among the Ghosts of Writers and Spies

TANGIER, MOROCCO

There was one more place that I needed to see to complete my Moroccan bucket list adventure—the Gran Café de Paris in Tangier. It's a special place where famous writers like Tennessee Williams, Paul Bowles, and William Burroughs penned some of their most memorable masterpieces.

It was also the hangout where secret agents and spies lurked to listen in on local conversations during Tangier's colorful International Rule of 1923 — 1952.

I've always been inspired to take the road less traveled, so we rented a car and ventured out on a road trip that would take us three hours north of Rabat, to the famous writer's retreat in Tangier.

We were definitely on a rural highway—one that separated two civilized worlds. Our route was lined with goat and sheep farmers. The homes in the villages looked like they were made of misshapen cardboard boxes. The village streets were not paved or even graveled. They were made of mud.

As we got closer to Tangier, the sky blackened and rumbled. It began to pour. We found a parking spot about a mile away. The rain was falling heavily as we briskly walked downtown to visit the famous café. The streets were busy with the hustle and bustle of hundreds of drenched locals who didn't seem to notice the downpour.

Six hours of driving in the pouring rain (round trip) just to sit in a café for an hour may sound preposterous to some people. But as a writer, I wanted to sit inside for a few minutes and inhale the writing genius that I knew would be lurking in the air. After all, famous writers once found inspiration in this tiny café. Now, it was my turn.

Not surprisingly, most of the patrons were men, but I entered without resistance. It was packed, and the small café was clouded with a murky layer of cigarette and cigar smoke.

The inside walls were paneled with rich, dark, ornate wood carvings. It reminded me of a gentleman's cigar bar you might find in a dark, secluded alley in 1920s Southside Chicago.

Several locals, all men, were seated in a dark round parlor-style room intently watching a soccer match on a big-screen TV that seemed out of place with the decor.

We were seated near a window in the front room and could see the activity of the wet locals outside. The waiters, all men, wore bright red wool suit jackets with white bow ties, white gloves, and black trousers. The small café was packed to capacity with mostly local men, and we had to share a table with other patrons.

A few of the older gentlemen sitting across from us wore suits, ties, and fedoras. With cigars clenched between their teeth, they looked like they had been sitting there since the 1940s.

Most of them were lost inside the pages of a book or a newspaper. They were all sitting shoulder to shoulder, but no one was engaged in conversation or even seemed to notice each other.

I ordered a homemade danish and Moroccan mint tea, which I had craved since we docked in Bouregreg Marina. I just sat there, smiling—soaking in the atmosphere. I felt inspired to write and tried to absorb the creative vibes of the famous authors that once frequented the historic café.

As we walked back to the car, even the pouring rain could not remove the stale stench of the cigar smoke from my clothes. I believe that the spirit of the writers and spies was not washed away either.

They will stay with me forever.

The Beginning of a Beautiful Friendship

Just as I was beginning to feel the transformation from tourist to local, my time in Morocco came to an end.

On the evening before my flight to Alabama, I leashed Cap'n Jack and Scout and took a quick walk with them to a nearby beach as a breathtaking sunset cascaded over the water.

I looked down to see the beagles with their noses to the ground, sniffing out all the stinky trash smells, which were never hard for them to find. It reminded me that the rubbish I had learned to overlook was still there.

I saw lovers walking arm in arm on the romantic beach, enjoying the colors in the sky, as they unconsciously stepped over piles of trash as if they were meant to be there. Some couples were sitting on the sand barely noticing all the garbage surrounding the perimeter of their blankets. I found this bizarre, but for the local Moroccans, it was the most natural thing in the world.

Despite feeling like an outsider at first, I had grown to embrace the culture and spirit of Morocco. But I had to accept that I was only a visitor in the spectacular place I had dreamed about my entire life.

Though the sky was clear, I gradually felt the air thicken as a cloud of fog surrounded me—just like in the last scene of *Casablanca*.

Rick was compelled to stay.

I knew it was my destiny to leave.

But there was no doubt that Morocco would hold a special place in my heart forever. Even in a culture that is not favorable to women or dogs, I knew it was the beginning of a beautiful friendship and that I would return one day.

As time has slowly gone by, I have learned that you have to look beyond the trash-lined streets to see the beauty of Morocco—but if you look closely enough, the beauty is there. Especially when you are walking armadillos.

CHAPTER 15

SWEET HOME ALABAMA

Exploring Morocco was a magical escape. I had allowed myself to let go of every anxiety and distraction and fully embraced the experience.

As I packed for a week in Sweet Home Alabama, I turned my focus to family. I had not seen them for four months and was excited for a break from the sailing adventure. I needed a reminder of what really matters.

NOVEMBER 19–26, 2018
With a little more than an hour drive to the airport, we left the marina at 04:30. The torrential rain we had battled the day before in Tangier continued to fall heavily.

At the airport in Rabat, there was a rigorous customs procedure. I always found it funny that when international customs officers would ask me about my profession, they always paused when I would answer, "I'm a journalist." Eyebrows would raise and interest would pique. When I explained that I mostly reported about pump technology for wastewater applications, they instantly felt less threatened.

As a seasoned international traveler, I had flown hundreds of time. But after three months at sea, it felt uncomfortable being on an airplane again. Eventually, I settled in and focused on the family connection I desperately needed

I had planned a surprise for my parents. They had no idea I would be there for Thanksgiving. First, I coordinated with Shelby and Bo. However, I couldn't let it be a surprise for them. With their busy 20-something lives, I was too afraid they would make other plans and not show up. It was absolutely essential that I spent time with my children.

We worked it out that Bo would pick me up from the airport in Atlanta and drive me to Birmingham (a less than three-hour drive). Then Shelby would meet us a day later and we would drive together to my parents' home in Guntersville (two hours away).

When I first saw Bo at the airport, I nearly burst into tears. It felt so good to see him and hug him. We had a lovely drive to Birmingham and got caught up on all the happenings in his life. I had missed my kids more than I can describe and was overwhelmed with emotion.

Trisha was in town visiting her son so we shared a hotel room and squeezed in some girlfriend time.

Trisha and I got comfy in our PJs and shared a bottle of wine, something else I had been missing. The skipper did not drink alcohol at all. It wasn't a moral decision or a health decision. He simply did not like the taste. He didn't mind if others drank around him, but for some reason, he didn't like it when I did. So out of respect, I never drank around him—except for the mini-bottles of champagne that I kept on board to toast the end of each challenging passage.

We sipped the crisp Chardonnay and talked and laughed into the early hours of the morning. It was exactly what I needed.

I never told her about what I had found on the skipper's laptop. She had always been my closest confidant when it came to my relationship challenges with the skipper, but I chose not to reveal to her that I was struggling and fighting the demons and ghosts of the past. I only talked about the grand adventures and exciting lifestyle.

Shelby arrived the next day, and then my precious children and I headed to Lake Guntersville to surprise my parents and all my brothers and their families.

We had the perfect plan.

We drove to my parents' house, and I hid behind the parked car. The kids went in and told their Nana and Pops (my parents) that they needed help bring in some things from the car. When they walked outside, I jumped out from behind the car and screamed, "Happy Thanksgiving! I came all the way from Morocco just to see you!" It was awesome! They were completely surprised!

My mom burst into tears. My dad hugged me so tightly I could barely breathe. He didn't want to let go, and neither did I. When I hugged my mom, she said, "Please don't go back." She had been worried about the journey. She was convinced that I would end up lost at sea, drowned by a hurricane, eaten by sharks, or murdered by pirates. I don't think she had any idea about the real battle I faced. And of course, I never told her.

Then my dad, the chef of the family, said, "I'm going to have to get another turkey!"

When I posted the video on Facebook, the rest of the family were let in on the surprise. My sister-in-law, Pam, and my niece, Allie, showed up a day early just to spend some extra time with me. The rest of the family trickled in during the next few days.

My heart was full!

I enjoyed the soft, comfy bed, the high-speed WiFi, the hot showers, and the ICE! It felt like I was in a five-star hotel. I enjoyed my first Auburn football game of the season, even though our rival Alabama beat us badly.

I especially loved just being with my family. We did our usual family activities—like competitive games of Pictionary and gin rummy. After Thanksgiving dinner, we all gathered in the living room for a family picture. All three of my brothers and all the grandchildren were there. I didn't know it at the time, but it would be the last picture we would ever take with the entire family together.

I tried to rest and focus on quality family time. The mornings were always my special time with my mom. We were both early risers, and it was our tradition to get up early while everyone else slept in. We would chat for hours while we drank coffee. I miss those moments with her the most—time alone while the rest of the world was still asleep.

I wanted to tell her what I had found on the laptop. I wanted to confide in her about the reservations I had about the relationship. But there are just some things that a mother shouldn't have to know.

If that wasn't enough, I could sense that Shelby was going through something difficult. I tried to talk to her about it, but she wouldn't confide in me. She was in a long-distance relationship, and I truly felt I could use my own experience to help her. But of course, I was not exactly setting the best example of a healthy relationship for her.

I knew that my voyage was stressful for her. Combined with the anxiety issues she had struggled with since she was a baby, she seemed especially sensitive and distant. I tried to reassure her about the voyage, but there was something deeper bothering her.

We had a few battles of will during the week, which was not unusual for us. But for some reason, these run-ins were especially dramatic. Maybe we both were fighting insurmountable demons that were just too difficult and too heavy to discuss. I couldn't discuss with my mom what I was going through. Maybe she felt the same way.

While in the States, I decided to call Sailboat Bob. He had untied the lines and headed toward the Florida panhandle on *Windy City* for his own liveaboard sailing adventure. I had tried to text him a few times from different ports, but at 80-something years old, he didn't adapt well to technology. Texting was not a comfortable form of communication for him.

He was in Key West and told me he was struggling to maintain his old ship. However, he was sailing close to shore and avoiding open ocean passages. He was loving the lifestyle and happy to finally be free from land life.

I told him of my adventures, and he told me how proud he was of what I had accomplished so far. He reminded me that he had never had the courage to cross an ocean or tackle challenging waters like the Bay of Biscay. I made sure he knew that it wouldn't have been possible without his patient teachings or the knowledge and wisdom he had shared with me.

The week went by way too quickly.

On Sunday, I sat on the bed in my parents' basement guest room. It was the same bed that the skipper was lying on when I discovered the truth about Julia and threw his phone at him a couple years before.

I didn't just *remember* the heartache of that discovery. I could still *feel* it.

I looked at my small carry-on suitcase and backpack sitting by the door and wondered what would happen if I missed my flight.

What if I just didn't go back?

It was difficult to leave the comfort and warmth of my family as doubts began to flood my already-confused brain.

Was I being selfish wanting this grand adventure? How would I get the dogs back home? What would the skipper do if I didn't return? Would he be happy or sad? Would he care at all?

Regardless of my doubts about the relationship, I was drawn to the adventure of doing something many people only dream about. The allure of destinations unexplored was strong and powerful. Meanwhile, my competitive nature was in full force, and my drive to challenge myself was at an all-time high.

There was a part of me that just didn't want to be a quitter. I was determined to finish what I had started.

I said I was going to sail that boat across the Atlantic to Alabama, and that's what I intend to do. I can't quit now. When would I ever get another opportunity to cross an ocean in a sailboat?

What would people think if I ended it now? It's only a few more months, and then I'll be back home. I've already gotten through all the hard parts. I made it through the freaking Bay of Biscay! I've come this far...How can I stop now?

It was almost impossible to compartmentalize the voyage from the relationship. They were connected in so many ways. As my mind focused on the relationship, I began to gaslight myself.

Is it worth it? Do the good times outweigh the bad? Yes, they do. Right? All the bad stuff happened a long time ago. I promised to push the reset button and start fresh. People can change. He's a different person now. He's not cheating on me anymore. How could he cheat from the middle of the ocean? He chose me over all the others.

It was amazing how I could convince myself of just about anything if I tried hard enough.

As I was rationalizing whether to go or to stay, I received a text from the skipper with a picture of him and the dogs. "We miss you and can't wait to have you back. Have a safe flight. I love you."

His timing was always impeccable. It was almost as if he could sense that I was wrestling with the demons that continued to haunt me.

I loaded the car and said goodbye to all the people who love me the most—assuring them that I would be safe and that I would come home soon.

Shelby drove me to Atlanta, and I could tell something still bothered her.

I gave her the biggest hug and reassured her that I would be home soon. Then I forced myself out of the car and onto the plane.

I spent the long nine hours on the flight back to Morocco in deep thought. I thought about the way the skipper had treated me all those years and wasn't quite sure what to call the situation I found myself trapped inside. I knew there were extreme highs and lows, but did the word "abuse" apply?

In hindsight, I can see clearly that abuse comes in many different forms.

However, it was difficult to see it while I was so close to it—especially when the abuse was verbal, emotional, and psychological. I didn't want to see it, and I didn't want to believe it. I tried to focus on the good and hoped that I was wrong about the bad.

There were no bruises, or black eyes, or bloodshed.

I know now that the scars on the inside are much more difficult to see and to identify. And, perhaps, they take longer to heal.

Just like with any kind of abuse, the victim tries to get out many times but continues to get pulled back in. I was feeling the pull all the way from the other side of the Atlantic.

I thought about how the skipper probably wouldn't cheat on me if I were prettier, or thinner, or smarter, or more cultured. He would have loved me more if I were a better sailor, or more talented. Or maybe I just didn't love him enough or treat him well enough.

I thought about all the times he stripped me of my confidence. It was little things, but in hindsight, I can see that the tactics were very strategic. He would never say I wasn't pretty, but he would say things like, "I don't have to be with a beautiful woman." If I showed him an article I had written, he would say, "I don't know why anyone would want to read this."

The manipulation was masterful. I think that deep down I knew I was being abused but didn't want to admit it—not to anyone else and especially not to myself.

I often hoped that he would just punch me in the face because at least I knew what that kind of abuse looked like. If he ever physically hurt me, I would leave him in a heartbeat and never look back. I think he and I both knew that.

But the slow burn of psychological abuse is much more difficult to identify. For me, it was disguised behind "I love you"s and exciting adventures. When close friends would advise me to leave him, I would brush it off and defend him.

This is just the way he is. He's from a different culture. He doesn't mean it.

What I didn't realize then is that behavior like that has nothing to do with culture—it is all about character.

My confidence was so low I didn't feel worthy of being with a better man. I honestly thought that he was the best I was going to get and would tell myself, "Nobody is perfect." Then I would remind myself of all of my own flaws and convince myself I was the lucky one.

I was blinded by love and loyalty. I'm quite sure he knew that and used it to his advantage—but I couldn't understand that back then.

I have often thought that perhaps it was my fault that the abuse continued. After all, I let it happen all those years and continued to go back for more.

It was a confusing and chaotic time as I fell deeper and deeper into a spiral that twisted me into an inescapable trap—stuck somewhere between the excitement of the grand adventure, the allure of all the exotic destinations, the promise of something better on the other side, and the struggle between my head and my heart.

CHAPTER 16

LIFE ON THE OPEN OCEAN

PASSAGE TO CANARY ISLANDS (PART ONE)

I returned to Morocco with a heavy heart—conflicted about leaving the comfort of my loving family and the excitement of continuing the grand adventure.

I must admit I was happy to see the skipper. He greeted me at the airport with Cap'n Jack and Scout in tow. All three seemed happy to see me, which warmed my heart.

The heavy rain continued to pour the entire week I was gone, so there was a lot of work to do before we could depart on our next passage—to the Canary Islands. But first, the skipper had a surprise waiting for me on the boat.

He had purchased a small Christmas tree and some twinkling white lights. He had gathered seashells to use as ornaments. I was amazed that he was able to find those items in a Muslim country that did not celebrate Christian holidays, but somehow, he did.

Sometimes he could be very sweet and considerate. Christmas has always been very important to me, and I knew I wouldn't be able to afford another flight home in a month to celebrate with my family. I appreciated his effort, even though I knew that the holiday meant nothing to him.

At least we would have a few festive decorations on *Seefalke*, and for that, I was grateful to the skipper. But before we could think about any serious celebrations, we had a long to-do list to get ready for the next passage.

We often compared our boat maintenance list to a roll of toilet paper. No matter how many squares were torn off, it would just keep rolling and rolling. When the end of the roll was reached, we replaced it with a fresh roll.

Two items were high priority before we could leave Morocco. First, water continued to enter the bilge from the anchor windlass. That required maintenance at least two to three times each week. The heavy rain from the previous week moved that task to the top of our never-ending list.

We worked the typical sponge technique, but this time, it didn't soak it all. The skipper rigged several creative tools to reach into the tiny crevices in *Seefalke's* belly. He placed some diapers on the end of a long stick to sop up the water in the crevices and corners that we couldn't reach with our arms, a sponge, or a water pump. Building creative rigs is essential for sailors.

The second priority was repairing the halyard at the top of the mizzen mast. To accomplish that task, one of us needed to go to the top of the mast—the crow's nest. On a ketch, there are two masts. The mizzen mast was the smaller one located on the stern about 10 m high. I eagerly volunteered.

I strapped myself into the bosun's chair, which is kind of like a sling that you can sit in. It was carefully rigged with the mast's built-in pulley mechanism so that I could be lifted to the top using a winch. I felt safe. But just in case, I wrapped my legs around the mast and squeezed as hard as I could with my thighs. Each time I heard the crank of the winch, I shimmied up the pole as the mechanism lifted me skyward.

I made it to the crow's nest and rigged the halyard.

From the top of the mast, I could see for miles and wondered what it would be like to climb up there while at sea.

The skipper cranked the winch to slowly bring me down while I continued my thigh-squeezing shimmies. When I made it safely down to the deck, the skipper said, "You're a real sailor now!"

I laughed and said proudly, "Make no mistake...I became a real sailor when I made it through the Bay of Biscay!"

Meanwhile, he was organizing another major repair. We needed to replace the zinc anodes on the bottom of the boat. A diver went underneath *Seefalke* in Lisbon and informed us that they definitely needed to be replaced, which meant pulling the 11-ton *Seefalke* out of the water on a crane. The marina in Morocco had no crane so we made arrangements to take care of that task once we made it to the Canary Islands.

The bad weather continued. We were trapped in port for a few more days because the swells coming in from the Atlantic at the entrance of the marina were too dangerous to execute a safe departure. But that gave us plenty of time to shop for more provisions and continue with the toilet roll list of repairs.

Sailing to the Canary Islands–Day 1

SATURDAY, 1 DECEMBER 2018

I could tell that Cap'n Jack and Scout were getting excited about another adventure. They saw us making preparations—securing the deck and the cockpit, entering the route on the plotter, filling out all the departure paperwork, and securing the cabin.

By now, they knew the routine. They would patrol the deck, trying to help like dutiful crew members. I believe that they could sense our excitement and would get excited, too.

At 08:30 I applied a Transderm Scopolamine Patch that my family doctor had prescribed while I was in Alabama. I had hopes that it would help me battle the recurring seasickness.

We left our mooring at 09:10 and cruised to the customs dock for the discharge procedures. A British couple on a beautiful sailboat, *Jack the Lad*, was moored next to us. The customs dock was small, so they moored *Jack the Lad* directly onto *Seefalke* on the starboard side and then climbed across our boat to get to the pier.

I asked the woman if they were full-time sailors. She told me that seven years prior, her husband had retired and they had begun sailing more regularly. About a year later, she was laid off from her job.

She said the management pulled her and a few other colleagues aside and told them that they were "redundant." She said everyone else was disappointed and upset, but she was cheering, "Yay! I've been made redundant! Now, we can go sailing full time!"

They had been living on *Jack the Lad* and sailing around the world ever since. Sometimes we would meet people who were weekend sailors or perhaps they were sailing while on vacations. Others were full-timers. They all had an interesting story to tell, and I found it fascinating to learn all the different scenarios that made it possible for a wide range of people to follow their dreams.

While in Morocco, we were moored next to a Dutch man and his Filipina girlfriend. He rented his home in the Netherlands and used the rent money to finance their sailing travels. They had been living on *Eastbirds* and sailing the world for four years with that small monthly budget.

Some sailors, like my German friend Yvi, would sell everything they owned and sail until the money ran out. Then they would go back to work until they could save enough money for the next sailing adventure. Many were retired and used their life's savings to fulfill their dream in their twilight years.

We also met sailors who were, like us, able to work remotely while sailing. We met very few, if any, sailors who were independently wealthy and able to just cruise along without any budget or limitations, although I'm sure there were some out there.

The Moroccan exit customs procedure was less tedious than the entrance procedure. Our drones were returned to us, and we were quickly cleared.

There were gigantic waves outside the mouth of the marina. We felt like we were on a roller coaster, but *Seefalke* handled them perfectly—gracefully surfing over them as we made our way into the open ocean. I immediately felt queasy and wondered if I should have applied the patch a bit earlier. Once we were into the open Atlantic, we hoisted the sails. I decided to rest and tried to fight off the early queasiness.

By afternoon, I was feeling better, and around 18:30 I took a short two-hour shift so the skipper could rest for the first long night watch. I enjoyed a spectacular red and orange sunset and was reminded of the old poem: *"Red sky at night, sailors' delight. Red sky in the morning, sailors' warning."*

I took photos of the remarkable sunset, but the images I snapped in my brain and in my memory were always so much more vibrant than the ones I captured on film.

Day 2

SUNDAY, 2 DECEMBER 2018

I slept from 20:00 to midnight then took my shift. My tummy was in knots and was cramping uncomfortably, which I didn't understand because the waters had been relatively calm. I could feel the nausea building and at 00:48, I surrendered and fed a few fish over the port side of *Seefalke*.

Afterward, I felt better and the nausea seemed to fade quickly. I wondered if the patch was either not working, or perhaps it was the medicine from the patch that made me sick. Either way, I decided to keep the patch and continue to give it a chance. One patch was designed to last three days.

It got cold during the night, and Scout joined me in the cockpit. I wrapped a sleeping bag around us like a cape and made it through the rest of my four-hour watch with no problems, no seasickness, not much traffic, and no drama. Just how I liked it!

In the morning, my head was hurting, and I felt like my body needed protein. I decided to make some scrambled eggs. It was enough to refuel, but not enough to ease my pounding headache.

All day the seas were relatively calm, and there wasn't much wind, so we motor sailed. However, swells came in from the Atlantic that continued to rock us occasionally.

We were about 25 nm from shore when we saw a small wooden, open-hull fishing boat. The boat couldn't have been more than 15-ft long, perhaps even smaller than *Protagonist*. My first thought was how seasick the four fishermen must be in the tiny boat that was being rocked by the huge Atlantic swells.

It also occurred to me that the little boat was their office and the sea was their livelihood. We had the freedom to sit in port and wait for favorable weather, but they had no choice but to be out there every day, no matter how severe the weather.

That was a long way from shore for such a small boat with nothing more than a small outboard motor and no cover to protect them from the heat or cold or rain. That little boat could get tossed and capsized very easily, but they kept working.

As the waters calmed, I decorated the little mini-tree and secured it in the cockpit, which made me feel festive and happy! I desperately wanted to feel productive at sea. I tried to read a little and write a little when I felt well enough. I desperately needed to break the sleep-watch-sleep-watch routine.

I wondered what 20—40 days of that at-sea routine would be like when we sailed across the Atlantic in a few weeks. I worried about how I would handle the loneliness and boredom.

I had the pups to keep me company, but I didn't have the most talkative human companion. When the skipper inflicted the silent treatment at sea, it was especially upsetting an unsettling.

Day 3

MONDAY, 3 DECEMBER 2018

We continued with our usual night watch shifts and had developed a good routine. I would take a short shift from 18:00 to 20:00 so the skipper could rest for the long night ahead. He was on watch from 20:00 to midnight. Then I would take over midnight to

04:00, and he would resume again from 04:00 to 08:00. He would then sleep from 08:00 until whenever he woke up, usually around 10:00.

We would both get eight hours of sleep, but his sleep was broken up more than mine. It was a good schedule for me. I only had one long overnight shift, and I got to see the sunset *and* the sunrise every single day.

During my midnight shift it was pitch black dark. There was no moon at first, but there were a zillion bright shiny stars twinkling in the black sky.

Sometimes I would love the silence, beauty, and solitude of night shifts, but sometimes it was hard work just to stay awake.

I missed the feeling of being productive, but I didn't miss all the heavy traffic. By the time the skipper relieved me at 04:00, I was exhausted and looked forward to a restful four hours off watch. I settled in with the pups and quickly drifted to sleep.

At some point, the wind changed and the skipper adjusted the sails. All of a sudden, the boat was rocking on all sides. I kept sliding off the bed and repositioning myself.

I thought about getting up and moving either to the floor or to the stern so I could stabilize my movement. I don't know why I didn't move. I ended up fighting the rocking of the boat for three hours and found it impossible to rest.

My head was splitting, but I didn't know if I could take ibuprofen as long as I still wore the patch. Around 07:45, exhausted and grumpy, I finally gave up and went to the cockpit.

That was the point during these passages—Day 3—when I would get frustrated with the tilt and the waves and the fatigue. I just wanted some normalcy. I wanted my house to stop moving and fighting with me.

Whenever I felt discouraged, looking at the beautiful scenery was the best medicine. We had the most magnificent sunrise, which made me happy. We were making good speed, which made the skipper happy.

At that point, we had 175 nm between us and Rabat. By mid-morning, I was feeling much better. I had calmed my own frustrations and embraced the beauty around me.

Day 4

TUESDAY, 4 DECEMBER 2018

We had traveled 244 nm—about halfway to our destination. Usually, night three was just before the day we would arrive at a destination. But on this voyage, we weren't even halfway.

Since the first night when I'd had a brief battle with seasickness, I had been feeling well enough to read books. The lonely, black nights were long. Sometimes I would listen to audiobooks or music, but mostly, I spent the time sharpening my Candy Crush skills.

When it was calm enough, I would write in my journal. It was very important to me to document everything about the voyage. If I didn't make notes, the days would all run together, and it would be hard to remember the details later. I would generally jot down details in my phone's "Notes" app, but on that passage, I was actually able to write and not just make notes. I could easily transfer the writings to the laptop when we made landfall.

However, even when we had calm waters and barely any traffic, it was important for us to not get too distracted from the watch. I would always make my perimeter checks every 10 minutes.

By the next morning, I had been wearing the seasickness patch for three days. I had only one brief episode of seasickness on the first night but had suffered a pounding headache the rest of the time. The cure couldn't be worse than the illness, so I decided not to use another patch. It seemed like the heavy conditions were behind us.

At sea, the calm never lasted for long.

Day 5

WEDNESDAY, 5 DECEMBER 2018

We had sailed 325 nm and had been at sea for 85 hours and 48 minutes. That was officially the longest amount of time we had been at sea on any single passage, so far. But there was still a long way to go.

There was a lot of activity on the radio that night. Some of it was the standard ships communicating with each other to avoid collision. One ship would radio another ship and ask them to make a shift to either the port side or the starboard side so they could pass safely. Sometimes I could just hear fuzziness and static.

On that night, for some reason there were several lonely sailors with too much rum in their bellies. They amused themselves over the radio with random comments and sometimes played music.

It was lonely at sea—especially in the black of night. So, if those guys wanted to talk to each other and find company on the radio waves, I had no problem with it. The authorities may have felt differently. However, in the middle of the sea, there was no judge and no jury.

I awoke with the sunrise and the bluest cloud-free sky I had ever seen. I fed the pups, and they did their morning business on the grass mat on the bow. They had made progress with their onboard potty training.

I shaved my legs using a bowl of hot water that I heated on the stove. I took what my mom would call a "spit bath," then Scout and I went onto the deck. I sat there for hours reading *Seraffyn's European Adventure* by my sailing idols Lin and Larry Pardey. I was so happy that I finally felt well enough to read on board.

Around 12:30 we were visited by a school of dolphins who played in the wake of our bow for about 20 minutes. The dolphins put on a show, leaping and jumping and diving deep below the surface. I was amazed at the clarity of the 3,000 m deep water.

When the dolphins swam away, I returned to my spot on the cold, steel deck. I had been searching for some sort of cushion to make the long passages more comfortable, but I'd had no luck finding anything in Rabat. I had asked the skipper to look for something for me, and his solution was a small piece of carpet, which helped a little, but didn't really provide the soft cushion I desired.

He reminded me that "sailing is not for sissies," and told me that I was less of a sailor if I required a cushion. I found this senseless since every other ship we had been on had many cushions available for its sailors.

I tried to get comfortable anyway. I leaned my back against a row of four fenders, cuddled with Scout, and once again got lost in the pages of the book, which told the story of the Pardeys' adventures on *Serrafyn*. The Pardeys spent 47 years living on small sailboats, circumnavigating the globe several times.

Earlier that morning I read to the skipper a quote from the book. Larry Pardey said, *"The most important tool or equipment you can have onboard is a well-trained crew."*

Apparently, he paid attention.

He stood up on the stern deck and said, "Hey, Michelle..." I looked up from my book just in time to see him toss one of our big round fenders overboard. "Man overboard!" he said. "What do you do?"

He loved to spring those little exercises on me. It generally happened when he was bored and I was content.

I was agitated that I had to stop reading mid-sentence and spring into action. I was really enjoying the opportunity to finally just relax onboard and read. But I also knew that those kinds of exercises prepared me for potential emergencies. It helped to build confidence so I reluctantly participated.

I went through the man overboard procedure—with a few mistakes—and in about 15 minutes retrieved the floating fender. That, of course, was not quick enough had I been trying to rescue a living thing rather than a rubber fender. The skipper pointed out my mistakes, and then we reviewed the procedure in detail.

After the training exercise, my already stinky body, which had not been showered in four days, was dripping in sweat. The waters were perfectly calm, so I decided to use the deck shower—a small bag filled with five liters of water, warmed by the sun. It felt so good to get clean and to wash my nasty, greasy hair.

The skipper showered after me. Five liters was more than enough for us both to have a full shower. Then we sliced open a fresh pineapple that was super yummy and refreshing!

At 13:55 we hit the 370 nm mark, making it the longest single passage of our voyage so far. At that point, we had been at sea for 98 hours and 58 minutes. The skipper took a brief nap while I cuddled with the puppies on the deck and once again got lost in my book. A few hours later, I cooked a warm pasta dinner, and we adjusted the sails for the night shifts.

Our dolphin friends returned that night. The sun had already set, but I could hear them porpoising in the water and breathing through their blowholes. When they surfaced, I could see their black silhouettes in the moonlight.

At the 20:00 shift change, we crossed the same latitude line that put us even with my hometown of Gulf Shores, Alabama—30° 17'N. The American South was now north of us.

That was by far my favorite day at sea, up to that point. It finally felt like we had something of a normal living-at-sea routine. For the first time, I believed we would be just fine living everyday life during the long Atlantic crossing.

I was grateful for the calm, boring, low-excitement day, but soon the adrenaline would be pumping again. A gentle giant of the sea was coming for a visit.

CHAPTER 17
WHALE OF A TALE
PASSAGE TO CANARY ISLANDS (PART TWO)

Day 6—THURSDAY, 6 DECEMBER 2018

The wind picked up and we sailed at about 3.5 knots. Four knots is the equivalent of a person casually jogging, while 3.5 knots is about the speed of someone walking briskly.

The drunken-sailor shenanigans continued on the radio and kept me entertained during my watch. The reporter in me wanted to talk to them and learn their stories. But the rules-follower in me didn't want to break the marine radio rules. I passively listened and crafted stories in my mind about the lonely sailors, so far from home, longing for a bit of company in the long, black night.

After a semi-restful sleep during the 04:00—08:00 watch, I settled into my favorite part of the day—the moment when the night becomes light and the sky reveals its special colors of the day. It was different every morning. That morning, the sky just above the horizon was bright lavender fading into cotton-candy pink and then melted into a warm buttery yellow.

Around 08:20, I heard a huge blowing sound that was unmistakably a whale. I looked to the starboard side to see a giant charcoal gray whale surface and then dive again not more than 10 m from *Seefalke's* beam.

I shouted to the cabin below, "Wake up! Come up here! It's a whale!"

We had an agreement that we would wake the other if there was something spectacular to see. This whale absolutely qualified! The skipper came rushing up to the cockpit in his underpants and bare feet just in time to see the whale surface again, this time on the port side.

At first, we thought our whale was about the length of *Seefalke* (12 m) but a closer look revealed he was about 10 m long. He circled around *Seefalke*—surfacing every 30 to 40 seconds—and was curious about us.

He swam so close to the boat we could see him diving through the crystal-clear water just next to *Seefalke*. If I had jumped into the water, I would have landed right on top of him. At one point, he was so close to the stern he actually sprayed the skipper with his blowhole.

The puppies were in the cabin below and could not have been less interested. Cap'n Jack had retrieved the wrapper of a package of cheese from the trash, and that seemed much more interesting to the beagles.

All the excitement was happening just as the sun was bursting over the port side horizon, blending magnificent tangerine and burnt orange hues with the already-brilliant pink sky.

We were not sure if he was male or female, but since we were headed to Spain and he appeared during a glorious sunrise, we named him Hijo del Sol—Spanish for "Son of the Sun."

Hijo del Sol continued to circle us and was very playful. At one point he swam right next to *Seefalke's* port side, turned onto his side, and made eye contact with us—which gave me happy chills all over. His eyeball was about the size of an American football. His underbelly was a much lighter gray than his back, and it was glowing underwater, reflecting off the fresh morning sunlight.

I noticed what I thought was a huge fin standing about a meter above the surface. But then we realized it was one side of his huge tail that revealed itself from his sideways position. He continued to study us curiously.

We knew the whale could swim much faster than 3.5 knots, but he stayed on *Seefalke's* pace for about 40 minutes. Sometimes he would circle us, and sometimes he would surf the waves behind the stern.

And then . . . Poof! Just like that, Hijo del Sol disappeared into the deep blue sea.

The skipper returned to the cabin and went back to sleep. Alone in the cockpit, I felt exhilarated and couldn't stop thinking about the playful mammal who seemed as delighted as we were for the play time. It was magical and exciting—so difficult to describe. I knew I would never forget it.

And I was reminded, once again, why I did this.

At that point we had been at sea for 117 straight hours and had sailed 440 nm. I thought about all the times I was miserably seasick, battling exhaustion and dehydration, or homesick.

Even when I felt like giving up, I kept coming back because of the gift of those rare and special glimpses of magnificence. At that moment, all those hours of being sick and uncomfortable were only a distant memory and were worth it for 40 minutes of a glorious encounter with that gentle giant of the sea.

Day 7

FRIDAY, 7 DECEMBER 2018

I had drifted into a deep sleep after my midnight watch. The skipper woke me at 05:30 and urgently told me to help him in the cockpit. I quickly threw on some shoes and pants and rushed up to help him, even though I was groggy and confused from being awakened so abruptly. The genoa reef line had gotten tangled into the furling mechanism. I stayed in the cockpit while the skipper went to the bow to try and untangle it.

It was one of those things that would have been easy to fix in port, but almost impossible to fix while at sea with heavy wind and waves. We got it under control, but the genoa was not quite all the way furled, and it flapped annoyingly in the wind.

All the commotion woke the pups, and it was a struggle to keep them from going onto the bow. Scout got nervous and promptly went into the stern cabin to pee on the cushion of the bed. I cleaned it the best I could and didn't scold her. With everything under control, I went back down to sleep. I was awakened again around 08:00 as we approached Arrecife.

As we got closer to port, the skipper returned to the bow to try to finish furling the flapping sail that could have impeded our mooring maneuver. I took the wheel and steered us in circles while he used our motion and the wind to wrap the remainder of the flapping sail around the stay.

We arrived in the marina at 08:20 and secured *Seefalke*. We both let out a sigh of relief. We had made it a full week at sea—520 nm in 145 hours.

I gave Cap'n Jack and Scout a much-needed walk while the skipper checked in with the marina and with customs. He is European, and we were in Spain, so his immigration procedure was easy. As a U.S. citizen, mine required more effort.

The next weeks required a focus on repairs and provisions. *Seefalke* had a date with a crane to replace the zinc anodes, and we planned to stuff her to the brim with food, water, and supplies in anticipation of our sailing passage across the Atlantic Ocean. I hoped we could find a little time to explore the fascinating Island of Fire.

And the skipper found time to book another flight.

CHAPTER 18

CHRISTMAS IN THE CANARIES

After our longest passage to date, we had an even longer list of chores, work, and provisioning with only a couple more stops until our Atlantic crossing.

For the first three days in Arrecife, the capital of the island of Lanzarote, we settled in and went to work. The marina was covered in festive Christmas lights, while holiday music played all day and into the evenings. Sailors were either hunkered for the holidays in the Canaries or preparing to leave their boats for their land homes all over the world.

Even though the seven-day passage from Morocco had been relaxing for the most part, we were exhausted and a bit overwhelmed with the amount of work ahead of us.

TUESDAY, 11 DECEMBER 2018
We immediately began prepping *Seefalke* for her date with a crane. Sailing a steel ship is a constant fight against corrosion. At every stop, we were married to a paint brush—constantly brushing rust corrosion prevention chemicals onto various spots all around *Seefalke's* steel frame. Under the surface, the zinc anodes protected the underwater hull from corrosion.

Any time two different metals that are physically or electrically connected are immersed in seawater, they become a battery. Current flows between the two metals. The electrons that make up that current are supplied by one of the metals giving up bits of itself—in the form of metal ions—to the seawater.

It's called galvanic corrosion, and if left unchecked, it quickly destroys underwater metals. It's hard to overstate the importance of maintaining the anodes on a steel boat. When an anode is missing or largely wasted away, the metal component it was installed to protect begins to dissolve—guaranteed.

Since we were in a popular sailors' port, the marina crew was equipped with a sophisticated crane system that lifts 110 tons out of the water easily. It would only take six to eight hours for them to lift our 11-ton ship, dock it on land, and replace the zinc anodes.

We cruised to the loading dock where we carefully positioned *Seefalke* on top of huge belts inside a concrete alcove and were lifted out of the water along with our heavy vessel.

With no home to rest on and no office to work in, we spent the day exploring the Island of Fire. The Canary Islands is a Spanish archipelago off the coast of northwestern Africa. It is known for rugged volcanic isles and for black- and white-sand beaches.

The Canary Islands are not named for the bird. In fact, Islas Canarias comes from the Latin term "insula canaria," which translates to "island of the dogs." Locals believe that the "dogs" were actually a species of monk seals, which in Latin means "sea dogs."

It is believed that the original inhabitants of the islands worshipped dogs. When the Romans first visited the island, it was given the name "canarii," which means "the ones with dogs." While the islands got their name from dogs, the canary birds got their name from the islands. The wild variety originates from the Macaronesian islands, which include the Canaries.

We started the adventure by stopping at a little café on the marina promenade for coffee and breakfast and began making our list of needed supplies. We took in the scenery, admiring the hundreds of sailboats moored in the large marina.

A sweet man and woman asked to pet the beagles. Cap'n Jack and Scout were always great magnets for attracting new friends. The lovely Swedish couple were retired and had been sailing the world full time for three years. They were going to Greece but wanted to sail through Norway on the way, which makes no geographical sense but proves that sailors often sail to wherever the wind takes them.

We took a short walk from the marina to the city center, where we found a huge bay with hundreds of anchored wooden fishing boats. Many of them were broken, neglected, and stuck in the mud on the low-water sides. I was intrigued about the stories behind old wooden boats, especially those that were in disrepair.

We walked to the shoreline where we saw the Museo de Historia de Arrecife, a history museum inside a castle on the waterfront. The Castillo San Gabriel was founded in 1593 when a square-shaped fort was built to create a defense against pirates.

While snapping photos of the castle and the fortress surrounding it, an American couple walked by me and said, "War Eagle!" I was wearing an Auburn t-shirt. No matter where I traveled around the world, it always made me happy to be greeted with my alma mater's battle cry.

The nice couple had arrived on a cruise ship earlier that morning. They were Florida Gator fans, so we had a great conversation about SEC football. They updated me on the first college football season I had missed in about 20 years.

We told them of our sailing adventures, and the man told us how he had crossed the Atlantic many times piloting large cargo airplanes—using only a sextant for navigation. We found this as fascinating as they found our impending Atlantic crossing in a small sailboat.

Back at the marina, we found *Seefalke* equipped with shiny new anodes on her hull. The huge crane lowered her back into the water, and we safely returned her to our mooring. That's when the skipper told me he was leaving again.

He would always disguise trips as opportunities to visit his young daughter, making it impossible for me to object without seeming heartless. I was deeply disappointed and, based on our history, suspicious about whether there were other people he wanted to see, as well. He softened the blow by agreeing to do more sightseeing the next day.

WEDNESDAY, 12 DECEMBER 2018

We worked half of the next day and then took a break to explore Timanfaya National Park.

Lanzarote is the northernmost and easternmost island of the Canary Islands. It was borne through fiery eruptions and has solidified lava streams as well as extravagant rock formations.

It is known as the "Island of Fire," and it's easy to see why. With hundreds of active volcanoes, some parts of the island's landscape are too hot to walk on or to touch. The layers of various textures and colors make visiting there a uniquely stunning experience—a mixture of sub-tropical beaches and lava fields.

The fire mountains of Timanfaya form part of a broad area affected by the volcanic eruptions that struck Lanzarote between 1730 and 1736. There were more eruptions in 1824. The long eruptive process drastically changed the island's morphology, leaving a quarter of it almost completely buried under a thick layer of lava and ash.

Scanning the landscape, we saw volcanic mountains that boasted colors of desert sand and dark chocolate brown combined with a rich, brick red that reminded me of the terre battue of the French Open clay tennis courts.

There were also layers of green varying in colors from a soft, almost yellow green to vibrant rainforest greens and even some tones as dark as a pine tree. When the sun would hit the mountains many shades of orange and yellow were reflected. The landscape was mostly black rock and charcoal lava fields, and I felt like I was visiting a distant, uninhabited planet rather than a subtropical island.

The next day was another full workday, but we took time to celebrate Cap'n Jack and Scout's second birthday with extra walks and extra treats.

We returned to our bilge project, which had been ongoing since our first week at sea way back in mid-August when we discovered a small leak in the bilge caused by water entering through the anchor windlass. We applied sealant in the places vulnerable to further leakage and then covered the entire bilge in a smelly orange rust preventer to protect *Seefalke's* steel belly. The thick substance would take several days to dry.

Meanwhile, I worked on a detailed provision list so we could shop efficiently. We needed to stockpile supplies for the Atlantic crossing. It required several hours for me to go through every locker, bilge, and crate in which we had stored food and supplies.

The main cabin was in complete chaos, and the floor was open because we were allowing the bilge to air out and dry. That's when the skipper said he wanted to relocate several supply crates that were on the upper shelves in the main cabin. We never slept in the bow cabin, so he suggested making the V-berth a pantry/closet so that our main cabin would be less cluttered.

I liked the idea, but I also knew that it meant more work for me. After four months at sea, I had finally put all the pieces of the puzzle together so that things were not flying around when we were underway.

It made sense to declutter our main living area and have one central place for the food and supplies that we needed the most often. The project provided me with a brand-new Rubik's Cube to solve while the skipper prepared to leave us alone again for a week in Germany with a side trip to the Netherlands.

I missed my family. It saddened me that I would not be home for Christmas. I felt more homesick than ever.

Since I was re-organizing the entire ship anyway, I asked the skipper if I could make some cosmetic changes while he was away.

The brown walls and dark wood in the main saloon made me feel like I was living in a depressing dungeon. I wanted to paint the walls bright white and mount some photos of all the gorgeous places we had visited. I also wanted to mount family photos that I felt would help to quell my homesickness.

The skipper quickly discounted my suggestions, telling me he didn't want to change *Seefalke's* original character. I made my argument. "You want me to make this my home and feel comfortable living here," I explained to him, "but you won't let me make it more comfortable and homey. Just think about how much brighter and happier it would feel with lighter walls and some colorful images."

His response was emphatic. "Do not paint the inside of this boat."

I struggled to understand. "Can I at least mount a few photos of my kids?"

He refused, saying, "The only thing I want hung on the walls are charts and maps. I won't feel comfortable having all those faces staring back at me all the time."

I confessed to him that I felt like I was suffering from a bit of low-grade depression spending so much time in the dark, dungeon-like cabins—especially since he left me alone every time we sailed into a new port.

His response lacked compassion. "When you feel depressed, sit in the cockpit or take a walk."

Feeling deflated, I reluctantly returned to my organizing project. I found some leftover postcards from a few of our destinations. It was important to me to send postcards from every port to family and friends—a simple gesture that helped me feel connected to home.

I also sent cards to the skipper's family, even though he told me that they wouldn't appreciate them. I heard from his delighted mother, sister, and son every time they received one—proving the skipper wrong.

Without asking for his permission, I taped the leftover postcards on the wall near the main bunk. At least I could add a little color and some life to the room where I spent most of my time. He immediately asked me to take them down, but I refused.

"A compromise," I said matter-of-factly, without opening the topic for any more discussion.

That day we had a visit from our neighbors just two boats down the pier. A sweet French couple, Alain and Alexa had been sailing the world for the past 10 years on their steel sailboat, *Et Puis Pas Plus*, which loosely translates from French to English as "That's all I have to say about that."

We swapped some rust-prevention steel boat maintenance tips, and then they invited us to their floating home for coffee. Hearing the stories of other sailors and how they made a transition from "civilized" life on land to a life at sea had always intrigued me. I was also excited to make new friends just before the skipper left me alone again.

As Alexa prepared strong French roast for the three Europeans and made fun of the amount of milk and sugar I used to "ruin" my American version of coffee, Alain told us how he had retired 10 years before and immediately transitioned to a full-time life at sea.

Alexa was 10 years younger than her partner. She had owned a gift shop in France, which she sold to join Alain on his sailing adventures. Ten years later, they were still out there sailing the world.

Their boat was a beauty! It was all white with a center cockpit like ours and also had two masts. Inside, it was much more spacious than our boat. Even though it was the same length as *Seefalke* (40 or so feet), it was almost twice as wide. It was amazing how much additional living space their boat provided.

Alain had bought the boat from a family friend when it was a steel shell. He hired a cabinet maker to design and build the inside with custom cabinets, three cabins, three heads, two showers, and a large galley and saloon with comfy cushions.

The main cabin in the stern featured a queen-size bed with a traditional mattress, fluffy linens, and beautiful duvet—pure luxury compared with the one-inch mat that barely provided any cushion on our wooden bunk that also served as our table.

What really caught my eye were the crisp white walls that made the space feel light, airy, and inviting. I remarked about the happy space and commented that it was exactly what I wanted to do to brighten *Seefalke's* living quarters.

The skipper sternly told me to drop it.

We had a nice visit and invited Alain and Alexa to have dinner with us on *Seefalke*. That's when they told us they were departing the next day to visit one of the other Canary Islands. I was openly disappointed. I wished they would be there to keep me company while I was alone the next week.

We said goodbye to our new friends. But goodbye was never really goodbye with sailors. There was always a chance we would meet again somewhere in the world.

While the skipper was still there to help me, we made a trip to the local market for provisions and filled four grocery carts to the brim. After unloading the second cart into the rental car, we learned that the store would deliver all of the supplies to the marina for only 4 Euros. I happily handed over the money.

When we returned to the marina, we made dozens of trips from the car to the boat to unload. Then I got busy updating the provision list while frantically trying to find a place to put everything. As soon as the first load was in place, the second load was delivered.

The cabin was in complete chaos. Groceries were everywhere, and we had to maneuver around the open floor because the smelly rust preventer was still drying. We walked into the city to eat local food at a restaurant by the water and enjoyed the most magnificent paella I had ever eaten.

Later, as we fell into bed, feeling exhausted and accomplished, a loud noise came from the discotheque in the marina promenade. An all-night party had started. Music blasted all night long, and the locals partied until 06:30 the next morning. The skipper was able to turn off his ears, but I struggled all night and managed to only get minimal rest.

The next morning, the pups and I drove the skipper to the airport. Then I took Cap'n Jack and Scout on a long walk into the city. When we returned to the chaotic, cluttered *Seefalke,* I got to work on my new Rubik's Cube project.

I worked on it the entire week while also finishing several articles for my clients. My goal was to stay busy and try not to worry about what the skipper was doing abroad. During the days, calm holiday music played, and I stayed productive.

Every night, the locals partied until 06:30 in the morning with banging bass beats and electric music booming throughout the marina.

I was so busy I barely left the boat all week. I only took breaks to walk the dogs. The day before the skipper's return, I decided to take the afternoon off. The pups and I took a long, relaxing walk into the city.

We stopped at a café by the water, and I enjoyed a refreshing mojito while basking in the warm sunshine for a couple hours.

It was nice to just relax for an afternoon and enjoy the gorgeous scenery and the wooden boats. I didn't want to leave that spot. Since the skipper was not there to object, I ordered a glass of white wine and splurged on a salad with grilled salmon. I stayed in the fresh, open air for a couple more hours—not yet wanting to return to the dark dungeon all alone.

As I walked back to the marina, I received a FaceTime call from my kids. I found a spot to sit and talk to Shelby and Bo for a while. They updated me on their lives, and I described the beautiful islands for them. It was such a lovely afternoon relaxing by the water, so I was in a happy place—made even happier by the sound of their precious voices and the smiles on their faces.

But it was also a harsh reminder that I would not see them for Christmas for the first time in their lives.

With the music blaring for the fifth night in a row, I closed all the hatches and tried to bear the heat and rust-preventer smell without any breeze coming into the dark cabin. But the music still made its way in, echoing into *Seefalke's* steel belly.

WEEK OF 21–24 DECEMBER 2018

We picked up the skipper from the airport and went right back to work, applying the paint overcoat in the bilge and continuing to organize and work on small boat projects.

We made plans to sail about 40 hours to Tenerife, another island in the Canaries. We had planned to depart on December 23, but the weather had something different in mind. The next morning, 30-knot winds rocked the island, so we stayed put.

Meanwhile, friends we had made while in Morocco—Jean Paul, who was born in France but grew up in the Netherlands, and his girlfriend, Annaleu, a lovely girl from the Philippines—had made their way to Arrecife, along with a Swiss couple, Ivo and Dajana, with whom I had been sharing Instagram communication.

We had coffee with Ivo and Daja on *Seefalke* and they invited us to join them, along with Jean Paul and Annaleu, on *Silkap* for a dinner featuring authentic Swiss fondue.

We did as much work as we could during the day, then walked over to *Silkap's* berth. It was a wonderful evening of fantastic food and new friendships as we enjoyed time with six sailors from eight different countries.

Jean Paul owned several cafés in Amsterdam but six years before, he had sold them all, along with everything else he owned, for a life at sea. He kept only his apartment in Amsterdam, which he rented out to finance the sailing journey. He sailed alone for two years, crossing oceans and traveling the world, but he wanted to share the experience with a companion.

He met Annaleu but had to warm her to the idea of leaving her home in the Phillipines to join him traveling the world on a boat. She told me that at first she wasn't sure, but when she saw the boat she realized it was nicer than her home in the Philippines. She began to fall in love with the charming Jean Paul and the idea of a life at sea. They had been sailing the world together for four years when we met them.

Ivo grew up in a small fishing village in Portugal and built a career in Switzerland as the manager of a government-funded program for people with disabilities. After a couple of decades, he grew frustrated with the corporate life and government red tape and began to dream of the freedom a life at sea could provide.

Dajana left her homeland of Slovakia with 40 Euros in her pocket and became an au pair in Switzerland. She earned a college degree while studying to be a digital nomad, then met Ivo when he enrolled in the LinkedIn course she was teaching. They had a passion for fishing and for deep sea diving. They took sailing courses, bought *Silkap*, and had been sailing the world since September 2018—just one month less than us. We swapped stories and compared sailing adventures late into the night.

I also enjoyed a quick tour of both *Silkap* and *Eastbirds*. I was more than a little jealous of the space and amenities both couples had on their boats. They had proper fridges and even freezers. Jean Paul had a washing machine, microwave, coffee machine, and even a TV onboard. The living space both boats had was much more expansive than ours. Both boat interiors featured bright white walls and plenty of comfy cushions.

The next morning was Christmas Eve, and we awoke to more severe weather conditions that would delay our departure at least another day. We continued with our work and preparations and began thinking about skipping Tenerife and sailing straight to Cape Verde on Christmas Day. That would mean an 8-to-9-day voyage rather than the 40 hours it would take to get to Tenerife. I had to wrap my brain around the change in plans, but I trusted that we were making the right decision.

The skipper had been agitated since returning from his trip. He would walk away from the boat without explanation and stay gone for hours at a time. Of course, he kept his precious phone in his pocket at all times.

His frequent desertions made me suspicious. During one of his disappearing acts, I noticed his iPad sitting on the navigation table. I knew it was linked with his phone and laptop. It had been almost two years since I had invaded his privacy by looking at his messages. I wasn't sure I wanted to know what secrets were lurking behind the screen, but my suspicions got the best of me.

I hated myself every time I did it. Maybe the skipper was right—perhaps the crime of invading his privacy was worse than whatever secrets I would find. However, my curiosity overruled my feelings of guilt. I opened the iPad and began to scroll his messages.

Unfortunately, my gut was never wrong.

As suspected, I uncovered countless messages of recent rendezvous with several women while he had been away all those times "visiting his daughter." I found shameless selfies of him having coffee or dinner with other women, and dozens of intimate text conversations.

They were all hurtful, of course, but one in particular sent a dagger to my heart—a message to Birgit, a German woman I recognized from the skipper's picture-hunting collection. He told her that he often thought of her while at sea.

My heart dropped, and I felt the color drain from my skin. I burst into tears, not wanting to believe it.

How could he think of other women while I was working my ass off, suffering from seasickness, missing my family, and making his dream come true?

Then my heartache turned to rage.

I was giving up Christmas with my family for THIS????

When he returned to the cockpit, I confronted him. I told him what I had found and asked for an explanation. He fell completely silent and became catatonic. I asked him question after question. He answered none of them and did not say a word. I screamed at him! I pushed him and shook his shoulders, trying desperately to physically force words out of his mouth.

He just sat there—perfectly still, silent, staring at nothing. He didn't even try to gaslight me. I continued to scream and didn't care if other sailors heard me. I called him every name in the book, but most importantly and most appropriately, I called him a lying, cheating piece of shit!

After about an hour, he stood up and walked away, but not before breaking the silence. "I never touched any of those women. I did nothing wrong." I continued to yell at him as he walked down the boardwalk. Screaming as loud as I could and for anyone to hear, I yelled that cheating with words is just as bad as cheating physically.

I went back to the iPad and continued to read conversations. I felt so alone and so trapped. I tried to remind myself that the voyage was now a personal quest—it was no longer about him and his dream.

I was no longer his life partner—I was now simply the first mate who was on a mission. When he returned to the boat, I calmly informed him of that fact. He never gave me an explanation for the evidence I had found.

However, he did find the words to accuse me of the crime of invading his privacy and reminded me that my invasive actions were worse than anything he had done.

I had scheduled a FaceTime with my family for Christmas Eve, so I told him to either act happy or stay away while I spoke with my family. My parents were busy cooking but took time to talk a little. My brother, Tim, walked through the house with the phone so I could say hello and Merry Christmas to everyone, but the scene was chaotic, and no one seemed too excited to talk to me.

I talked to Bo and his girlfriend for a few minutes, but Shelby and her boyfriend were not there yet. The skipper put on a happy face and turned on the charm for my family's benefit.

When the call was over, he returned to his catatonic state and cruel silent treatment—again making me feel guilty for the invasion of privacy. That night, I lay next to the skipper and felt sick to my stomach just being near him.

I asked him to sleep in the stern cabin. He agreed.

I stared at my little tree that he had bought for me in Morocco. It was such a sweet gesture. As the lights twinkled, I realized it was the only Christmas I would have that year.

The next morning, Christmas morning, we prepared *Seefalke* and made a quick visit to say farewell, for now, to our new friends on *Silkap* and *Eastbirds*.

I was able to reach Shelby on FaceTime to tell her Merry Christmas and briefly talked to Bo again. The family was having a wonderful celebration, and they were all too busy to talk very much.

I understood and was grateful for the brief opportunity to see their faces and tell them all how much I loved them and missed them.

At 16:00 that afternoon, we untied the lines and departed toward Cape Verde.

CHAPTER 19

FREE POWER OF THE WIND

PASSAGE TO CAPE VERDE (PART ONE)

Day 1–TUESDAY, 25 DECEMBER 2018

W e set sail on Christmas afternoon for the more than 1,000 nm passage to Cape Verde, Africa.

After the horrible fight the day before, the skipper and I were not speaking at all. He only barked the most essential sailing orders as we left the beautiful Canary Islands.

It was a particularly rocky departure. I don't know if it was the huge Atlantic swells that seemed to rock us from all sides as we left each marina or if we truly did lose our sea legs every time we sat in port for so long. Perhaps it was both.

I stumbled to the bow to untangle the genoa furling mechanism and could barely keep from falling overboard in the dangerous conditions.

When I made it back to the cockpit, I took a peek through the companionway just in time to see my newly organized cabin fall apart like a house of cards. I watched the books fly from the shelves and join all the rubble that was already on the floor.

Then a frightened little Scout peed all over her bedding, and I knew it would be up to me to clean it. It was not the best start to a week-long voyage.

We had barely left the marina, and I was practically in tears—frustrated with the clutter and mess and also with the queasiness for which I couldn't seem to find any relief.

I glanced at the skipper in desperation—I needed to tell him what I was thinking and feeling, but I worried that he would make me pay for it if I did.

He was queasy, too, and went below to rest. I took the first shift and fought through the uneasiness. We were still close enough to shore to have a slight internet signal, and I heard his phone ping. I picked it up without hesitation, without worrying whether he saw me do it, and without any guilt about spying on him.

The message was a photo from a pretty Polish sailor wearing nothing but a Santa hat. The caption said, "Merry Christmas, love."

I was furious!

I went down to the cabin and shook him awake. "Come up to the cockpit right now," I said sternly. "We need to talk, and it can't wait another minute."

"I'm not feeling well," he said.

"I don't care. Get up here."

He followed my orders.

I looked at him directly in the eyes. For some reason, I wasn't crying. I was pissed! But I tried to be calm.

"Are you really thinking about other women while we are out here?" I asked him desperately.

I waited for an answer and did not allow my eyes to leave direct contact with his. He looked concerned and perhaps even a bit remorseful.

Uncharacteristically, he broke his silence.

"Of course not, Michelle," he said sincerely.

"But I saw the message to Birgit. Why would you tell her you think of her when you and I are out here together? This isn't easy for me. I'm working hard. I'm battling through the seasickness and the homesickness and all the bullshit with the other women. I'm still here. I'm helping you sail this ship and doing everything I can to fight for our relationship.

"I have been utterly and completely faithful and loyal to you even through all the cheating and the lying and all the secrets I found on your phone. I'm doing all this for you. For us. I believe in us, but you are making it impossible for me to stay."

I showed him the photo that had just popped up on his phone.

He laughed at me.

"It's just a photo," he said flippantly.

"I didn't ask her to send it. I've done nothing wrong. But you continue to spy on me and gather all this evidence against me. I'm not having sex with these women. You are obsessed with these other women, but they mean nothing to me. It's just a game."

I refused to let him gaslight me. I looked him directly in the eyes and stayed firm.

"You are humiliating me! It's not okay," I said, fighting back the tears. "Why would these women think it's okay to send you photos like this? Why do you tell them you think about them while I'm here helping you sail this fucking ship? And why do you leave this shit on your phone when you know I look at it? Are you testing me? Are you trying to force me to leave you? Are you trying to torture me?"

He stayed firm.

"If you don't want to see it, maybe you should quit spying on me," he said. "I've done nothing wrong. It's all harmless. I haven't touched these women—well, maybe in the past, but not since our reset. I've given up a lot for you."

What?????

"Okay, I want to hear this," I said. "I've given up my family, my friends, my home, my business, my self-confidence, my life savings—all for YOU and for your dream of sailing forever. What exactly have YOU given up for ME?"

He sat in silence for a few seconds, but it was long enough for me to wonder if he would just torture me with the silent treatment again. Then he surprised me with a response.

"Yeah, I gave up the picture hunting," he said. "And I don't have sex with other women anymore. I don't delete all these messages because they are just harmless flirting. I have done nothing wrong, and you should be ashamed of the way you learned of all this information anyway. Spying on me is worse than anything I've done."

My response was quick.

"That's all bullshit," I said calmly and firmly.

I remembered a conversation I had with my mother several years before. It was right after I found out my former boyfriend had cheated on me. She wisely said, "Michelle, you deserve to be with a man who will honor you." I could see her face and hear her voice as clearly as the day she said it.

She was right. I did deserve that, even if this man had made me believe all these years that I didn't.

"Let me try to explain this to you," I said to the skipper. I looked him right in the eyes. "If you put me in a room with all these other women and you were forced to choose, I honestly believe that you would choose me 100 out of 100 times."

"Of course, I would," he said.

"Well, I need you to choose me even when I'm *not* in the room," I tried to explain. "It's as simple as that. And every time you have an intimate conversation with one of these women, or when you tell them you think about them when you are with me, or when you let them believe that it's okay to send a naked picture to you, you are *not* choosing me.

"And I don't really give a shit whether you touched them or had sex with them or whether in your warped disloyal mind you think you've done nothing wrong... Let me assure you that you have done a lot that's wrong. Just by having these conversations and receiving the pictures, you are *not* honoring me. You are not choosing me."

He didn't respond, and I couldn't tell whether I was getting through to him. So, I continued.

"I absolutely love sailing! I love all these sailing passages, and I love exploring all these new places. But when you leave me alone at every port, and then spend your time making other women feel special ... Well, it's just not okay. That is not what I signed on for. I realize that your dream is to sail forever, and I want that for you. I'm proud that I'm the one who is giving that to you.

"But my dream was to be with you. And if that's not what you want—to have me, and *only* me, by your side—then I need to jump off at the next port and we can just call it a day. I've been putting up with this shit for six years, and I just can't do it anymore. If this is what forever is going to be like for me with you, well, I just can't live my life as your consolation prize."

I couldn't stop.

"Maybe one of these other women will bust their ass on this boat and sail through the lonely night and battle the seasickness for you and sacrifice their family and friends and career, and maybe they will be okay with your addiction to all the other women. If that's the case, then I'll step aside and let them have it. But I can't live like this anymore."

It all just poured out of me.

"Michelle, I love you," he said. He took both my hands in his and looked me directly in the eyes. It was the first time he had touched me in months. "I want you here with me. This has been our dream and now it's coming true. Don't give up on me now."

He never said he was sorry. That wouldn't be his style.

"We'll see," I said, unconvinced. "Go back to the cabin. I'll take this shift."

Day 2

WEDNESDAY, 26 DECEMBER 2018

I felt uneasy and tired—worn out from the conversation and the drama. I made it through my shift, but I didn't sleep well after it. The skipper deployed his greatest weapon and remained silent after our deep conversation.

When I took over again at 08:00 I felt the familiar tightening in my abdomen and knew it wouldn't be long before the contents of my belly found their way into the deep blue waters of the western African Atlantic—a premonition that came true with brutal force around 09:00.

I felt icky all day and wondered how I would make it another week at sea.

Just before sunset, I snapped a picture of the southern coast of Fuerteventura Island, the last land we would see for the next 10 days. The sky was a gloomy . . . like my mood.

A few dolphins came to play, and I rewarded them with some chum over the side of *Seefalke*.

Day 3

THURSDAY, 27 DECEMBER 2018

The swells grew larger and the waves got choppier as we left the wind shadow of the last Canary Island. I continued to struggle to get comfortable.

But as I settled into my midnight watch, I got distracted by the black sky and the spectacular full moon that was rising at *Seefalke's* port side beam, casting a brilliant light onto the black water. The choppy waves, however, continued to rob my body of its sense of balance.

The skipper and I had not exchanged a single word since our intense conversation.

Around 10:30, I was lying flat in the stern cabin trying to rest and get through the queasiness when an alarm sounded in the cockpit. It was an engine coolant alert.

The skipper went down into the engine room, which is inconveniently located under the floor of the cockpit well below sea level. He discovered that the cooling fluid loss was actually a leak. At first, we thought it was coming through the casing bolts.

We felt uncomfortable running the engine without further investigation. We didn't use the engine much, especially when we had good wind on offshore passages. But we needed to run it occasionally to charge the batteries.

The batteries keep the instruments—most importantly the auto pilot and plotter—running when the solar panels and wind generator did not produce enough energy.

We fired up the portable generator—a last-minute impulse item we purchased the day before we left Stralsund. We used it to charge the batteries. Meanwhile, the gasoline fumes wreaked havoc on my already splitting headache and queasy tummy.

The bad news was that we had no functioning engine, something we didn't realize until we were deep into the Western African Atlantic, almost 300 nm from shore with more than 700 nm to go.

The good news was that we were in a sailing boat, not a motorboat.

We had sails and the free power of the wind.

The skipper made the wise decision to manually steer during the warm, sunny afternoons and save the autopilot for the night watches. We were finally talking to each other, but only about essential sailing details.

Day 4

FRIDAY, 28 DECEMBER 2018

I began my midnight watch as the wind picked up to 21 knots. The skipper was happy about the speed, but I preferred to go slower and remain more comfortable. The sails seemed to be absorbing some of the wave movement, which also tempered my queasiness.

I finally got a little rest, and by 09:30 I noticed we had sailed 265 nm in 65 hours.

The skipper went into the engine room again and after closer inspection, he found a crack in the casing of the heat exchanger.

That was where the engine was leaking water. He began to read all the manuals and texted our mechanics in Stralsund through our satellite communication device.

He received a lot of advice and suggestions. Our friend Dean did some research and suggested adding finely ground pepper into the casing.

An old sailor's trick, the pepper would separate itself from the water and rise to the surface of the cast iron, temporarily filling the crack. He said this worked like a charm with cracked radiators and thought it might work for us.

The skipper wanted to think and study more before taking action. That was his way—if he had time to think, he liked to think. And we had nothing but time.

Meanwhile, the genoa furling line tangled again as we were trying to tack. It had been an ongoing problem that was fairly easy to fix while in port but almost impossible to fix while at sea with heavy wind and rocking waves.

Day 5

SATURDAY, 29 DECEMBER 2018
350 NM – 80 HOURS AT SEA

I didn't sleep at all during the skipper's 20:00 shift. I couldn't sleep in the main cabin because I kept sliding off the bunk due to the starboard tilt. I moved to the stern cabin but couldn't sleep there because of random noises and generator fumes.

At that point, we had not had a proper meal, shower, or any relaxation since our departure. The seasickness hadn't been as bad as some of our other passages, but in my exaggerated mind at that time, I felt like it was even worse than the grueling Bay of Biscay. At least that passage was over in four days. We were not even to the halfway point on this voyage, and I was miserable.

I could also tell that the stress of the engine situation was wearing heavily on the skipper. When he was worried, it always added to my anxiety.

I also told myself to drink more water. I noticed that my pee was bright orange, which meant that I was dehydrated. *I had to take care of myself if I wanted to feel better.*

As my mood began to improve, a beautiful half moon rose just off the port side beam. Its bottom half was stark white with just a faint ring around the top half of the circle. It looked like a teacup and reminded me to think "cup half full."

After some rest, I took over the morning shift and reminded myself that as bad as things would sometimes get, it still beat going into an office every day and working for someone else.

We hit 400 nm and passed the 3,000-mile mark for the complete voyage. We sailed at an average of 5.5 to 6 knots—a fast speed for our heavy, slow but sturdy steel vessel. My body was finally adjusting to the waves and to the tilt, and the sailing soon turned from uncomfortable to completely pleasurable and fun.

We began to get a taste of the trade winds we expected to experience when we crossed the Atlantic Ocean. I remember thinking, *Ok, I can handle this kind of sailing for several weeks at sea.*

Then I made a big decision. I was not going to take any more seasickness meds.

I had tried every pharmaceutical prevention and so-called remedy out there. I had often heard that the only real cure for seasickness is to sit under a tree. In other words, as long as you are on the water, you are vulnerable. If my body was going to react to the motion, the medicine wouldn't really help. In fact, by that point I believed it was making it worse.

It made me groggy and reduced my appetite, which in effect caused me to deprive my body of nutrients and vitamins, which gave me a splitting headache. And I was still spending time over the rail.

The skipper spent most of the morning in the engine room. First, he drilled two holes at the beginning and the end of the crack to prevent it from cracking further. He then tried to apply emergency leakage paste to the crack, which was not designed for hot environments under pressure, but was generally effective.

We filled the cooling system with fresh water and cranked the engine. The water found its way through the crack almost immediately.

We wanted to use liquid steel, but we didn't have any. He then applied the only other kind of sealant we had on board, Sikaflex. We let it dry for about two hours. Then we cranked the engine and held our breath.

After about 20 minutes, water again began to drip, but at a reduced rate. Considering the slow drippage rate, we calculated that we had about 1 to 1.5 hours of running time before the engine would overheat.

We worried that if we tried to use the engine, we could cause further damage. We decided to save what little functionality it had for when we would arrive in Cape Verde. We would need it for the mooring maneuver.

But that was still 600 nm and about a week away. We continued to manually steer during the days and use the generator to charge the batteries so we could use the autopilot at night.

The waves began to calm as the day went on and so did my mood. I was finally able to read for a couple of hours even though the generator was a loud but necessary annoyance.

Now that my attitude and health were improving, it was the skipper's turn to not feel well. When he wasn't in the engine room, he was in the cabin reading the engine manuals from a 3-inch-thick white binder. I could tell that finding a solution to the engine problem weighed heavily on him.

As I was reading, a passage from Lin Pardey's book, *Taleisin's Tales,* really spoke to me.

"Truly memorable days were vastly outnumbered by those days when sailing was merely pleasant, or other days that were utterly mundane, or hard work, or even downright difficult. I knew this would be the case as we voyaged onward."

She went on to describe some of her truly spectacular days at sea that made the difficult days not only worth it, but forgettable.

It helped me put things into perspective as I recalled some of our memorable days—like when we saw landfall after a grueling passage across the Bay of Biscay, or when we played with our curious whale, or the day I saw Africa for the first time.

Even more spectacular moments would outweigh the difficult ones as soon as in that current passage, although I didn't know it yet.

Day 6

SUNDAY, 30 DECEMBER 2018
 485 NM – 105 HOURS AT SEA

Just before midnight, we crossed over the Tropic of Cancer, putting us officially into tropical waters. But it didn't feel tropical yet. It was a cold night. I buried myself inside a big winter coat.

Around 01:45 we lost connection with the wind indicator. It was an obvious result of low batteries as electronic systems began to shut down. To save energy, the skipper spent his next four-hour shift steering manually through the black night.

As I took over at 08:00, we hit the 500 nm mark, officially making it halfway to our destination.

I started a new book, *Atlantic,* and settled into the cockpit with Cap'n Jack and Scout.

We took shifts manually steering to hopefully save energy so that we could continue to use the auto pilot during the night. We steered about four hours each, and then I decided to take a shower. Deep into our sixth day at sea I was starting to smell my own stink. The deck shower felt great in the hot sun even though the water in our shower bag was only lukewarm and the wind was freezing.

We were speaking to each other a little more, but not about anything important. At one point, I asked the skipper if he wanted to talk about the conversation we had started the day we departed, but he said he wasn't in the mood to be lectured.

We worked more on the genoa and got the furling line repaired . . . we thought.

Sometime during that afternoon, we noticed a small, black petrel circling the boat. Petrels are birds that live at sea and only come on land for breeding. They are some of the least known birds because they can only be studied at sea.

They can't walk well on land because they have weak feet and legs and struggle to carry their own load. Some are shy and stay away from ships, but others have been known to seek ships and stick around for a while.

Many people believe that petrels carry with them the souls of dead sailors.

A little more than halfway through the long passage, the equipment issues and the drama of our intense relationship often took a backseat to the starry nights, magnificent sunsets, and the small, black petrel with the stamina of an albatross who guided our way for the last 300 miles of our journey—all the way into Mindelo, Cape Verde, Africa.

CHAPTER 20

SEABIRDS, SUNSETS & THE SOUTHERN CROSS

PASSAGE TO CAPE VERDE (PART TWO)

Day 7–MONDAY, 31 DECEMBER 2018 – 600 NM – 128 HOURS AT SEA

Even though there were no ships in sight, there was a lot of activity on the radio in the wee hours of the morning—lonely sailors longing for a little company. It was entertaining to listen to their conversations. I felt well enough to spend the shift writing in my journal, but as always, I continued to diligently make my night watch checks every 10 minutes.

I had not been seasick since I stopped taking the medicine, but that morning I felt congested and achy. I took Zyrtec to help with the congestion and ibuprofen for the body aches. I wondered if the cold deck shower might have given me a chill, but even if it had, it was worth it to be clean.

Sometime during that night watch, I spotted the Southern Cross shining brightly in the black sky. I woke the skipper and asked him to come to the cockpit to confirm the sighting.

The Southern Cross is a five-star constellation that is only visible in the Southern Hemisphere and in the winter of the Northern Hemisphere. You can only see it, theoretically, from 25 degrees north in the northern winter, and only right above the horizon.

The Southern Cross is to sailors in the South what the North Star is to sailors in the North—it's the main point of orientation for celestial navigation. The North Star never moves, at least not from the perspective of the Earth. It is always pointing North.

But the Southern Cross moves, making a semicircular voyage across the sky. However, the two stars at the long leg of the cross always point to the celestial South Pole.

It was another beautiful morning, and I made a batch of eggs and bacon for the crew. I felt great, so I got busy working on the cabin organization.

When you live in a house that doesn't move, you place books and other items on the shelf, and they will stay where you put them. When you live in a house that moves, you have to also consider that the air around you is moving, and the water beneath you is moving, and it's all moving in many different directions. Placing a book on a bookshelf becomes less about organization or decoration and more an issue of the physics of space and balance.

I was finally able to create a rig for the books on the shelf above the lockers. On one side, I placed a wooden silverware tray right next to the upright row of books and anchored it with our heavy brass ship's bell.

On the other side, I used a heavy technical manual placed on its side to anchor the other books. It was just the right size—31 cm—to squeeze tightly in between the wall and the edge of the shelf, turning the book into a bookend. It worked.

Then I used an empty egg carton as a locker door buffer, attaching it to the inside of the door, hoping the rig would help with some of the clankety-clanking that would happen when all the locker contents shook, rattled, and rolled with the choppy sea.

It was amazing how ingenious we had become, by necessity, while at sea. There was no Walmart or Home Depot that we could rush off to for supplies. We were forced to use what we already had onboard, and we had to get creative.

With each onboard puzzle I put together I would think of my high school algebra teacher, Ms. Frickie (she was Ms. Hill back then). I was an energetic and ambitious 15-year-old girl who thought I knew everything about life but actually knew nothing. I remember telling her that I didn't need math skills because I wanted to be a writer. "I will be in the business of words, not numbers," I would tell her emphatically.

In her sweet, patient way, she would then explain to me that algebra was less about math and more about learning how to solve problems. With every challenge that would present itself onboard, I would think of her and appreciate the problem-solving skills she taught me all those years ago.

While I was computing the value of x down below, the skipper was solving problems of his own. He hoisted the mizzen stay sail so we could pick up an extra knot of speed, and we continued to find ways to utilize natural energy and perhaps find a temporary solution for the cracked casing that haunted us from deep below the cockpit.

There was not a cloud in the glorious blue sky. We hadn't seen another ship for days . . . only the horizon. I relaxed with a book on the deck. The skipper joined me in the hot sun, the cool breeze in our faces, and finally, after seven quiet days at sea, we began to have a conversation.

I told him how lucky I felt to be challenging myself and getting through the voyage.

I soaked in the sun. I felt free and happy in that moment.

"It's moments like these that make all the hard work and seasickness worth it," I told him, fully appreciating the magnificent day.

His response . . . "You've earned it."

It was so rare that he would compliment me. Even the slightest bit of encouragement or recognition from him always made me smile. He wrapped his arms around me, and I cuddled up next to him. It felt good to be in the warmth of his arms. It had been a while.

However, I had not forgotten about our conversation on Christmas Day—the day we departed from Lanzarote. And I wasn't ready to let him forget it, either.

"We have a lot to work out," I told him. "If you truly want to be with me and continue the voyage together, I need you to do me a big favor."

He waited for me to continue.

"When we get to Cape Verde, don't leave me alone again. Stay with me. We can't work things out if we are apart. And I don't trust that you will not see other women. It's not going to work if you continue to give them the attention that I need so badly from you."

"Okay, I promise," he said. "But you have to quit spying on me."

"I'll quit spying on you when you prove to me that I can trust you."

Then we sat in silence, cuddled, and listened to the waves. We tried to ignore the annoying sound of the generator charging the batteries.

After we ate dinner, the skipper went below for his early evening rest while I enjoyed the last sunset of 2018. I had seen hundreds of sunsets at sea, and each one was special and unique. As long, smooth 3 m swells rolled underneath us, the golden sun melted on the horizon like a scoop of ice cream that had dropped onto the hot pavement on a warm summer day.

The golden fireball fizzled in a flash, leaving behind brilliant hues of ruby red, tangy orange, and golden yellow that reflected off the silvery blue water and faded into the cloudless sky.

We had enjoyed orange sunsets all week. But somewhere in the Western African Atlantic with nothing in our 360-degree view but the glorious horizon, the sky on the last night of 2018 was as bright orange as *Seefalke*.

Just before 21:00, I saw a shadow through the glow of the green and red navigation lights on the bow. It was the small black petrel circling us again.

The German word for petrel is *sturmvogel*, which means "storm bird." They are called that because they are seen at sea flying around in all kinds of weather. In fact, some seasoned mariners believe that petrels possess the souls of lost sailors. They have often been known to guide sailors safely to land.

With a busted engine, a mangled genoa furling mechanism, and about 500 more miles to go, that little petrel became part of our crew—a flying compass guiding our way.

It would not be the last time we would see that tiny little black bird with the white crescent on her back.

Day 8

TUESDAY, 1 JANUARY 2019
695 NM – 152 HOURS AT SEA

I would normally begin my night watch at midnight, but it was New Year's Eve, so I joined the cockpit a little early. The radio came alive with greetings from sailors all over the world, all in their own languages.

The skipper joined in and offered our New Year's wishes on behalf of the two-person, two-beagle *Seefalke* crew in English, German, and Russian. We hadn't seen a ship in several days, but with the many greetings over the radio, we were reminded once again that we were never truly alone at sea.

I grabbed a mini bottle of champagne from the bottom of the cooler. I popped it and enjoyed the crisp sparkling treat, even though it was lukewarm at best. The skipper held me tight and told me he loved me. He asked me to be patient with him.

He didn't want to talk about all the things that we needed to discuss, and I agreed that we shouldn't spoil the nice moment as we brought in the first minutes of 2019 together. I had no idea what the next year would bring. I still had hopes that we could work things out, but those hopes were outweighed by doubts.

For now, I was happy for a little companionship out in the middle of the ocean.

When the skipper went down to sleep and I took over my watch, I felt all alone again. It could feel so isolating out there at times. I thought about how in normal, everyday on-land life, I would be surrounded by other humans. I wouldn't always speak to them, and I often wouldn't even notice them because seeing other humans was just part of my everyday fabric.

At sea, the skipper and I would go for days and weeks without seeing another human being.

The next morning, I enjoyed the glorious first sunrise of 2019 some 700 miles off the African Atlantic coast. The golden sun boasted more bright orange and yellow hues as it lifted gently from the horizon, hidden at times by 4 m swells.

I noticed that Cap'n Jack had crawled onto our bunk and gotten a little seasick all over our bedding. So, for me, New Year's Day became laundry day.

I decided to use the burst of energy I had to completely clean the entire main cabin and sweep away the massive amounts of dog hair that had accumulated during our week at sea. The beagles would shed so much hair that sometimes I wondered how there was still any left on their bodies.

The swells continued to roll in all day, and it got uncomfortable at times. We continuously adjusted the sails and the course trying to soften the blows. I remained firm in my commitment to no longer use seasick medicine. I felt fine. Even though we were being rocked from all sides, my sea legs were becoming firmly planted and my resolve solidified.

Meanwhile, our little petrel continued to circle *Seefalke* with great interest. We would see her during the day and night, flying around us and occasionally gliding along the top of the water. We believed she was guiding us all the way to Cape Verde, so we named her Lotse (pronounced lōts-sa) which is the German word for "pilot."

At 16:08, we officially hit our one-full-week-at-sea mark at 767 nm.

Day 9

WEDNESDAY, 2 JANUARY 2019
800 NM – 176 HOURS AT SEA

I've always been a morning person, but I especially loved the mornings at sea. I relieved the skipper from his 04:00—08:00 shift and made all the necessary watch checks. When he went down at 08:00, I let him sleep as long as he wanted, generally two or three hours.

After making my checks, I would settle into a little nook I created in the cockpit. I sat on my piece of carpet and would nestle in the corner with some soft pillows. I cuddled with Cap'n Jack and Scout and got lost in the pages of a book. Of course, when on watch, I still made my checks every 10 minutes so I could never get fully distracted with my book. I would read a few pages, make my checks, read a few pages, make my checks....

When the skipper awoke, I cooked breakfast. If conditions were good, we would sometimes sit in the cockpit and talk for hours. I missed that.

That morning, I asked the skipper if we could just sit and talk. I desperately needed companionship. We talked about our kids and the places we dreamed of sailing to one day. We shared stories, ramblings, and musings from each other's night watches and also discussed politics and philosophy, stories from our youth, and plans for the future.

I enjoyed the conversations so much, but the skipper would often get restless and find something to keep him busy. That day was no different. The skipper spent the day configuring the sails in many different ways trying to gain us a little more speed and to soften the blows of the increasing swells. *Seefalke* is a ketch, which means it has two masts and five sails—theoretically 60 possible sail configurations.

Meanwhile, I relaxed on the cold, hard deck in the sunshine in nothing but a ponytail and found inspiration from my book about the Atlantic, in which the amazingly talented author, Simon Winchester, reminded me of a famous quote from Arthur C. Clarke, who said: *"How inappropriate it is to call this planet Earth, when clearly it is Sea."*

I took advantage of the beautiful day and had another deck shower as our lovely little navigator, Lotse, circled around us slowly guiding us closer to Cape Verde.

Day 10

THURSDAY, 3 JANUARY 2019
 889 NM – 199 HOURS AT SEA
The midnight watch began with heavy, gusty winds and big, choppy waves. It seemed the closer we were to shore—on the front end and the back end of those long passages—the bumpier and more uncomfortable the ride.

By mid-afternoon, we were about 100 miles from landfall, but there were still no other ships in sight—only our sweet little Lotse, who continued to fly with us and guide us toward the Cape Verde archipelago.

Day 11

FRIDAY, 4 JANUARY 2019
 991 NM – 223 HOURS AT SEA
After a long night of rocking and rolling seas, restless sleep, and still no ships or land in sight, we reminded ourselves that we would not have the use of the engine to help us work our way into our mooring position.

We studied the charts and prepared to maneuver the channel and the bay into the marina under sail. We planned to take down the mizzen, the main, and the genoa sails and use only the small jib to make the maneuver under sail more controllable. In the early morning, after 233 straight hours at sea and 1,030 nm, in the distance through the morning fog we finally saw the mountaintops of Cape Verde.

Land ho!!!

It was at that point that we couldn't find Lotse. After flying with us for more than 300 nm, she was not there anymore. She had brought us to within sight of land, and then had quietly flown away to new adventures—perhaps to keep other sailors company on the expansive Atlantic.

We missed her, but we understood that petrels want to be at sea. They are not land birds. She had piloted us to within sight of land, and now it was time for her to glide away.

Meanwhile, we had some new visitors. I saw something floating in the water, but I couldn't figure out what it was because of the glare of the rising sun. I thought it might be a bottle or some other kind of trash. But then we began to see more of the floating objects and decided to take a closer look.

The small, bubbly, colorful objects were about the size of a small bottle decorated with purplish-blue and pink features. They glistened as the sun reflected their colors onto the surface of the clear water that was beginning to take on an aquamarine tint as we got closer to land.

We later learned that they were Portuguese man o' war. Beautiful, but deadly. The creatures are found in the Atlantic, Indian, and Pacific Oceans. With tentacles floating beneath them that are typically 10 m in length (but can be as long as 30 m), they can deliver a painful and even deadly sting. The tentacles are venomous and powerful enough to kill fish, and sometimes humans.

They are not actually jellyfish, although that is what they resemble. Portuguese man o' war swim in large groups, sometimes with more than 1,000 individuals, and have been known to deplete entire fisheries.

We sailed into the bay just outside of Marina Mindelo. We made a sharp port side tack and marveled at the detailed layers of remarkable brown mountains and small island formations that just a few hours before were only a faint silhouette on the horizon.

We waited until the last possible minute to use the engine. I checked the fresh-water funnel to be sure it was full. It was time to focus on keeping the engine cool. We had three spare 1.5 liter bottles on standby in case we needed to refill while we were maneuvering into the marina.

As we made our way into the bay and inside the wind shadow of the islands, we began to furl in the genoa. But the furling mechanism decided to give us one more aggravating challenge. It tangled again in the gusty wind and turned us in circles as we tried to furl the sail manually while balancing on the bowsprit. The mission was unsuccessful. We finally had to slice the sheet. The skipper wrapped the genoa as best as he could around the stay, but a small corner was still flapping violently.

We brought in the jib and then took our chances with the engine. It started.

As the clock on our depleted engine capacity ticked away, we quickly made a straight shot into the marina entrance. But our challenges didn't end there.

Although I didn't know it at the time, one end of the sheet the skipper had sliced to untangle the genoa furl had dropped into the water on the port side and found its way into the propeller where it wrapped itself around the blades and the shaft—putting a harsh halt to our ability to control the boat.

We slid haphazardly into the fueling station like a baseball player sliding into second base trying to break up a double play. The four attendants yelled at us in Portuguese telling us that we couldn't moor there.

We ignored them and moored *Seefalke* anyway. Frankly, we had no choice. We had no control of the boat and slammed our ship's starboard beam into the pier, scraping a huge strip of orange paint from her hull. Fortunately, an 11-ton steel ship wins against a floating wooden pier every time. *Seefalke* suffered only cosmetic damage.

At that point, I was on the bow securing the lines and was unaware that the sheet was tangled in the propeller. I knew something had happened that made us lose control of *Seefalke*, but I naturally assumed the engine had died.

I looked back to the cockpit at the skipper. He was stripping down to his skivvies. My first thought was that maybe he was just overheated, like the engine, and was layering down. I was confused. Then he grabbed his scuba mask and worked his way to the stern.

When I got back there with him, he told me what had happened. He grabbed a sharp knife and dove underneath *Seefalke*. It took some effort and several dunks under the boat to release and retrieve all the pieces of the mangled line from the propeller.

As he was climbing back on board, I heard something in the distance . . . *"Michelle! Michelle!"*

It was a familiar voice. I looked over toward the marina entrance and saw our friends Molly and Baxter, along with their dog, Kala, motoring toward us in their dinghy. We had met the fellow American sailors a few months ago in A Coruña and had been trying to reconnect with them ever since. We barely missed them in Vigo and almost connected in Lisbon. It was so cool to finally see them again that I forgot about our equipment troubles for about five seconds.

The engine came through for us, and the drenched captain navigated us safely into our slip. Then we met with our friends at the floating bar on the pier. We were exhausted, but we couldn't miss another opportunity, especially since they were setting sail for their Atlantic crossing the next morning.

Molly and Baxter had been sailing the world on *Terrapin* for the past seven years. It's rare to see a boat sailing under an American flag in Europe, so when we saw their boat in Spain, we hunted them down and began communicating with them regularly—always trying to find an opportunity to get together.

They were both seasoned sailors, and I had especially appreciated all the advice that Molly had given me during the past few months—everything from living on a sailboat to fighting seasickness to sailing with dogs. Our time together was short but meaningful. As we would always say, you never really say goodbye to sailors.

Case in point: as we moored *Seefalke* into her slip earlier that day, I noticed the boat next to us looked familiar. Just as we were tying the lines, out popped Alain and Alexa, our French friends from Arrecife who were sailing the world on *Et Puis Pas Plus*.

Meanwhile, we also connected with Maria and Fredrik Rovik (and their Jack Russell terrier, Tulling)—a Swedish couple who had a gorgeous catamaran, *Limitless*. They had also grown tired of the corporate life after working many years with a major automobile manufacturer in Sweden. They sold everything they owned and began their worldwide sailing voyage earlier that year.

I was excited to connect with a few friends—just in case the skipper was planning on leaving me alone again. I wondered if he would keep his promise.

After a 242-hour passage that spanned 11 days and covered 1,058 nm, we were exhausted.

But there was no time to rest.

Our next mission was the biggie—a sailing passage across the Atlantic Ocean. But first we needed to repair the cracked heat exchanger and furling mechanism. We knew that it could take several weeks since we would likely need to have parts shipped to us on the remote island from other parts of the world.

We spent the next several weeks working on those and other projects and completing our final round of provisioning to get *Seefalke* and ourselves in tip-top shape for the Atlantic crossing.

And perhaps we could find some time for another exciting adventure exploring the many colors of Cape Verde.

CHAPTER 21

EXPLORING THE MANY COLORS OF CAPE VERDE

W hen I first walked through the streets of Mindelo on the Cape Verde island of São Vicente, it didn't take long to fall in love with the spectacular scenery and friendly, relaxed, colorful culture that was bursting with rhythmic music.

Vibrant street art added local character to the buildings painted in bright purple, yellow, orange, and green. Dozens of stray dogs adopted by the community roamed the streets and the wild beaches. The water was as blue as Windex.

The beautiful, caramel-skinned Creole women of Mindelo casually strolled through the city wearing bright colors and easily balancing heavy bins full of fruit and vegetables on their heads.

Every day, they would find a street corner and peddle the fresh produce for hours—until long after the tangerine sun dropped behind the horizon of the lush brown mountaintops. For an offer of just about any number of escudos—the local currency—we were able to buy lettuce, potatoes, tomatoes, gigantic carrots, rhubarb, zucchini, huge papaya, squash, fresh coconut, and bananas.

There were open markets full of more vegetable peddlers. At the Mercado de Peixe, shoppers could choose from fresh fish wrangled directly out of the Atlantic that morning by local fishermen.

In the city center, easy walking distance from the busy harbor, there was a small replica of Lisbon's famous Torre de Belém and a bronze bust of Diogo Alfonso, a 15th century Portuguese explorer who discovered São Vicente and several of the other islands of Cape Verde.

Tucked away in the mid-Atlantic Ocean, the 10-island cluster of Cape Verde is located more than 1,000 miles from the northwestern coast of Africa. It's landscape includes inactive volcanoes, miles of dry wasteland, and unbelievably beautiful beaches.

The sea water reflected a medley of every shade of blue and green imaginable. It felt like I was viewing it through the sparkling mirrors inside a kaleidoscope.

Cape Verde (or Cabo Verde) is known for its Creole Portuguese-African culture and continuous beat of traditional lifting and rhythmic morna music. It also has close to perfect weather, rarely shifting up or down from 25°C (77°F) at any time of the year. It hardly ever rains.

The islands were uninhabited until Portuguese and Genoese sailors stumbled upon them in 1456. Many describe the archipelago landscape as the "unspoiled alternative to the Caribbean." Cape Verde stretches across 1,500 square miles of the Atlantic.

We spent three weeks in São Vicente, which has a population of just more than 80,000. Most live in the heart of Mindelo.

Monte Verde dominates the landscape with its highest peak at 750 m. Even though the name implies that it's green, the mountain is a mixture of brick red, chocolate brown, and every shade of red and brown in between with a few faded green sprinkles on top.

The architecture of Mindelo features unfinished brown stone buildings in slum-like, dilapidated condition and vibrant buildings painted bright purple, blue, yellow, orange, green, and red.

Handshakes among locals were nowhere to be found. Instead, the friendly Cape Verdeans greeted each other with a fist bump with their neighbor followed by an in-sync fist pump to their own chest. The people of Cape Verde always seemed to be outside, and every second of every day they were playing lively, upbeat music.

On the streets of the city center, there were plenty of locals begging for money—mostly men and children. The practice was a bit annoying, but not threatening, and it left me wondering if it was more of a habit than a necessity. Although the beggars were ever present, the employed Cape Verdeans we came in contact with in the marina, at the markets, and in the boat repair workshop were hardworking, kind, and friendly.

I realized quickly that the dozens of stray dogs were an important thread of the fabric of the island of São Vicente. They were friendly for the most part, well fed, and seemed to have been adopted by the community. They obviously had no permanent home. Because the weather is so temperate and dry, they seemed content living in the streets and eating random food trash discarded by the locals and tourists or found while scavenging around the markets.

There were open-air buses that seemed the perfect fit for the mild, comfortable climate. They were nothing fancy—simple, old pickup trucks with wooden benches in the bed.

The beaches on the island of São Vicente were completely wild and undeveloped! There were no tall buildings blocking the coastline view. No restaurants. No hotels. No condos—and hardly any people. No lifeguards or flag signals were there to warn swimmers of heavy waves or dangerous wildlife. It was nature and beauty in their purest form.

A walk through the city center was always filled with color, life, and energy. There were often free concerts in the main square performed by well-known Cape Verdean musicians.

Because of its remote location, everything in Mindelo was expensive. The internet was weak and sketchy. When we were able to find local data cards that helped us stay connected, it was ridiculously pricey—they charged per megabyte and per minute.

As was the case for many sailors, especially those on an Atlantic crossing voyage, our month in Cape Verde was filled primarily with boat maintenance.

Our first priority was to repair the engine's cracked heat exchanger. At Boat CV, the local repair shop, we found a good engine mechanic, Cesar. The machine shop's motto was, "If it is made by humans, we can fix it."

We hoped this was true in our case, because we feared that ordering a new heat exchanger from Germany would take much longer than we wanted to wait—and the expense would be significant.

The repair shop was full of hardworking local men, all in either flip flops or their bare feet. The equipment, machinery, and tools looked ancient—old, rusty, disorganized, and dirty. It was amazing the quality they delivered laboring in that kind of environment. We were grateful to find high-quality mechanics. There were not many options in that remote part of the world.

The last possible stop on an east-to-west Atlantic sailing crossing, the marina was generally full of battle-worn ships. Almost every sailor in the marina was busy making repairs after long sailing passages and in preparation for even longer voyages.

It's not typical for sailors to stop in Cape Verde unless they are crossing the Atlantic or sailing to southern Africa. Some would find their way to the remote islands when some sort of boat-related malfunction would occur at sea after departing the Canary Islands. Others would use the archipelago as a break point when sailing from the Canaries to the Caribbean. We stopped at Cape Verde for all of these reasons.

The marina was active with the sounds of buzzing drills, scratchy sanders, pounding hammers, and multilingual conversations among international sailors helping each other get their ships fit to return to sea.

Cesar's team came to the marina and climbed onboard *Seefalke* to inspect the cracked casing. To repair it, they needed to remove the entire heat exchanger and take it to the shop. They could not estimate how long it would take or how much it would cost.

Meanwhile, since we were completely out of clean underwear, I dropped off the last five weeks of dirty clothes at a local laundry service shop and splurged on the wash/dry/fold option for about $42 USD.

Following a mediocre lunch of a very thin fish burger at a local café, we spent the evening with Maria and Fredrik on *Limitless*—a huge, beautiful catamaran. Once again, I was reminded that boat living doesn't have to be uncomfortable.

Limitless was more spacious than my Gulf Shores apartment with plenty of comfy cushions. Cap'n Jack and Scout had a blast running all over the boat playing with their new best friend, Tulling. It had been a while since we had come in contact with a dog that could compete with the energy of our beagles.

The next day, I decided to take a short walk to a nearby beach. Tulling's humans were not feeling well, so I offered to take all three dogs on the adventure.

Tulling loved the water and wanted to jump right in. Cap'n Jack and Scout loved to be *on* the water but didn't particularly love to be *in* the water. They weren't quite sure about the waves that would trickle onto the shores of the beach. Rather than let them run off in three different directions, I kept the dogs leashed as we walked the entire length of the small beach, Praia de Laginha.

We sat for a while on the sugary white sand. I admired the amazing blue and aqua colors of the water while all three pups dug holes in the sand for a few hours.

Several of the local strays approached my canine crew, but most of them just plopped on the sand nearby and slept in the warm sun.

It was cool to get a different view of Monte Cara, a 490 m peak that we could see every day from the marina. When looking carefully at the top of the mountain, one can see a human face looking at the sky. That is how it got its name, which means "face mountain."

Walking back to the marina, I caught a glimpse of some of the local graffiti, which was something I loved to see in all the places we would visit. São Vicente markets itself as the home to some of Cape Verde's greatest musicians, writers, and thinkers, and Mindelo is considered the cultural hub of the island.

I walked by the Universidade do Mindelo, which is one of only seven institutions of higher learning on Cape Verde. The university has only been around since 2003 and consists of one gray building on the corner of one square block.

The next day, we continued with boat repairs. We needed to climb back up the mast to repair the courtesy flag line, but the skipper had thrown out his back while mooring *Seefalke* upon our entrance into Marina Mindelo.

We had plenty of tasks that weren't so physically demanding, so he tackled those. Since I had a recurring bulging disk that often left me with considerable lower back pain at times, I was empathetic to his suffering. I thought about reminding him about the time he didn't believe my back pain was real when we were in Italy a few years before, but I stopped myself from opening old wounds.

We kept chipping away at our long to-do list and spent an entire day working on *Seefalke's* flesh wounds from when we slid into the fuel station pier. The ship had suffered mostly cosmetic damage. I inflated our dinghy, *Nela*, and while floating in the water alongside the ship, I sanded the affected area. I then applied rust preventer, followed by primer, and then *Seefalke's* signature bright orange paint.

While the paint dried, we ventured far beyond the city center. That's where we found many local people out in the streets, listening to music, enjoying the amazing weather, and peddling fresh vegetables.

As with most of the world's remote destinations, the best food is found in local hideaways. While meandering down a secluded alley, we discovered a very cool local dive that we returned to many times during our stay in Cape Verde.

Were it not for its small black awning over the royal blue door and the chalkboard menu sitting on the window sill with scribbles of the day's catch, it would be easy to miss Pastelaria. However, the lively music booming from the diner could be heard blocks away. It filled the alley with audio entertainment for all the locals who gathered outside daily.

At this traditional family-owned restaurant, the fishermen father and son would bring in the fresh seafood directly from the Atlantic each morning. Mama was the cook, and the daughter was the hostess/waitress. They lived in an apartment above the restaurant, which was open every day.

Other than the windowsill chalkboard, there was essentially no menu. They would serve what they caught each morning. The entire restaurant was smaller than our sailboat, with only four small rickety square tables that had tattered mis-matched chairs. The service and the food were both fantastic. The warm mood reminded me of Sunday dinner at Nana's.

Each time we went into the restaurant, I would tie up the hounds outside and pay a local man one Euro to watch them. That was necessary due to random conflicts with the dozens of stray dogs that roam the streets. Even in such a poor nation, I was amazed how happy the man was to earn 100 escudos (1 Euro or $1.25 USD).

Cachupa was often served, but I also enjoyed the garupa, a fish commonly found in the local waters.

The family was important to the extremely poor community. Locals sat on the dirt street outside the restaurant for hours each day listening to the vibrant music. Some of them would come inside and buy one cigarette at a time because they couldn't afford a whole pack.

The portions of food were huge. Our leftovers, which we always had, were wrapped up and distributed to the hungry locals waiting outside. Our total bill one day for two home-cooked meals and two sodas was around 600 escudos—less than $7 USD.

The skipper's back still bothered him, so we couldn't tackle some of our more physical boat tasks. I wanted to see some of the surrounding beaches, so we rented a car and drove all around the island of São Vicente. We first drove to Praia Salamansa and enjoyed spectacular views of the surrounding mountains, crystally dynamic blue waters, and pounding waves while several local kite surfers put on a show for us.

As the hounds were enjoying their unleashed time, we launched our drone and got some amazing footage from high above us. A young local boy from the nearby rural village approached. He was amazed by the flying camera and was eager to learn more. He was probably about 12 years old with huge, round, deep eyes that were as black as night. He didn't speak English, but we were able to communicate.

It was obvious that the boy was fascinated by seeing his hometown from a completely different view. It would be a safe bet that he had never seen a drone before. Based on his fascination and curiosity, I wondered if he had ever seen a video camera of any kind.

Soon, about 10 other young Cape Verdeans came running toward us as the drone was landing. The boy became animated as he told his friends of the flying camera in the native, blended Portuguese/Creole dialect. They all became wide-eyed and curiously looked to us with anticipation, waiting for us to show them the magic machine. Unfortunately, the battery needed to be charged so we couldn't launch it again for the new spectators.

One of the kids had a small tray of seashells he had gathered from the beach. He had used the shells and a little glue to create trinkets to sell. I bought a small turtle and a shell bracelet. Total price—5 Euros, which was probably more money than he had ever seen at one time before.

We set out to explore more of the island. We found a huge wasteland with a giant mountain sitting virtually in the middle of nowhere and decided to try launching the drone again. Thanks to the drone footage, we were amazed to discover that the mountain was actually a volcano that had been inactive for millions of years. From there, we drove to Praia de Sarangaca, another totally wild and uninhabited beach with spectacular views and even more brilliant shades of blue, green, and aqua.

The next day we decided to drive to the top of Monte Verde and see the island from its highest peak. We could see many of the surrounding islands and noticed the overall dryness of most of the islands as seen from a distance.

Many places were desert-like with mostly sand, rocks, and mud. There was not much grass anywhere and not much natural vegetation. But the beaches that surround the island highlighted the amazingly brilliant azure waters of the Atlantic.

We then ventured to the other side of the island. São Pedro beach featured vibrant water of gorgeous blue and green hues. It also featured golden-blackish sand and was surrounded by another small village with buildings as colorful as the contents of a Crayola box. The wooden boats that lined the shore were also painted a multitude of bright colors.

We were welcomed by about 10 stray dogs who served as a built-in alarm system for the village. They were no match for two howling beagles. Cap'n Jack and Scout joined in the bark fest as we made our way to the cold water for a refreshing dip.

That evening, we left the exhausted dogs on *Seefalke* and found a local restaurant that served the traditional Cape Verdean dish, cachupa. The slow-cooked stew includes corn (hominy), beans, cassava, sweet potato, and fish or meat (sausage, beef, goat, or chicken). Each island has its own variation.

Nautilus, a restaurant on the main street right outside the marina, was known for its cachupa, and did not disappoint—it was hearty and delicious. The skipper had pizza covered in fresh tuna, cheese, and artichoke—an unlikely combination, but it was tasty.

We accomplished a lot, and I was having a lovely time exploring Cape Verde. With the great food and the welcoming culture, I found myself in a happy place. But while we were walking back to the boat after dinner, the skipper broke some bad news to me.

He had booked a flight to Germany for the next day. Another broken promise.

He explained that he was attending a family funeral following the death of a distant cousin. It was someone he had never mentioned to me, and I'm not sure he even knew this person had existed before.

I challenged him. In the six years that we had been a serious couple, I had never known him to attend a funeral—not one. In fact, he didn't even attend the funeral of my biological father a few years earlier.

I had begged him to come to that service with me, but he said, "Why should I come? I didn't know him." I had explained to him that I needed him there to support and to comfort me. He told me to lean on my family and insisted that there was nothing he could do or say that would help me.

I asked him if he knew the distant cousin who had died. He said he didn't. I reminded him the reason he didn't attend my father's funeral.

"That was your family," he said unsympathetically. "This is my family."

It was impossible for me to not be suspicious. "When did you learn of his death?" I asked him. "When did you book the flight?"

"Two days ago," he responded.

"Why did you wait until now to tell me about it?"

"I knew you would get upset," he said matter-of-factly. "And I didn't want to deal with that for two days."

This time I was silent.

He was right. I was upset. We didn't speak on the long walk back to *Seefalke*. I cuddled with the dogs while he packed. Neither of us said another word.

Chapter 22

ATLANTIC CROSSING PREPARATION

14–17 JANUARY 2019

With the skipper gone again, I fell back into a lonely, sad state of depression.

The Roviks and their dog had departed for the Caribbean so I couldn't hang out with them anymore. Alain and Alexa were in the slip right next to ours, but they ventured out exploring the islands every day.

I mostly used the time to work for my clients. But I also found time to give the main cabin floor some attention—a project I had wanted to tackle for a while.

I sanded and cleaned the raw wood floor panels and applied a few layers of polyurethane. I couldn't find wood stain anywhere in town, but the clear coating moisturized the boards and brought out the natural wood tones.

I removed the stained, worn-out blue fabric that snapped to the floor and served as something of a "carpet." I think that fabric floor coating had been in *Seefalke* since it was built in 1974.

It was nasty and impossible to keep clean. I hated it and was happy to dispose of the smelly carpet so that the skipper couldn't make me re-install it later.

Beyond that, the wood floor required more coats of varnish. With each coat, warmer natural tones began to shine through the wood. It was a worthwhile project and kept me busy and distracted while the skipper was away.

One evening, Alain and Alexa invited me to join them for dinner along with other French sailing friends. Everyone spoke French, but charades skills often came in handy in situations like that. I never felt left out because those lovely people continuously tried to include me in conversations.

One of the women taught English at a school near Madagascar, so she translated some of the more interesting conversations for me and was very kind to speak to me in English for most of the night.

It was almost 23:00 before we ate dinner, and a lot of delicious French wine was consumed by all. I had never learned to adjust my digestive schedule to European dinner times. But I realized that I would have to if I wanted to continue to hang with my French friends!

Alexa was so sweet to me, even though we didn't speak the same language. She was closer to the age of my mother (maybe mid-to-late 60s) but she became like a big sister to me.

Her English was about as bad as my French, but we agreed to make an effort to learn each other's language. We each down-loaded the same language app and tried every day to say a new phrase to each other in the other's native tongue.

One day I took a pair of scissors to Alexa's ship and pointed to my hair. She got the message and gave my ratty, tangled hair a good trim. Then she smothered my hair in coconut oil and communicated to me that my salt- and sun-damaged hair needed some heavy conditioning.

She was very sweet, and I appreciated her honesty.

Sensing my continued loneliness during the skipper's absence, Alain and Alexa invited me for dinner again. They bought a beautiful, fresh mahi mahi at the fish market.

Alain was a trained French chef and prepared an amazing meal. He spoke English a little better than Alexa and asked me why the skipper left me alone so often. He remembered how disappointed I was when the skipper left me alone in the Canaries.

Too embarrassed to reveal the real truth, I said, "He just doesn't like to stay in one place very long." It wasn't a lie.

"I would never leave Alexa alone," he told me. "She is so beautiful. I would not want other sailors to keep her company. As we get older, I want to spend all the moments of my life with her. We go on adventures together and share our lives, and I cherish each day I get to spend with her."

As he said it, he glanced across the room at his love. She was washing dishes. Their eyes met and they both lovingly smiled at each other.

Then he walked across the cabin, embraced her, kissed her tenderly, and whispered something in her ear. Even though he said it in French, I could easily understand.

He told her how much he loved her.

Even though they had been together for more than two decades, they were like a couple of teenagers experiencing love for the first time.

It warmed my heart, but I became overwhelmed with emotion and started to cry.

I wished with all my heart and soul that the skipper felt that way about me. But he didn't.

And I knew that most likely, he never would.

The skipper returned from Germany around 13:00 the next day, just in time for the repaired heat exchanger to be installed at 15:00. We ran the motor for about 20 minutes. The engine performed perfectly. No leaks.

The next morning, we ran the engine for 90 minutes and it passed our test with flying colors. As the skipper continued to nurse his sore back, I woke up with a huge stye in my left eye, perhaps caused by the very dry, windy weather. It was very painful and annoying.

While squinting with one eye, I finished my floor project and applied some varnish protection to the wooden trim surrounding the cockpit. The skipper never said anything positive or negative about the improvement on the cabin floor, but I didn't need his approval. I was thrilled with the results.

I never asked him anything about his trip. I also chose not to look at his phone. I was upset, but even moreso, I was worn out. I couldn't have that same conversation again.

My stye continued to get worse, so we walked into the city in search of a pharmacy. We found one with a line that was all the way out the door and into the street. I stood in the queue for about 10 minutes before I realized I needed to take a number like in a bakery.

In Cape Verde, and in most other countries outside the U.S., I had learned, it was not customary to just walk into a store like Walgreens and get over-the-counter drugs—not even antibiotic ointment or saline eye drops.

All the medicine, ointments, and other things Americans can usually grab off of a shelf are stored in locked cases behind a huge counter manned by licensed pharmacists. It was impossible to even purchase aspirin without first consulting the pharmacist.

While walking back to the boat, we stumbled upon a cool classic car show in the middle of one of the busy streets in the city center. Once again, Cape Verdeans enjoyed an afternoon of free entertainment in Mindelo.

That evening, there was a free concert in the city square. One of Cape Verde's most famous pop stars performed. It was such a lively and energetic atmosphere as the locals and tourists enjoyed the entertainment into the early hours of the next morning.

Even though I didn't want to discuss it with him, I was irritated that the skipper had broken his promise and left me alone again. I informed him that he needed to take care of the dogs because I was taking a day for myself. I grabbed a towel and a book, jumped off the boat onto the pier, and walked away without giving him an opportunity to object.

I walked to the nearby beach in the city center and rented one of the cabana chairs. I promptly ordered a glass of white wine. The skipper didn't like it when I would occasionally drink alcohol. He said that he could taste it when he kissed me.

For that reason, and out of respect, I never drank around him. But I told myself that since he never kissed me anymore, it might be nice to treat myself to a glass of pinot grigio. I sipped the refreshing drink, got lost in the pages of a book, and relaxed in the warm sun.

About half an hour later, I ordered another glass. I tried to relax, but I was still upset. I wanted to believe that the skipper really had attended a funeral, but it did not make sense. I texted Trisha and told her that I was having a bad day but didn't feel like sharing any details. She tried to comfort me, but I was just feeling blue.

I was enjoying Cape Verde, but my incessant suspicions made me miserable. At that point, I just wanted to get the boat fixed and get the hell out of there. I was ready to cross the Atlantic Ocean and finish the voyage. However, I had to admit that I looked forward to the crystal blue Caribbean waters that we would surely find in Barbados.

It was a confusing and chaotic time for me as I tried desperately to balance my constant teeter-totter of emotions. The loneliness and uneasiness about the relationship were counterbalanced by the lure of exciting destinations and the thrill of the sailing voyages.

As the day turned to night, I wasn't ready to return to the boat. It was a mild evening, so I stopped at the marina's floating bar.

That's where I met a lovely couple from the Netherlands. Caroline and Fred had been sailing for a while and had been in Cape Verde for several months. They had visited eight of Cape Verde's ten islands and would not leave again until after the famous Cape Verde Carnival on São Vicente, which is a colorful spectacle of music, dance, and street processions.

While we were enjoying a lovely chat, I noticed the skipper walking toward us with Cap'n Jack and Scout. He sat down and introduced himself to my new friends. As usual, he turned on the charm and soon made Caroline and Fred forget that I was there.

Feeling invisible, I grabbed the beagles' leashes and walked back to the boat alone.

23–31 JANUARY 2019
Many ships had come and gone during our time in Mindelo. Boats came into the marina with battle scars and many required repairs. Then a few days later they would head west toward the Caribbean or south toward the southern points of Africa.

We had no fewer than six different neighbors on our port side who had stayed a few days and then continued on their journeys. We had been in Cape Verde for three weeks but thankfully Alain and Alexa were still there, too. They had a much bigger problem than us—a broken mast!

I continued to learn French phrases so I could communicate with Alexa, and she continued to work on her English. One night we joined them for dinner, and while Alexa and I looked at her photos from Panama, the Caribbean, the South Pacific, and other places they had visited, the skipper and Alain were busy plotting.

We all realized that such a busy sailor's port should have a marine shop, and we wondered why there was not a proper one in Mindelo. When any of the sailors needed supplies or parts, they were forced to have the items shipped from somewhere else in the world—a logistics nightmare that was ridiculously expensive.

The skipper was a businessman with a knack for concocting business ideas that made sense, but he was terrible at following through. As he and Alain began to plot the idea of opening a marine shop on Cape Verde, my heart began to sink.

I thought this one was a horrible idea—just one more reason for the skipper to leave me when we were in other parts of the world. I mentioned that to him, but I presented it in a different way.

"Yes, the island needs a marine shop, and perhaps we could make money doing this," I began. "But one of the four of us would always have to be here. It would be difficult to sail here regularly and expensive to fly here regularly. We would need capital to invest in all the shelves and shelves of supplies needed to keep a marine shop well stocked. And frankly, I'm not interested in running a retail shop even if I lived here full time—which I also do not want to do."

It fell on deaf ears. The skipper was determined, and nothing I did or said could change his mind.

He and Alain spent the next few days researching business licenses in Cape Verde and what it would take to open a bank account. They even spent a day looking at properties in the city center.

I was irritated and completely uninterested in the idea.

So I turned my focus to trash.

Trash had been on my mind since before we left Gulf Shores. Where would we possibly store three weeks of trash on a boat during the Atlantic crossing? We couldn't throw it overboard, and it would take up far too much space on *Seefalke*, not to mention the problem of the smell.

I worked hard to find solutions. Anything organic would be thrown overboard (egg shells, banana peels, etc.). Any major packaging of food and/or supplies would be thrown away before we left the marina (for example, cereal boxes).

Ziploc bags and a sharpie became my new best friends as I identified all the insides of the dozens of boxes I threw away. Plastic bottles would be smashed and crushed to take up less room in the garbage bags. We had a Diaper Genie for the head to handle waste paper. Then I came up with something brilliant....

We had several 8-liter jugs of water that we would use to refill a couple of smaller reusable bottles for drinking. By not using too many smaller water bottles, we could eliminate the large number of bulky bottle trash on board.

Then we could use the empty 8-liter jugs for paper trash. A lot of trash could be stuffed inside the jug, and then it could be sealed. It would be much more compact, and less smelly than trash bags.

With that problem under control, I spent the rest of the week focused on work and small boat projects. My stye had cleared, but the skipper's back still bothered him.

However, he did find time to work on his marine shop project—something that continued to irritate me. I kept my focus on preparing for the crossing.

We had already consumed most of the food we had gathered in Arrecife, so we needed to replenish our critical provisions. Food and supplies were much more difficult to find in Cape Verde, and they were more expensive.

We bought what we thought was reasonable—eggs, canned tuna, cereal, dog food, canned veggies, and 100 liters of water. We would wait to purchase fresh produce and potatoes until our last day before departure.

I had to accept that we would basically be vegetarians during the crossing because fresh meat was too expensive in Cape Verde.

We had canned meat and canned tuna but decided not to buy any ham, bacon, or luncheon meat. Plus, we had the added challenge of very limited refrigeration.

1–8 FEBRUARY 2019

Our sights were set on a late-week departure, but with the skipper's back still not strong, and with the distraction of his ongoing business project, we were delayed at least another week.

As I continued to focus on preparing for the voyage, he continued to try to sell me on the idea of the marine shop business.

"I just think logistically it doesn't make sense," I told him one afternoon. "How can we run a business from the other side of the world? And why do you need me to be involved? I seriously have no interest in it."

"We need you to build the website and do all the marketing," he said. "You are the only one with the skills to do that."

"I'll do all that for you guys," I relented. "But I don't really want any part of owning or running the business. And I'm definitely not interested in coming back to Cape Verde several times a year when there are so many other places in the world I want to see. And it's just more time I would have to be away from my family. How will you fit this in with all your other traveling? If you do this, it will mean even less time that we get to spend together. Is that the point?"

"No, of course not," he countered. "I see it as a business. We can make a lot of money for our future."

I threw my hands in the air and could no longer hide my agitation.

"It doesn't matter," I argued. "You'll never follow through with it anyway. As soon as we leave here you will forget all about it. You are notorious for never finishing what you start."

It was true, but I shouldn't have said it.

My comment hit a nerve.

He grabbed his water bottle and threw it across the cabin, almost directly hitting Scout while splattering water in all directions. She whimpered into a corner, and I immediately went to her and held her.

She was trembling. So was I.

It wasn't the first time I had seen him explode and throw something violently in a fit of rage. It definitely wouldn't be the last.

I leashed the dogs, and the three of us swiftly left the boat, giving him some space and time to cool off.

As we walked down the pier, a German couple was mooring a large white catamaran about two berths from ours. I wanted to keep walking, but they were juggling two small children and a large dog, so I offered to help with their lines.

They were very sweet and offered me a beer as a thank you. The beagles immediately became friends with their dog, Rocky, as I boarded the ship. It was just the distraction I needed.

Like all the sailors we met, they had an interesting story to tell. Dieter and Claudia had decided to take a sabbatical from their jobs in Hamburg. They rented their house, bought a boat, and decided to sail for a few years with a dream of crossing the Atlantic.

The day after they bought their boat, they learned they were expecting their first child. They delayed the departure but then set sail with their daughter when she was three months old.

A couple years later, baby number two arrived. The children (now 4 and 2) had never known a life that was not at sea.

It was the first time I had met sailors who couldn't wait to return to life on land. They told me the renters of their house had 18 months left on their lease at which time they planned to return home and go back to their jobs in Hamburg as an airline pilot and a teacher.

I was curious as to why this family would return to life on land because most of the sailors that we encountered were addicted to the liveaboard lifestyle. They told me that they simply had other things on their bucket list—for example, a walking journey across Antarctica.

They decided to take the kids and Rocky for a walk. As we were disembarking their ship, we ran into the skipper. He had calmed down and turned on his usual charm. He began talking to the couple in German, deliberately leaving me out of the conversation. He loved to do that.

However, I understood more of the language than he ever gave me credit. They told him that their next stop was Cabedelo, Brazil and spoke of the beautiful marina there and a remarkable remote island along the way—Ilha Fernando de Noronha.

We met another sailor headed for Brazil a couple weeks earlier, and I had told the skipper that I would really love to go there one day. Neither of us had ever been to South America.

As we continued to discuss it, we talked about how sailing to South America would give us an opportunity to cross the Equator into the Southern Hemisphere. With some research, I began to get excited about the possibility of sailing on the Amazon River.

We continued to research and began seriously thinking about changing our route and setting a course to Brazil rather than to Barbados as originally planned.

There were many good reasons to make the switch. With so many delays and extended time in various ports, we were way off our original schedule of being in Barbados by early January. To avoid hurricane season, we would need to rush our way through the Caribbean to Alabama, and it would be a pity to miss out on exploring so many gorgeous islands.

The next morning, I told the skipper I would stop in the marina while walking the dogs and check out the courtesy flags. We agreed that if they had a Brazilian flag, we would sail to Cabedelo. There was one flag in stock, and they had the electronic charts, so I purchased them.

It would delay our arrival in Alabama since we would make a detour around the northern South American coast and then wait out hurricane season in Panama.

I was lukewarm about going to Barbados but became ecstatic about the prospect of Brazil. I felt an amazing sense of freedom as we opted to go where the wind would take us rather than sticking to a schedule.

I was so caught up in all the excitement that it didn't occur to me that the change in plans would add months to the journey. The original plan was to return to Alabama by March. It was already February. But in that moment, I didn't stop to think about all that.

With the new plan in place, I spent the morning working on our final checklist. I climbed up the main mast to untangle the courtesy flag line and also scrubbed the ladder and dinghy of all the barnacles and muck that had accumulated during our time sitting in port in Cape Verde.

We also arranged for a man to take a dive underneath *Seefalke* and scrub the barnacles from her underbelly. With renewed energy, I wanted to scrub the cabins and head to be sure we had a fresh clean boat to begin our long journey. We visited all the street vendors for fresh produce—apples, oranges, onions, peppers, cucumbers, and potatoes. We planned to set sail the next morning.

But we woke up to a dense fog. We still had work to do and some boat preparation and just couldn't get it all done. Even around 16:00 and 17:00 I was still hopeful. But the fuel station would close at 18:00, so we finally gave up and decided to relax and depart on Friday morning—two days later, on February 8, 2019, the skipper's 42nd birthday.

Since his outburst, I thought the skipper had forgotten about the marine shop idea. I was wrong.

The next day, he dragged me to the local Chamber of Commerce and forced me to sign the business license with him and Alexa and Alain. To keep the peace, I gave up the fight and signed the paper. But I knew I would never actually work in the business. In fact, I knew that as soon as we set sail for Brazil, the skipper would lose interest in the project.

This time, I kept my comments to myself.

At that point, we had only made a 7 Euro investment for the business license. Alexa smiled and said, "We are bound forever by 7 Euros." A dear friend, she always made me smile. I knew I would miss her.

Swimming with Loggerhead Sea Turtles

As our preparations for the cross-Atlantic sailing voyage neared their end, so did our time in Cape Verde. I craved one more local experience before leaving the island we had grown to love so much.

Together with Alexa and Alain, we boarded a bus to São Pedro. We donned our diving gear and swam in the warm water in search of tortuga—local loggerhead sea turtles that swim in the wild in that area. One local diver noticed that we were on the hunt. He swam out to greet us and offered to show us where to find the tortuga.

The water was so unbelievably crystal clear it was barely blue—so transparent we could see easily without a diving mask. However, we opted for one to help us dive to the ocean floor where the sea turtles liked to play, which was about 20 ft below the surface.

Through the crystalline water, we saw the brilliant creatures swimming and playing with each other as tiny bubbles gurgled upward. Some of the turtles were huge—as big as 3 ft long.

Adult loggerheads can weigh as much as 250 pounds. All of them featured variations of earthy brown and dark gray tones on their armored backs. They had large heart-shaped heads and yellow bellies, and their flippers were dark brown with white edges.

I was hesitant at first to disturb their natural habitat, but they didn't seem to mind. They curiously and playfully swam directly toward us and all around us, as if encouraging us to join their party. I was mesmerized and for a few moments felt like I belonged in their world, although deep down I knew that we were only brief visitors in their majestic home.

After what seemed like hours, one of the magnificent creatures swam directly toward me and touched my video camera with its face. It was like he was kissing me goodbye as we left this vibrant place full of wildlife, spectacular scenery, beautiful people, and the many colors of Cape Verde.

After years of dreaming and planning, and months of sailing 3,798 miles across five bodies of water and through eight countries, we were finally ready to untie the lines and cross the Atlantic Ocean in our tiny sailboat. I prayed that three or more weeks alone together at sea would help us work through our considerable relationship obstacles. After all, the sea was our happy place.

CHAPTER 23

RITE OF PASSAGE FOR BLUEWATER SAILORS

ATLANTIC CROSSING (PART ONE)

"Following the light of the Sun, we left the Old World."
Christopher Columbus

Many sailors dream of crossing an ocean—only a few of them actually do it. It was finally our turn to untie the lines for three nonstop weeks at sea.

Day 1

FRIDAY, 8 FEBRUARY 2019
  Departure 11:40

I had been searching all month in Cape Verde for some sort of cushion to use during the long passage. The cold, hard steel of the deck and the wooden cockpit bench had become increasingly uncomfortable. The skipper had refused to bring something back from his trip to Germany, reminding me that "sailing is not for sissies."

"I wouldn't exactly call Alain a sissy," I said of our French friend, a very seasoned sailor. "His ship has plenty of comfy cushions."

"I don't care," he would say. "If you find one, fine. But I'm not helping you."

I wanted to find a lawn chair cushion, or a blow-up raft, or even a yoga mat—anything to provide the slightest bit of relief for my bum. I had popped in every shop on the remote island with no luck, and now I was out of time. Sometimes, I really missed Walmart.

It was difficult to say goodbye to Alexa and Alain. They reminded us that we would spend a lot of time together organizing the marine shop business. I smiled sincerely but knew that as soon as Cape Verde was in our backwater, the skipper would never think about it again.

It was almost as if our French friends were another one of his picture-hunting victims. The skipper used them as a distraction until he got bored, and then he disappeared without another word. It was his way.

This time, I don't think he did it on purpose. But the end result was the same.

Our friends waved from the pier as Cap'n Jack and Scout sang in the melodic howl that's so unique to their breed. Alexa and Alain got smaller and smaller, and I wondered if we would ever meet again.

I already missed my friend.

When we hit the open water, the wind blew through the sails and through my horribly neglected hair. It felt wonderful to be back at sea, but I was nervous.

I knew all of our previous sailing adventures had prepared me for that moment. There was no turning back. There would be no stops along the deep blue waters of the Atlantic for at least three weeks.

It was the skipper's birthday, but I knew better than to acknowledge it. He hated it when anyone, especially me, wished him a happy birthday—a strange quirk that I never understood but tried to respect.

Every year, for 24 hours, he disconnected his phone and refused to accept well wishes from anyone. One of the biggest fights we ever had was the year I sent him a happy birthday text.

I learned my lesson and never did it again.

I took an early-afternoon nap and was awakened by choppy waters. We both felt queasy. Determined to beat seasickness without medication, I refused to take anything while the skipper swallowed a couple pills and went down below to rest.

I felt queasy then fine, queasy then fine.

It was strange, but I noticed that there were no colors in the sunset—just a gray sky and silvery water.

Out of nowhere, an enormous dolphin jumped completely out of the water. He performed a complete flip before making a huge saltwater splash that drenched the cockpit. It happened too quickly to get the camera, but I'll never forget it. That's how it was at sea . . . some moments were special and just for me. My memory snapped a photo.

I continued to battle the queasiness and finally emptied my belly just before the end of the shift. It was violent but brief. I tried to swallow some water. The first few sips came back out, but I didn't give up. *Damn you, seasickness!!!!!*

I was determined.

Day 2

SATURDAY, 9 FEBRUARY 2019
  33 NM – 13:20 HOURS AT SEA

I felt better when I returned to the cockpit for my midnight shift. I nibbled on some crackers and was able to eat most of an apple. I knew it would take a while to get back into a sea rhythm, so I continued to power through without the aid of any harsh medicine. Luckily, I made it through the night.

The next morning, I ate an orange and some more crackers. But after about 30 minutes I found myself over the side of the rail again. Still, I refused to take medicine. I was more determined than ever to beat it.

It was a long, hot day, and though I was never quite 100%, I continued to rest and hydrate. The skipper was feeling a lot worse than me. We passed the baton each shift and didn't engage in any conversation. Two days in, I was already feeling lonely.

I had asked many other sailors how they spent their time at sea. Some played cards, read books, or played music. Those who didn't get seasick would watch videos or play games on their phone or tablet. Most important, they would talk and keep each other company. I was so jealous.

It should be such a fun experience. I didn't notice it as much on heavy passages like the Bay of Biscay when it was a constant battle with the elements. But on those long open ocean passages, it was hard to overlook the extended stretches of silence.

Sometimes the skipper would spend days without saying a word to me. I tried to understand that it was simply how he enjoyed the experience—lost in his own solitude.

But for me, it was torture. I craved human contact and conversation. I talked to the dogs, and I talked to myself. But it didn't fill the void of human interaction that I wanted and needed so badly.

Even though I wasn't alone, being at sea with the skipper was sometimes the loneliest place in the world. At least at sea, I could enjoy the sailing and embrace the experience. When the skipper would leave me alone at port, I felt abandoned.

That night, I remembered an adventure we had taken a few years before. We were on a four-day trip to Iceland and had a fabulous time driving around the famous loop, bathing in the natural hot springs, climbing to the top of the waterfalls, and enjoying the exquisite calving glaciers.

It was a magical experience in a gorgeous place, but four days was apparently one day too many for the skipper.

On the last day, we were in the rental car and I said something that agitated him. I honestly don't remember what I said, but I remember with detailed clarity what happened next.

He screeched on the brakes and pulled over to the shoulder. He reached across my body, opened the passenger door, and pushed me out of the car.

Then, he squealed away, leaving me on the ground. I rose to my feet and brushed the dirt from my clothes. That's when I realized I had no phone, no purse, and no money. It was a busy four-lane highway and cars were speeding past me, honking at me to stay clear of the road.

I kept thinking he would turn around and come back to get me. But he didn't.

He drove to the airport, boarded a plane, and flew home to Germany.

I wandered the streets of Reykjavík for several hours, bawling my eyes out. I had no phone to call anyone, no GPS to help me find my way, and no money for a cab or a bus. I walked in the direction that I thought was toward the hotel.

I finally made my way to a bus stop, but the driver would not let me board without any money. A cab pulled up. The driver only spoke a little broken English, but he could easily tell that I was lost and upset. I told him if he would please take me to the hotel, I would be able to pay him when we got there. He agreed.

I continued to sob uncontrollably.

When we reached the hotel, I asked him to wait so I could go get some money to pay for the fare. "It's going to be okay," he said. "No charge for the ride."

The stranger showed me more kindness in that one moment than the skipper had shown me in years.

I expected the skipper to be waiting for me in the lobby or in the room. He wasn't there. I cried all night, and the next morning I boarded a plane back to Alabama.

I swore I would never speak to him again.

Of course, he convinced me otherwise. I asked him to at least say he was sorry for abandoning me on the side of the road in a foreign country. It wasn't his style to say he was sorry. He honestly didn't think he had done anything wrong.

"You were getting on my nerves," he said. "I just couldn't be with you another minute."

"Can you at least promise me that you'll never do that again?" I needed something—anything that demonstrated even the slightest bit of remorse or a sliver of acknowledgement that what he did to me was wrong. He refused.

However, he did say, "Perhaps I need to leave you in more random places so that you can work on your survival skills."

I didn't speak to him for months. But in the end, he was able to manipulate me into coming back to him—again.

As I sailed into the night, longing for human companionship, I felt just as abandoned as I did on the side of the road in Iceland.

Day 3

SUNDAY, 10 FEBRUARY 2019
105 NM – 37:20 HOURS AT SEA

The next morning, it was foggy with no color and no wind. I felt much better and was able to read a book for a couple of hours, but I struggled to find a comfortable spot to sit and relax.

The conditions were slow and calm, just the way I like it! We were averaging about 2.5 knots. Even with no wind, there were still constant swells in the Atlantic that were causing a lot of side-to-side motion—my Achilles Heel.

I was queasy at times, but I took no medicine and was able to fight off the seasickness with only hydration and pure will.

Day 4

MONDAY, 11 FEBRUARY 2019
  176 NM – 60:48 HOURS AT SEA

It was bright and hot—a perfect day to bask in the sunshine with a good book and eliminate my tan lines.

A huge school of dolphins showed up to play with us. The pod was one of the biggest we had ever seen. There were at least 100 of them, and they stayed with us for more than an hour.

The skipper and I had begun to have short conversations during the day, mostly about sailing.

There was still no color in the sunset, which disappointed and intrigued me.

Day 5

TUESDAY, 12 FEBRUARY 2019
  270 NM – 84:49 HOURS AT SEA

During my night shift, the sky was as black as I had ever seen it. There were a few stars, but they were not as bright and spectacular as usual.

The wooden bench was as hard as ever. I tried to cushion my bum with a piece of carpet and some pillows, but it didn't help.

I couldn't sleep that night.

The wind was gusty, and the waves were choppy. By 08:00, we shifted all the sails to the port side and took a westerly course to try and pick up some of the trade winds. It worked, but then we were on a heavy tilt.

The sea had become angry. However, we cruised at 5 to 5.5 knots, which seemed to make the skipper happy.

I relaxed and started a new book, but the entire day was rocky and uncomfortable. I refused to take seasick medicine and focused on hydrating. My plan was working, and my sea legs felt strong.

Day 6

WEDNESDAY, 13 FEBRUARY 2019
  376 NM – 108:49 HOURS AT SEA
During my night shift, a little petrel flew into the cockpit. I was startled by the noise, and before I knew what was happening, it slapped me right in the back of the head and then got stuck in the corner of the cockpit floor, unable to fly away.

The commotion woke the skipper, and he came up to help. He used one of my shoes as a ledge. She climbed on board and then he lifted her into the air, and she flew away.

It was so sweet.

On long passages, we found entertainment wherever we could. I finished my book and began reading another one, although I continued to struggle to find a comfortable place to sit.

I enjoyed the calm, smooth seas and the gorgeous weather. I realized I didn't need much company from the skipper and instead found contentment reading book after book after book.

But there is always a calm before the storm.

Day 7

THURSDAY, 14 FEBRUARY 2019
  477 NM – 133:04 HOURS AT SEA
During the skipper's night shift, the wind and waves had picked up, and it felt like we were back in the Bay of Biscay. The boat was rocking in all directions. I could hear the skipper on the deck bringing down the main sail. I was awake, so I went up to help. It was a struggle to fight the heavy gusts of wind and the rocking boat.

The next morning, we realized that we had been spoiled by the many days of calm weather. We were out of practice for heavy conditions. It was always easier to deal with the wind and waves and constant rocking in the light of day. In the black of night, it was grueling.

Day 8

FRIDAY, 15 FEBRUARY 2019
577 NM – 158 HOURS AT SEA

That night, the moon was amazingly bright! It was directly above the boat and looked like a huge lightbulb that was casting a magnificent glow into the cockpit.

I actually enjoyed the night shift. I spent almost the entire night texting with friends and family through our satellite tracker. Finally, I was able to get some human company. I was so grateful to have that communication system on board. The next morning, I thanked the skipper for making the investment and told him how happy it made me during the night shift.

He was in a bad mood. He told me that the pinging of all the messages kept him up all night. I apologized and told him I would turn off the notifications but emphasized how much it meant to me to be able to communicate with friends and family.

He didn't care and told me to limit the messaging at night. I made a mental note to not tell him the next time something made me happy for fear he would take it away from me.

I reminded him that if we could have more conversations and interactions, I wouldn't need to talk to other people so much. He reminded me how much he hated chit chat.

With continued silence from the skipper, I started reading my sixth book of the passage, *The Old Man and the Sea*. I think it was the tenth time I had read it, but it had probably been 15 years since the last time. Only 20 pages in, I quickly remembered why I loved it so much.

Day 9

SATURDAY, 16 FEBRUARY 2019
   676 NM – 181 HOURS AT SEA
   I woke up to 17-knot winds and 6-knot speed. During the night we had hit the halfway mark of the passage, putting us closer to America than Africa with 700 miles to go to Ilha Fernando de Noronha, the small remote island off the coast of Brazil. We planned to make a quick stop there on our way to Cabedelo.

It was another perfect day of fantastic 84° sunny weather with trade winds sailing. We averaged 5.1 knots, which was speedy for our heavy, steel ship.

We closed part of the canopy in the cockpit, even though I wanted to suntan a little more. But I was reminded that we were close to the Equator and then slathered my body with sunscreen.

The skipper and I began talking a little more, even though I had become more interested in my books and less interested in his company. That afternoon, the mood between us lightened a bit. We listened to music and talked about how much we would love to have an ice cream cone. I told him I missed the spectacular sunsets I was so used to seeing at sea. I later researched why we had not seen much color.

At low latitudes, the sun sets perpendicular to the horizon, while at higher latitudes, the sun can set at a more oblique angle, allowing it to remain close to the horizon after sunset for a longer period of time.

The farther south you travel, the farther and quicker the sun will dip below the horizon at night. Eventually, once you get to the tropics, Polaris is on the horizon, and the sun sets directly down below the horizon. Since it has very little movement horizontally with respect to the horizon, the sun quickly leaves the horizon behind after sunset, making for a very quick twilight.

Then, as you proceed southward from the Equator, the effect is reversed—twilights become longer and longer.

Day 10

SUNDAY, 17 FEBRUARY 2019
802 NM – 205 HOURS AT SEA
The skipper became more restless. I became more content with my books. But he had only allowed me to bring 12 books on the crossing. I originally thought that was fair—not believing I would ever read that many. But when I opened my final book, I realized I needed to pace myself or I would be forced to start reading maintenance and equipment manuals. We relaxed and showered, but the seas were too choppy to cook. The skipper was seasick, but I was fine—still no medicine for me.

Day 11

MONDAY, 18 FEBRUARY 2019
913 NM – 229 HOURS AT SEA
As we got closer to the Equator the heat intensified—95°F. We listened to music, danced in the cockpit, and cruised at a steady pace. We had fun together and embraced the time alone at sea. I was grateful for human companionship but also content if I needed to bury myself back in a book. The doldrums were close, which would slow us and make the blazing heat even more intense. The sunsets remained colorless, but the moonlights were incredibly bright.

Day 12

TUESDAY, 19 FEBRUARY 2019
1,016 NM – 254 HOURS AT SEA
Scout joined me for every night watch. She slept and cuddled right next to me. It was so sweet and great company on those long nights.

As the skipper pulled in a bucket of water to clean dogs' grass mat, he noticed some of *Seefalke's* orange paint was peeling on the starboard side. A closer look showed a *lot* of paint had peeled. Perhaps when we had the hull scrubbed in Cape Verde, the guy may have been too aggressive. We added the task of sandblasting and painting the ship to our long to-do list.

The skipper considered painting her a different color, but I talked him out of it. *Seefalke's* bright orange color was part of her character and personality. I reminded him how he wouldn't let me change the interior to bright white.

It was swelteringly hot as we cruised directly toward the Equator. The doldrums were taking a toll on our bodies and on our progress through the water. The doldrums are famous for long slow days of intense heat and no wind with tropical squalls in the evenings.

As a storm began to brew, we hustled to get the main sail down and pull in the genoa. We struggled as rain poured heavily and enormous waves swept us from side to side. It had been broiling hot all day, so the cold rainwater was welcomed. But the conditions were challenging as we fought to stay on course. The short squall cooled us, and our salt-encrusted deck and gear definitely needed a freshwater bath. We used the rainwater to clean our bodies, which needed it after sitting in puddles of our own sweat all day.

Day 13

WEDNESDAY, 20 FEBRUARY 2019
1,116 NM – 278 HOURS AT SEA

I woke up with just three hours to go before reaching the Equator. We had fun preparing our Neptune-style ceremonial proceedings. The traditional Equator-crossing superstition involves getting into full costume. We took turns playing the part of Neptune. We each asked Neptune for permission to pass across the Equator and enter the Southern Hemisphere. We each had to answer three questions and then make a sacrifice. The skipper sacrificed piece of fresh fruit, and I sacrificed our last fresh vegetable.

The seadogs also participated. We asked them questions for which the right answer was always "yes." We asked the question and then said, "If the answer is yes, eat this treat. If the answer is no, reject this treat." Cap'n Jack and Scout passed with flying colors! But they weren't too happy when a treat was thrown overboard as their sacrifice to Neptune.

Next, we made our equatorial vows—to respect the sea and its creatures and to keep our crew safe on the passage. Lastly, we needed to take a dip in the equatorial waters. We wanted to jump in, but the swells were dangerously high. So, the skipper dumped a bucket of sea water on the pups and me. Then I dumped a bucket on him. It was goofy and the most fun I had had on any passage so far.

Later, the skipper lifted me up the main mast to rethread the courtesy flag line through the block. It was scary, but I loved being up there while underway. Fortunately, the seas were calm, but I still suffered some minor rope burn on my thighs and arms on the way down. We barely had any wind all day, and it was brutally hot with nowhere to escape for relief. I felt dizzy and had a headache, and the skipper thought I might be suffering from heatstroke. We continued to douse ourselves with seawater to cool off.

Day 14

THURSDAY, 21 FEBRUARY 2019
1,205 NM – 301 HOURS AT SEA
Night watches had been calm and peaceful with cooler temperatures and only short patches of rain—a nice break from the sweltering heat of the day. During the days, it was blisteringly hot! I retrieved several 8-liter bottles of water from the stern bilge. We were working our way through our generous supply. We mostly just relaxed and hydrated. It was difficult to exert too much energy in the broiling heat.

As we got closer to land, I began to think about the reality of working again. The skipper began talking about what it would look like if we just continued to sail forever. I told him I was not interested if he was going to continue to leave me every time we got into a new port. "That's not what I signed on for," I reminded him. "And I miss my family."

"I promise we can sail to Alabama often, and you can see your family."

I knew it was a promise he would never keep, but he was a gifted salesman.

"Can you be faithful to me?" I asked directly.

"I am faithful to you," he lied.

I had not checked his phone since we were in the Canaries, and I didn't want to. But one thing was certain—I knew I didn't trust him.

"I'm out of money," I told him. "The condo is costing me every penny I make, and my savings account is empty."

"We could rent out the condo longterm, and you could sell your car," he suggested.

I loved my little royal blue Beetle convertible. But perhaps he was right. I wasn't using it. It didn't make sense to keep paying for it if we were going to live full-time on the boat.

Wait! What was I thinking? I want to go home and return to my normal life! I want to see my family and friends and sleep in a regular bed and play tennis and take a hot shower and have ice!

He was determined to reveal his plan.

"You are paying for a storage unit and don't need anything in it," he said. "You could sell all that stuff, sell the car, and then contribute some money for the sailing kitty."

It all made sense, but I still wasn't so sure. As usual, he was manipulating me, and I was getting caught up in the excitement of the idea.

"So," I said. "What are *you* going to sell?"

Silence.

Day 15

FRIDAY, 22 FEBRUARY 2019
  1,299 NM – 325 HOURS AT SEA

Scout and I settled in for our night watch and continued to stay on alert for squalls. I texted with Trisha and ignored the skipper's rumblings about the pings. We talked about an idea of her renting our condo, but decided it was better to just keep it on Airbnb. Something told me not to give up my land home just yet. However, she agreed to buy my car.

In the morning, the wind had picked up to 20 knots. We had made our way through the doldrums and were back in the tradewinds. That afternoon, even with the steady wind, it was HOT! We were melting!

I love hot weather. I can play a three-hour tennis match in 90° weather and 100% humidity and be fine—sweaty, but fine. But the equatorial heat was overwhelming. It was like sitting in a sauna for 10 hours a day with the sun shining directly on your face from about 10 ft away. Walking on the deck scalded the bottoms of my feet, even when wore shoes. We had no air conditioning onboard, no fans, and no ice. The drinking water was lukewarm. It was unbearable even for someone like me who loves the heat and the sun.

As we got closer to land, the sunsets revealed brilliant shades of color again, which made me happy.

Sailing Directly into the Eye of a Storm

Later in the evening, we saw another batch of thunderstorms. It was the tropics, after all—extreme heat all day and then thunderstorms at night.

While we prepared for an oncoming squall, the skipper tripped over the piece of carpet that I used to cushion my bum. Furious, he grabbed the carpet and violently slung it out into the sea. I was caught off guard by his sudden burst of rage and found myself slinking into the corner of the cockpit.

"Get control of yourself," I said calmly but firmly.

"Don't bring that fucking cushion in the cockpit again!" he screamed at me with fury in his eyes.

"Well, I can't now," I said matter-of-factly.

"You deal with this fucking storm! I'm going to bed."

The skipper left me all alone, and I was not happy about it.

Through random flashes of lightning bolts, I could see the batch of storm cells ahead of us. I didn't try to maneuver around them because there was nowhere to go. The only option was to plow straight through them.

The sun had already set, and the sea was angry. In the darkness, we sailed into what felt like a black cave. I could hear loud claps of thunder every few seconds. The heavy rain drenched me, and I couldn't see anything. I held my breath and fought to keep *Seefalke* on course.

I asked the skipper for help, but he refused to join me in the cockpit. It felt like he was leaving me alone again on the side of the road in Iceland.

There is not much you can do when looking directly into the eye of a storm—except go through your checklist. Adjust the sails. Check the emergency positioning radio beacon tracking device to be sure it's on and functioning. Secure your life vest. Strap yourself in.

Make your peace with God. And hold on.

Feeling abandoned and terrified, I looked to the black sky and asked God to help me make it safely to the other side.

Then I forged straight ahead into the dark sea—directly into the cluster of raging storms.

CAPTAIN
OF MY SOUL

LIVING LIFE SIDEWAYS SERIES
BOOK 3

MICHELLE SEGREST

CHAPTER 24

CONFRONTING STORMS & MAKING LANDFALL

ATLANTIC CROSSING (PART TWO)

"Confronting a storm is like fighting God. All the powers in the universe seem to be against you and, in an extraordinary way, your irrelevance is at the same time both humbling and exalting."—Francis LeGrande

I held the wheel with clenched fists and kept *Seefalke* steady through the darkness. With each bolt of lightning, I could see the storm cells all around me but only for a couple seconds. I stayed strong, even though I was afraid. I pushed directly through the patch of storms that were emerging into one right in front of me.

It reminded me of a NASCAR race. Many years ago, I was a sports reporter and covered races. Whenever there was a huge wreck, the other cars were safest if they drove right through the pileup rather than trying to swerve around it.

I had no choice but to push straight through and pray that *Seefalke* would stay afloat. Capsizing had always been my biggest fear. I talked to God. I asked him to keep the mast intact. If the mast and the keel stayed steady, we would not tip over. I asked him to give me the courage to make it through.

The storm didn't last long, but it seemed like an eternity. Somehow, we made it, and I found peace on the other side.

I thanked God.

Then, I vowed I would never again let the skipper tell me I was not a good enough sailor. I pulled my weight, even if he didn't acknowledge it. I was not a passenger or even just a first mate.

I am a sailor.

I had sailed that ship 50% of the time from Germany to Brazil—the exact same amount of time that the skipper had sailed it. Even when I felt weak, afraid, and debilitated, I never missed a shift. I remembered in that moment what I had already learned in the Bay of Biscay. The mind is stronger than the body. If I want to do something badly enough, I can do it.

The sea calmed, and so did I.

The sky cleared. The moon began to shine, providing me with light. Stars twinkled in the black night. I let the sea settle my nerves as I tried to relax on the hard, wooden bench. I thought about the skipper's outburst and for the first time allowed myself to be a little afraid of him. I felt unsettled, but I knew I needed to just make it to Brazil and then I could plan my escape.

Did I really just use the word "escape?"

At the shift change, I passed the skipper in the companionway. I wasn't going to say anything, but I couldn't help myself. I looked him directly in the eyes and gave him a warning.

"Don't you ever leave me alone in a storm like that again."

"Sailing is not for sissies," he said, sarcastically, under his breath.

If looks could kill, he would be dead right now.

"The only sissy I see on this boat is a captain who abandoned his crew during a storm. And why? Because he slipped on a silly cushion."

I was pissed.

"The next time you call me a sissy, I'll show you what growing up with three brothers taught me about not being a sissy."

It was a threat, and I meant it.

He recognized the seriousness of my expression and tone. He paused for a moment.

But then he laughed at me. "You are fine," he said, flippantly. "It was not fatal."

Day 16

SATURDAY, 23 FEBRUARY 2019
1,391 NM – 350 HOURS AT SEA

When I came up for the midnight shift there was a sweet little petrel sitting on one of the fenders near the cockpit. When Scout joined me, she promptly chased her away. The little bird made a circle around the boat and came right back to her perch. I wouldn't let Scout chase her this time, but my sweet little guard dog stayed on alert the rest of the night, loyally protecting me.

At about 06:00, after 15 straight days at sea, we saw land! About four hours later, we arrived in the bay of Ilha Fernando de Noronha. After sailing 1,430 nm in 360 hours, we dropped anchor in a cove surrounded by lush green mountains and a vibrant rainforest. It reminded me of Jurassic Park.

The plan was to stay a day or two and explore the hidden gem, a national park located about 250 nm from the eastern coast of Brazil's mainland. After a week of blistering heat while sailing the doldrums on the equatorial line and into the waters of the Southern Hemisphere, we welcomed the overcast weather and even the rain that began to fall and cool us.

We were in need of some relief from the intensive heat, as well as a little rest. It took a while to get the anchor set, and we felt completely unsettled. Something just wasn't right.

In addition, we had received an alert that our engine was running hot. With the sweltering heat, it wasn't much of a surprise. *Seefalke* was built for sailing in North Sea conditions. She wasn't used to temperatures in the high 90s directly under the blazing equatorial sun and with no wind. We had only motor sailed 2 of our 15 days at sea, but that was enough to put stress on the engine.

It was, by far, our longest passage ever. I was ready to pop our traditional celebratory champagne and toast the accomplishment. But the skipper refused. He was not comfortable with the anchorage. While a steady rain fell, we blew up the dinghy, lowered the outboard motor using the mizzen halyard as a crane, and the skipper went to the island to check into customs and secure our berth.

When he returned, he told me that as an American citizen, I needed a visa. I kicked myself for not checking on this sooner but excused myself since going to Brazil was a last-minute decision. I was usually so organized. I jumped online with the little bit of weak internet we had and took the necessary steps to secure the visa. However, I learned it would take five business days to be approved.

Meanwhile, I cooked dinner and hung out the sheets, blankets, and towels to let the pouring rain do some laundry for us. I took a refreshing deck shower in the fresh water falling from the sky. But I still had not put my feet on land yet.

The skipper could not shake his feelings of uneasiness. Always trust the gut of a sailor.

We were excited about our accomplishment and about the opportunity to explore the beautiful island. But Mother Nature had a different plan for us.

The wind was howling and gigantic 3 m swells from the open Atlantic were pounding into the bay and rocking our anchored ship in all directions. The island had no marina, so anchoring was our only option.

Sometimes, I would soon learn, your worst night at sea is the one you spend at anchorage.

We needed rest badly, but we were floating about 200 m from massive rock formations and mountainous cliffs. If the anchor dragged, *Seefalke* would be slamming against those rocks in minutes. We made the decision to keep our night watch schedule to be sure that if the anchor didn't hold, we could quickly do something about it.

The night was brutal. I could hear the heavy anchor chain scraping against *Seefalke's* steel hull, making haunting sounds that echoed throughout the cabin. The swells were lapping against the ship and jerking and jolting us in all directions. The rain continued to pound us as lightning flashed all night. I couldn't remember a night passage at sea that was as uncomfortable or as downright scary—not even the storm I had just battled my way through.

At sea, there was room to move. There was plenty of space to maneuver off course to avoid storms and other obstacles. In that small bay, the rocks were right there, taunting us, daring us to come a little closer and face their wrath.

Day 17

SUNDAY, 24 FEBRUARY 2019

Anchorage, Ilha Fernando de Noronha, Brazil

It was a long night for all of us.

The next morning, we decided to skip our island adventure and get back in the open ocean where we felt safe. The skipper got in the dinghy and went to shore to check us out and pick up a few provisions while I cleaned the cabin and prepared the boat for departure.

Then the sun came out, and we could truly appreciate the beauty that surrounded us. In deep contrast to the brown and silver mountains of Cape Verde, the formations were covered with lush green vegetation. Hundreds of long-tailed birds hovered around the island.

Dozens of dolphins played and leaped from the water to the delight of the sailors sitting in anchored ships, the tourists on charter boats, and the kayakers and paddle boarders that had populated the bay under the bright Brazilian sunshine. Huge sea turtles swam alongside *Seefalke*, piquing the interest of our sailing dogs.

The skipper was enjoying the sights in the small island community and learned that the island would accept no more than 400 visitors per day. He decided to take the dinghy to go check out another anchorage. He thought that since the weather had improved, perhaps we would stay another day and explore the island after all.

But after checking out the anchorage, he changed his mind. His gut continued to tell him it was dangerous to risk another night at that anchorage. We didn't want to have another night like the last one.

It was blisteringly hot—almost 40°C (104°F). I cooked a hearty meal, but it was so hot that I had to jump in the water before I could eat the food I had just prepared.

The water felt fantastic! After we ate, we both took a break and swam for a while. We jumped in and enjoyed the cool aquamarine tinted water that was so clear you could see all the way to the bottom of the ocean floor, more than 8 m below us.

We showered off all the salt water and then went back to the business of preparing the boat for departure. Neither my feet, nor the pups', had touched dry land. It was about that time that the skipper realized that he had not properly closed the waterproof bag he took with him onshore. His cell phone was completely waterlogged and no longer functional. I downloaded the much-needed weather and navigation apps to my phone.

We finally got the boat prepared and were ready for departure. But even more drama was looming.

We were ready to set sail, but as we tried to pull in the anchor using the electric windlass, we couldn't get the hook to dislodge from the ocean floor. The constant pounding and dragging from the previous night had wedged the anchor deep into the ground.

It was stuck. No matter how we tried to maneuver the ship, we couldn't get it loose.

Finally, the skipper went into the bow and released the chain. We left the anchor and the chain on the ocean floor and got the hell out of there. We needed to return to sea.

When we were finally back in the open ocean, we felt safe again. The temperature dropped about 10 degrees. It was still in the 90s, but combined with the wind propelling our movement, it felt cool and refreshing.

However, the engine was still not happy about the heat. The alert sounded again, and the skipper checked it out. We pulled out all the maintenance manuals and checked in with our mechanics back in Stralsund. The consensus was to let the engine cool some more and then we would head back down to check out the thermostat, which we guessed was what was broken or stuck.

Meanwhile, the conditions were breezy and comfortable. Several huge petrels circled us as we cruised around the island to get glimpses of what we were unable to see up close. I was exhausted from the long ocean passage combined with no sleep at anchorage. When it was time for the skipper's first night watch, I crashed hard and fast and slept soundly in the safety of the open Atlantic.

Day 18

MONDAY, 25 FEBRUARY 2019
1,456 NM – 398 HOURS AT SEA
Well rested, I enjoyed the pleasant midnight shift. There was a cool, steady breeze with calm, relaxing waters—a refreshing contrast from the previous night at anchorage. Early the next morning, we continued to fight the heat.

The skipper spent time in the engine room dealing with the raw-water circuit alert and performed an oil change. He confirmed that the temperature sensor was stuck, and the engine was fine to use.

We had calm seas most of the day, but it remained blisteringly hot. And as we were growing accustomed to these conditions, we knew that the extreme heat during the day would likely produce tropical thunderstorms in the evenings.

Day 19

TUESDAY, 26 FEBRUARY 2019
  1,535 NM – 422 HOURS AT SEA

As expected, we had thunderstorms and lightning all night. The sky lit up like fireworks on New Year's Eve. It was a long night followed by another extremely hot day. The hours from 10:00 to 15:00 were the toughest. We would try to exert as little energy as possible during those hours and do whatever we could to beat the heat. We drank lots of water. I wished so much that the water had been cold. I would have been happy if it was even slightly above room temperature.

I would have given anything for just one cube of ice. Every 30 minutes or so, I doused myself with a bucket of cool sea water, which quickly evaporated from my sizzling skin.

Cap'n Jack and Scout generally stayed in the cabin and laid on the cool wooden floor to beat the heat. I struggled to be in the cabin and preferred to have the fresh air and breeze. I read some, but the heat made it difficult. Usually around 15:30, it would begin to cool and then it would be pleasant until the sun began to set. That's when the stormy cloud formations would build on the horizon, and we braced ourselves to fight the tropical storms at night.

Day 20

WEDNESDAY, 27 FEBRUARY 2019
  1,628 NM – 446 HOURS AT SEA

My early sleep shift was rough. We were on a heavy tilt, and I struggled to find a comfortable sleeping position. Gusts during that shift reached 42 knots as *Seefalke* rocked and rolled but kept us afloat. When I began my midnight shift, conditions had calmed. I embraced the cool breeze of the evening as we approached our destination of Cabedelo, Brazil.

I thought a lot about our accomplishment. Not many sailors have crossed the Atlantic, and fewer have sailed across the Equator and faced the doldrums. In my opinion, the extreme heat was our biggest challenge—even more so than the length of the journey or the tropical squalls. And I had sailed alone through a brutal storm and conquered another fear.

Yes, I am a sailor!

We made landfall at 10:08. As the large city skyline of Cabedelo came into focus, I felt the conflicting feeling that I would usually get when long passages came to an end. I was ready to be on land, but I was not ready for the journey to end.

We made our long list of work and boat-repair tasks and dreaded what awaited us back in the real world.

The skipper reminded me that the actual Atlantic crossing was technically Morocco to Brazil—mainland to mainland. All our other stops—Canary Islands, Cape Verde, and Ilha Fernando de Noronha—were just island hops along the way. From Rabat, Morocco, to Cabedelo, Brazil, we covered approximately 3,400 nm.

We arrived in Jacaré Village at the banks of Rio Paraiba in beautiful Brazil at 15:10. After finally reaching South American mainland, we had successfully finished our first Atlantic crossing and completed an important rite of passage for sailors. I proudly reviewed our stats:

- It had been 192 days since we set sail from Stralsund, Germany on August 19, 2018.

- We had sailed 5,475 nm through the Baltic Sea, the Kiel Canal, the North Sea, the English Channel, the Bay of Biscay, and the North and South Atlantic Oceans.

- We had visited 10 countries on three continents.

- The longest single passage (1,690 nm) took us from Mindelo, Cape Verde, Africa, to Jacaré Village, Cabedelo, Brazil in 462 hours (three weeks).

- The coldest temperature we experienced was 6°C, the warmest 39°C.

- All four crew members were safe.

I was so happy to have made it across the Atlantic, and was ready to focus on the primary reason we sailed to Brazil—a passage through the Amazon River. But I had no idea how long we would be stuck in that port, or how much my mental and physical health would suffer in the process.

CHAPTER 25

CARNIVAL, SAILOR STORIES & MOSQUITO SOUP

27 FEBRUARY–8 MARCH 2019

As we entered Marina Jacaré following our cross-Atlantic passage, we heard from some old friends on the radio. Dieter and Claudia were the German sailors traveling on their catamaran, *Whitebird,* with their two small children (Charley and Nicholas) and their big black dog, Rocky. I was excited about seeing old friends in a new place.

No slips were available in the small marina, so we had to settle for a mooring buoy about 200 yards from the pier while waiting for an open berth.

We no longer had our main anchor—it was sitting on the bottom of the bay in Noronha—but the mooring buoys were well secured and the marina was protected from open ocean swells.

We inflated the dinghy and went into the small village to eat and explore. After three weeks at sea, Cap'n Jack and Scout were excited about a long walk and all the amazing smells of a new unexplored land. I was ready for a walk, too, and craved two things—a cheeseburger and ice!

We couldn't find a cheeseburger and instead settled for meat on a stick at a small restaurant located outside the marina. It wasn't a restaurant in the traditional sense—it was an open tent with a couple of coolers, a small grill, and a few plastic folding chairs and tables.

It was owned and operated by a sweet Brazilian family who lived in a small shack next to the marina. Felipe also worked as a night security guard in the marina. Ellen was seven months pregnant. We were only seven degrees south of the Equator, so it was well over 100°F even after sunset. I couldn't imagine how uncomfortable Ellen must have felt, but she flashed a beautiful smile and cooked our meat sticks over the small open-fire grill. There were no sides on the menu—in fact, there was no menu. They only served grilled chicken or beef on a stick. After three weeks of the vegetarian life, my body craved protein.

When I asked Ellen for something to drink with lots of ice, she suggested in very broken English that I try a caipirinha—the traditional Brazilian cocktail. Usually, I would not drink alcohol in front of the skipper, but I was no longer worried about offending him and drank the entire plastic cup of sweet nectar in one gulp. It was the first cold drink that had touched my lips in weeks.

Caipirinhas are made with cachaça, sugar, and lime and are prepared by mixing the fruit and the sugar together, then adding the liquor. I ordered another one, this time with extra ice, and ignored the scowl on the skipper's face. In the intense equatorial heat, the ice cubes melted faster than I could chew them.

I was uncomfortable in the plastic chair, but for a good reason. I had been experiencing pain in my hindquarters since about midway through the Atlantic crossing. That evening, I had considerable discomfort while using the bathroom and realized that a recurring hemorrhoid had surfaced. Since my first pregnancy, it was not unusual for me to suffer from the pain they often caused.

268

I knew that sitting on the hard wooden bench and the steel deck combined with not getting much fiber in my diet were most likely causing the flare. Generally, Preparation H would minimize the swelling and the pain in a couple days. I had some onboard and began the treatment, vowing I would go on a hunt to find a suitable cushion somewhere in Brazil.

Was it really asking too much to have cushion onboard?

As soon as the sun rose, so did we. We got busy!

I washed three weeks of sweaty clothes and linens. Then I scrubbed and organized the boat while the skipper went into the city to get his waterlogged phone repaired. That afternoon, we all piled into the dinghy and went into the marina to visit with Claudia and Dieter. The men rented a car and drove to the customs office and then to the market. They were able to score some fresh fruit, but the customs office was already closed for the day.

While the men ran errands, I spent the afternoon with Claudia and her sweet kids. Claudia and Dieter were about seven months into a two-year sabbatical. Claudia wanted to continue the sailing journey, but Dieter was counting the days until they would return to civilization.

I learned that she had sailed her entire life and was the captain of their ship, *Whitebird*. Dieter was the first mate and had less sailing experience than me. It was so nice to have a friend to spend time with, especially since the skipper had already informed me of a flight that he had booked for a week later.

I no longer had the energy to be surprised or upset about being abandoned when we reached a new port. However, this time, I responded by booking a flight of my own. I scheduled a two-week trip to Alabama—a getaway that would begin shortly after the skipper returned from his trip to Italy. I put the cost of the ticket on the same credit card that still had a balance from my Morocco flight.

The marina had strong WiFi, so I found a comfy spot and worked for a couple hours. I completed an article that was due the next day, and then we had pizza for dinner at the marina canteen.

The marina lobby was completely open, but it had a grass shack ceiling that provided shade from the blazing sun. The floor was covered with terra-cotta Spanish tiles.

In addition to picnic tables and comfy lounge chairs, sailors often relaxed in the many hammocks that hang throughout the space. Restrooms with showers are available to all sailors.

The skipper spent the entire next day in the city getting us processed through customs. My visa was finally approved, so he was able to get all the paperwork secured for a three-month stay in Brazil. We had no idea at the time that 90 days might not be long enough.

I continued to catch up on work and looked forward to my flight home. I had been so homesick and couldn't wait to spend time with Shelby, Bo, and my friends. I also needed to take care of several things like annual checkups at the doctor and dentist and renew my expired driver's license. And I knew that my wooden sailboat, *Protagonist*, needed some maintenance.

It was inexpensive to eat out in Cabedelo, so one night we went to a rodízio restaurant—the traditional Brazilian style with a buffet of salads, sushi, and other sides. Servers offered huge sticks of barbecued meat and shaved off as much as we wanted. We stuffed ourselves until we were miserable.

Our taxi driver, Marco, spoke no English but had a fantastic translation app where we could speak to an actual person who would then translate our conversation. One thing we had learned quickly in Brazil was that very few people spoke English. We began learning a few key phrases in Portuguese.

The next day, we explored the village near the marina, which was covered by dirt streets. Stray dogs and cats roamed freely. With no air conditioning, all the locals were always outside—sitting in rocking chairs, hammocks, and swings—hoping to catch any breeze that might blow from the water's edge.

My skin looked polka dotted from all the mosquito bites, and the humidity felt like it was about 900%. The sticky air was so thick you wouldn't be able to carve through it with an Indiana Jones-style machete. I could see steam rising from the streets. My hair was soaked, and my clothes dripped from the sweat. The only living things not suffering from the intense heat and heavy humidity were the thousands of mosquitos that clearly enjoyed my delicious American blood.

I called the atmosphere "mosquito soup."

We found a local street market and treated ourselves to an ice cream cone. Even in the uncomfortable climate, I enjoyed looking at all the crafts in the local shops.

We asked the few locals who spoke English where we could find a good mechanic, painter, and handyman to help us with our long list of boat projects. They directed us to a small shop about three blocks away. That's where we met, Christoph, an amazing craftsman, carpenter, and sailmaker. Christoph was a German sailor who had a local company, Orca Deck. He had sailed into Brazil 18 years prior, started his business, and settled there permanently. He lived with his wife on a beautiful catamaran, which was anchored near our mooring buoy. However, his workshop was in the village.

We talked with him about our repairs for *Seefalke*. The list was long, so we were happy to find him, and even happier to discover that skilled labor was very inexpensive in that part of Brazil.

His workshop was amazing. He handcrafted small wooden sailboats and gorgeous custom-crafted teak tables with perfect compass roses carved into them.

While I was admiring some of his displays and current projects, something caught my eye that excited me. He made beautiful cockpit cushions out of durable sail material, which protected them from the saltwater and high temperatures. Each cushion was super comfy, very attractive, and folded for easy storage. They were hand sewn and only cost $50 USD each. Without asking the skipper's permission, I promptly ordered four of them.

The skipper was irritated, but I didn't care. I was still struggling from the pain in my bum and vowed I would get cushions for the boat no matter how much the skipper objected. "I'll pay for them myself," I said, and didn't leave it open for discussion.

We needed to take *Seefalke* out of the water to get her completely sandblasted and repainted. She also had considerable rusted areas and rotted wood that required attention. We ordered a new anchor and chain and more solar panels.

20 Things I Would Rather Do Than Attend Carnival in Brazil

Since we happened to be in Brazil during Carnival season, we called Marco and asked him to drive us two hours to Olinda so we could experience it.

I went in with an open mind but learned quickly that not everyone loves a parade.

As I walked through the streets of the quaint city, I began to feel claustrophobic. I was outside, but the walls were closing in on me. Trapped in a mob of literally tens of thousands of colorfully costumed, more-than-slightly-inebriated people, I was being stampeded from all directions.

It was as if Mardi Gras had exploded in the middle of Comic-Con, but without the reward of Cajun food, colorful beads, or a selfie with William Shatner.

Street vendors were passing out free fans, bandanas, and condoms. I took two of the three.

I was only there about 20 minutes, and my head was already throbbing in sync with the ridiculously loud, never-ending banging drums.

As I was getting drenched in booze and sweat thanks to playing bumper cars with thousands of drunk Brazilians, I began to think of about all the places I would rather be at that moment:

1 In a Turkish prison
2. At Navy SEAL boot camp
3. Knee-deep in a swamp full of crocodiles
4. On a Trojan battlefield with no weapons
5. In shark-infested waters with an open, bloody wound

6. Face to face with an overprotective mother bear

Big crowds, loud drums, and naked old men dancing in the streets are just not my thing. But it was important to me to experience the historic Carnival, so while my mind was racing with activities that I considered more fun, I looked around and realized that we were probably the only sober people in the dense crowd.

"Maybe I need to be drunk to enjoy this," I said to the skipper and Marco. "Everyone else seems to be having a blast."

I scanned the crowded streets for anything containing alcohol. There were many options—hundreds of street vendors selling cocktails and pure-grain alcohol. I bullied my way through the maze of bodies to get to the closest one. I found a piña colada served from a real coconut. Perfect!

About that time, the sky opened and began to pour onto an oblivious crowd. I was actually happy for the opportunity to wash all the splashed booze out of my hair and clothes. As I stood in the rain, getting pushed and pulled by the crowd, I held tightly to the belt loop of the skipper's jeans, and we muscled our way through the pack. He was like the offensive guard blocking for his tailback while I clutched my purse tightly in my right arm like a football.

I tried to convince myself that I could enjoy the experience.

But my mind wandered again as I thought of other activities that seemed like more fun:

7. Washing a sink full of week-old, crusty dishes
8. Doing laundry for a team of sweaty, pubescent teenagers
9. Scrubbing a filthy floor with my toothbrush
10. Cleaning a clogged toilet with my bare hands
11. Poking myself in the eyeball with a sharp stick

Thousands of people were having the time of their lives. Through the masses of glittery superheroes, sequined tutus, mermaids, and togas, I caught glimpses of the beautiful colonial architecture.

Olinda is an UNESCO World Heritage Site and a hub for local artists and musicians. I longed for the opportunity to explore the city that was hidden somewhere in the sardine can I found myself stuffed inside.

Masses of partiers joined in what became 10 or 12 conga lines of intoxicated, costumed people dancing and jostling their way through the narrow streets.

The street party made Mardi Gras look like an afternoon of tea with the queen.

Rather than the large samba parades, huge figurines are paraded throughout the town representing saints and spirits, known as *mamulengos*. One of the most famous of these huge dolls is the 10-foot *Homem da Meia-Noite* (Midnight Man) who is carried through the streets at midnight to symbolize the beginning of Carnival. The street parties (*blocos*) feature large crowds of people following a slow-moving truck that meanders through the streets blasting music.

The first official Carnival street party is *Sábado de Zé Pereira*. It begins with a huge parade of street puppets and live music and is represented by a large rooster figurine on the city's bridge. It attracts a crowd of about two million people.

I get it. This is fun for most people. But for me, I could still think of things I could be doing that would be more fun:

12. *Doing my taxes with an IRS auditor watching me*
13. *Taking the SATs while nursing a hangover*
14. *Picking up litter on a busy highway in a fluorescent vest*
15. *Moving heavy furniture for someone I barely know*
16. *Attending a defensive driving class on a Saturday*
17. *Watching paint dry*
18. *Experiencing childbirth with no drugs*
19. *Standing in line at the DMV*
20. *Chinese water torture.*

I was happy to have experienced Carnival in Brazil. I can't recommend it, but I am clearly in the minority. There are millions of other people who feel differently.

As for me, I missed the Bay of Biscay.

Endless Projects and Beating the Heat

4–7 MARCH 2019

Dieter offered to take us into town in his rental car, so we went on a hunt for an internet data card and provisions. We found a card, but it only had 5GB of data. We needed it at the anchorage but knew we could use the marina internet for the bulk of our work.

As the skipper's flight approached, I was nervous about how I would manage to get the dogs off the boat and into the dinghy every day by myself so that we could go for walks and work in the marina. I begged the skipper to work with the harbor master to find us a berth, at least for the week that he would be in Italy.

He refused, so I took matters into my own hands. I went to the harbor master and pleaded my case. He was very sweet and understood my plight. He and his crew repositioned some of the moored ships to make room so we could squeeze in *Seefalke*. That made it possible for me to easily get the dogs off the boat each day.

I was pleased with my initiative, but the skipper became enraged while reluctantly moving *Seefalke* into the berth. He was scheduled to fly to Italy that night. For an entire hour before Marco arrived to drive him to the airport, he yelled furiously at me for taking action against his wishes. I stood my ground but didn't participate in the argument. I just let him yell. He was so loud that Dieter walked over to our boat and told him in German to "take it easy."

Embarrassed, the skipper grabbed his bag, stormed off and then waited at the end of the pier for Marco. He didn't contact me the entire week he was gone. Not one text.

Even though tensions were high between us at times, it was always lonely when the skipper left me. However, this time, with so many sailors in port, it was less lonely than usual.

I stayed busy and productive, but the mosquito soup sapped my energy.

During the daytime, I borrowed one of Claudia's three electric fans, but her family needed them all in the evening. It was stifling—practically unbearable—on the boat with no air circulation, no wind, and no breeze. It was like sitting in a sauna. The dogs also suffered.

I tried to sleep in the cockpit, but it was too hot and uncomfortable on the wooden bench. I downloaded movies onto my laptop while I was in the marina, and the distraction helped a little. One evening, just as I thought I would roast to death, a guardian angel knocked on the side of the boat. It was Claudia. She brought me a fan, awakening me from a hot coma. She said she couldn't bear to think of me not having any air at all. They had two other fans, so she kindly lent me one. I wouldn't have been happier if she had given me a million dollars.

The next day, the dogs and I spent half the day working in the marina lobby. I took the dogs on a long walk, but the heat took its toll on all of us. Dieter and Claudia went into town to shop, so I asked them to pick up two fans for me. They cost $25 USD each, but the investment was worth it. Even though it was not cool, I finally had a steady flow of circulating air in the boat cabin. I placed one fan directly in front of my face and positioned the other directly on the dogs.

Meanwhile, I met two sailors who had sailed in from a 40-day crossing from Cape Horn. Robin and Philemon were flatmates in Switzerland and had been sailing the world for about a year at that time. They had a very old, rusted, green, steel ship that made *Seefalke* look like a luxury cruiser. Robin was Swiss, and Philemon was French. They both spoke English and told amazing stories of their sail down the eastern coast of South America to Patagonia.

One morning, Christoph came to the boat to pick up our cockpit benches and floorboards to have them sanded and oiled. Left behind was a disgusting mess of dog hair and muck. I spent several hours scrubbing the steel cockpit with hard brushes. There was a lot of rust, which needed to be sanded before treating. We added another messy project to the list.

The dogs and I had settled into a routine. We would take an early morning walk before it was too hot, then spend at least half the day working in the marina. The dogs would sit at my feet on the cool tile floor, enjoying the occasional breeze and the shade.

I kept up with work but found it difficult to concentrate in the severe heat. I loved the marina lounge area. It was a great atmosphere for meeting and socializing with other sailors and provided a brief escape from the mosquito soup.

After a week of silence, the skipper contacted me on the day he was scheduled to return. He had trouble on his flight back from Milan. Customs officials wanted him to produce a return flight ticket back out of Brazil, but since he was traveling by boat, he didn't have one. I had to scan and text him mountains of ship documents to prove that he had transportation out of Brazil.

He arrived back on *Seefalke* after midnight.

More Sailors and Their Stories

8–14 MARCH 2019

We worked in the marina lobby every day and continued to meet interesting sailors. Emeline and Felix were French engineers who worked offshore jobs six months of every year and sailed the world the other six months. Emeline told me that one year she only spent 10 days on land.

Sophie was in her mid 20s and had spent the previous two years circumnavigating the entire globe by hitchhiking. She started in Martinique and had been onboard six different ships who needed extra crew. She had been sailing with a German captain for six months and said her favorite spot in the world was French Polynesia, where she spent an entire year. She would pick up random jobs at each port and at that time was sailing with Tobias, a young English sailor. Within the next month, they planned to sail back to Martinique to complete her circumnavigation.

One day, we saw Robin and Philemon working on boat repairs. Their cool steel ship was named *Bekwaipa*—a French word that Robin had learned from his grandmother. Loosely translated, it means "the opposite of not stable."

They invited us onboard for a tour. It was not a bright, shiny, or fancy boat. The green and white steel structure was covered in rust, and in some parts of the cabin there were no walls, only open insulation. But it was a stable ship. The name fit.

Their inside layout was similar to *Seefalke*. It had the appearance of being messy and cluttered, but it was organized for them. They had creative rigs everywhere, including a long board with their depth sounder attached to the end. They would hang it off the back stern when they needed to test the depth of the water. It was simple and unsophisticated. It worked.

They had surfboards and looked like typical vagabond surfer dudes. They enjoyed a minimalistic, free lifestyle. They planned to return to Europe for a month, then fly back to Cabedelo and sail across the Atlantic to the Azores.

One evening we ate dinner at our favorite outdoor meat-stick tent and eventually drew a crowd. We were joined by Robin and Philemon, Sophie and Tobias, and Felix and Emeline. We drank caipirinhas and talked for hours about the addiction of the sailing lifestyle. We felt an instant connection among the sailors even though each one had a unique story to tell.

The next day, we met another sailing couple, Mer and Dan. Mer was French, and Dan was British. They had been in Brazil for three months and were headed toward French Guiana. They were in their mid-to-late 20s and had an apartment in London that they rented out for what they called a "ridiculously obscene price"—income that supported their cruising kitty.

They always stayed at anchor, never ate out (only cooked on the boat), and did 100% of their boat maintenance themselves. With every new sailor I met, I was fascinated that those who truly wanted to sail the world could find a way financially.

A Sailor's Work Is Still Not Done

We had started many boat projects but had not finished any of them. One morning, Christoph showed up unexpectedly and delivered our finished cockpit boards. They had been sanded and oiled and looked brand new. It felt like a milestone.

We continued our usual daily routine. We rose early, and I prepared coffee and breakfast. The skipper would go to the marina and begin working while I walked the dogs. There was a sweet Brazilian woman, Annabella, who ran a laundry service. For a small fee, she would wash clothes and hang them to dry in the boat yard behind the marina. I was grateful for her service.

There were a few shelves of books in just about every language in one corner of the lobby. The sign read, "leave one and take one." I donated most of the books I had read during our ocean crossing. Occasionally, I found something interesting to read in English.

Sailors hung out in the lobby to get relief from the heat and to socialize. The small bar served beer and caipirinhas and some food items. The harbor master was also the bartender and the short-order cook. There was always upbeat music playing, which we had trained ourselves to tune out while working.

With time, more of our smaller projects were completed. Christoph had made a custom, navy blue lazy bag for the main sail. A lazy bag is a device designed to wrap itself around the main sail with lines attached to the mast spreader, creating a bag to capture the sail when the halyard is released.

In addition to looking clean, lazy bags are a safety feature when at sea. We would no longer have to fight the sail that may be flapping in heavy conditions when we tried to bring it down, nor would we have to hand tie it on the foredeck. The sail dropped into the bag and then we zipped up the bag when conditions allowed.

When I asked Christoph about the status of my new cushions, the skipper rolled his eyes. They were being hand sewn in the same navy-blue sail material as the lazy bag, and they were on pace to be ready for me when I returned from Alabama.

I was excited to go home for only the second time in the past eight months. I was determined to make the most of it.

CHAPTER 26

GOOD OLE USA &
A SAILBOAT TREE
HOUSE

24 MARCH–8 APRIL 2019

Eight months is a long time to be away from home. I had not been in Alabama since Thanksgiving, and had not been to my Gulf Shores condo since July.

My friend Michele picked me up from the Pensacola airport. I stayed two nights with her and her husband, Doug, while Airbnb renters occupied by home. I had a long list of boat supplies to find while in the States—things we couldn't get in Brazil. So, Michele and I began the hunt at Walmart and Lowe's. I had missed those great American super stores!

Once in Gulf Shores I struggled to settle in. It felt unfamiliar. Sometimes, it's difficult to get your land legs.

I had plenty of projects to keep me busy. The condo required several repairs—the byproduct of having so many renters. I found some time to hang out with Trisha and my neighbors, Krista and

Tom. I didn't reveal anything to any of them about my struggles with the skipper. I told them tales of the Atlantic crossing and the exciting places I had explored.

I had a doctor checkup and had my bum inspected. He warned me that things didn't look great back there and without treatment it could get worse. He advised me to eat more fiber, take stool softeners, and sit on a donut or comfy cushion. I prayed the skipper would not cancel my order for the new custom-made cushions while I was away.

I took *Protagonist* for a solo sail and worked on her wooden hull. I went to the dentist and then got my driver's license renewed. I had plans to spend time with Bo, but Shelby was in Memphis with her boyfriend and was unable to come down while I was there. I was so disappointed. I volunteered to drive to her, but she didn't want to see me. I was devastated. She was still upset about Thanksgiving but wouldn't share the details with me.

I was also disappointed that I wouldn't get to see my parents. I wouldn't have time to drive six hours to Guntersville, and they didn't want to drive six hours to Gulf Shores. They would often drive to nearby Mobile to visit my brother and his family, so it upset me that they wouldn't make the effort for me.

I made several trips to West Marine for supplies as the skipper continued to send me lists of things we needed—lines, blocks, and other necessities to build the dinghy davits, instrumentation drives for the new solar panels, and more. The Amazon River charts had arrived, and the dining room was overflowing with items to take back to Brazil.

I asked my neighbors for old suitcases they didn't want any more so that I could fill them with all the supplies, check the bags at the airport, and then throw the old luggage away when I returned to Brazil. That would be less expensive than shipping heavy boxes to a remote village in South America. By the end of the two weeks, I had filled five large suitcases.

One of my main tasks was to sell enough from my offsite storage unit to move to a smaller, cheaper unit. I put most of the old furniture items on Facebook Marketplace and brought a few things back to the condo to use there.

During the two weeks stateside, I downsized from a 10 x 10 storage unit to a 5 x 10 unit, cutting my footprint and the monthly payment in half.

Then I sold my Beetle convertible to Trisha. I loved that car, and it was hard to let it go. But it was just sitting there all those months, and the insurance was expensive.

Trisha paid me $7,500, which I thought would provide me with some financial cushion for a while. I convinced myself it was okay, even though the skipper didn't sell any of his possessions.

By the time I sold half of the items in my storage unit and my car, I barely had enough money to pay for all the boat supplies, my prescribed medications, the condo repairs, and the two international flights that were on my credit card. I had $200 left—just enough to pay for the four cushions that Christoph was making for me.

Even though I stayed busy, I struggled to find a good rhythm at home. I enjoyed the long, hot showers, air conditioning, strong WiFi, and the unlimited supply of ice, but found it hard to concentrate on real work.

My amazing son, Bo, came to visit for the weekend. It was fantastic to have very high-quality one-on-one time with him. I missed my kids terribly! It was definitely the hardest part of being at sea.

Bo and I spent the weekend talking, catching up, and watching all the Oscar-nominated films. It was our tradition. Every year we binged on all the movies and predicted who would win the Academy Awards.

I had a lovely dinner with friends Lynn and Mike, and then my sis-in-law, Pam, and my niece, Allie, drove all the way from Decatur to visit me for a couple days. We went to the beach and took a quick trip to Mobile to have dinner with my other sis-in-law, Dana, and my niece, Ashton, and nephew, Wells, at their restaurant, *Dumbwaiter*.

Otherwise, I stayed in the condo all alone.

It was very strange to be separated from the dogs. Except for Thanksgiving and the one week I went with the skipper to Germany, I had been with the dogs every single day for eight months. They had kept me company on more lonely nights than I could count.

I missed them.

Except for a few visits with friends and the many projects and errands, I rarely left the house. I spent most of my time alone and distant. I'm sure Trisha would have kept me company every night if I had asked her to, but for some reason, I wanted to be alone.

It's hard to explain. I think I had become accustomed to being by myself. Loneliness felt more natural. Continuing to act happy around the people I loved seemed insincere and dishonest.

I was ashamed and embarrassed about what was going on between the skipper and me, and I didn't want anyone to know about it.

Time in Gulf Shores was productive and went by fast. Unlike at Thanksgiving in Guntersville, this time, I didn't even stop to consider whether I should return to the boat. I was numb about the relationship with the skipper and, frankly, too tired and confused to fight for it anymore.

I had developed a very mechanical attitude about the sailing journey. It had become something that I *needed* to do rather than something that I *wanted* to do.

I tried to assess my feelings. I was dedicated to the journey, still loyal to the skipper, looking forward to sailing the Amazon, missing the dogs, and upset about Shelby. I wished I could be a better mother to her and give her a better example of what a healthy relationship looked like. But how could I possibly do that?

I didn't really know where I belonged anymore.

I loaded my huge suitcases full of boat supplies and headed back to Pensacola for my last evening with friends. I put on a happy face and tried to convince them (and myself) that returning to Brazil was the right thing to do.

After an early flight out of Pensacola, I had another long layover in Orlando, which allowed me to catch up on all the work I hadn't finished during my hometown visit.

Back in Brazil

9–14 APRIL 2019

While I was in the U.S., the skipper and the marina crew had moved *Seefalke* onto the dry dock in the Marina Jacaré Village shipyard. They were extremely busy with repairs and upgrades.

As Marco drove me into the marina, I didn't recognize *Seefalke*. Her bright orange paint had been almost completely scraped from her hull and there were little bits of orange paint peelings all over the dirt ground in the shipyard.

As soon as I got out of the car, Cap'n Jack and Scout sprinted toward me from the other side of the boatyard. They squealed with delight and licked my face. I was so happy to see them. The skipper actually gave me a hug and said, "Welcome home." It was an unusual but nice greeting from him.

The skipper and the dogs had gotten used to living on dry dock since the day after I left for the U.S. I had to learn quickly what it was like to live on a sailboat on dry land.

We had access to electricity and water, but we couldn't use the head at all. There was a bathroom in the marina lobby just a short walk from the shipyard. However, it was a major project to climb in and out of the boat.

A swimming ladder was attached to the back of the stern, but it was not long enough to reach the ground. A traditional ladder leaned against *Seefalke's* stern. We climb a few steps on the regular ladder, then switched to the swimming ladder to climb the rest of the way to the top.

On the way down, we used the swimming ladder and then switched to the regular ladder. A huge oil can was positioned below the swimming ladder, providing us one last step to the ground. The system worked, but it was especially inconvenient when I needed to go to the potty in the middle of the night.

Living on dry dock, I realized quickly, was like living in a tree house.

Then, there was the issue of maneuvering Cap'n Jack and Scout on and off the boat. *Seefalke's* deck was about 3 m off the ground. It was not safe to carry the beagles up and down the ladder.

The skipper engineered a puppy crane for them. It was similar to the one we used in Helgoland and the one we rigged to get the dogs off the boat and onto the dinghy. We strapped them into their incredibly safe life vests. Safety straps with D-rings connected the life vest handles to a line rigged with a block to the mizzen boom. Then we lowered or raised them safely and securely.

It required a lot of effort from the humans, but the canines didn't seem to mind. Their tails wagged the entire time.

As I began to adjust to the sailboat tree house, the skipper informed me that he booked another trip to Germany. I didn't even ask him why. It didn't matter. I was now accustomed to being alone. However, I did wonder how I would manage the puppy crane by myself twice a day, every single day.

After unloading the five suitcases, we returned to the rodízio restaurant that night and had a nice dinner. The next morning, Marco showed up to drive the skipper to the airport.

While I was continuing to nurse my bum, I suffered another minor injury the very next day. I missed the last step of the ladder on an early-morning bathroom run. My hind end broke the fall when I crashed onto the cement ground. I twisted my ankle slightly and scraped the flesh from the palm of my left hand. The additional wounds did not make it any easier to get myself or the dogs on and off the boat. However, I managed.

While I was in the U.S., the skipper had finally ordered a proper fridge for *Seefalke*. It was a wonderful surprise. He called me from Germany and told me it would be delivered that day. Our new best friend and taxi driver, Marco, was very sweet and offered to pick it up from the store for us and deliver it to the marina.

Then I had the challenging task of finding a way to get the fridge up the ladder and into the boat. It was not much bigger than our little cooler, but it was bulky and heavy.

Scraping and sanding was performed on the boat every day. One of our daily workers, Anderson, saw me wrestling with a way to attach the heavy fridge to the puppy crane. He was so sweet. He picked up the fridge, hoisted it onto one shoulder, and then climbed the ladder to transfer it onboard for me.

I was grateful and immediately got it hooked up and running. I was thrilled to now have cold drinks and a place to store meat and other items that required refrigeration. After nine months living onboard with only lukewarm drinks in the broiling heat, I felt like I was in the lap of luxury.

Every day was the same. The workers showed up at 07:00, and I lowered the dogs in the puppy crane. Anderson helped me every single day. I climbed down the ladder with my backpack and walked the dogs before it got too hot. Then we settled into the marina lobby and worked all day.

I completed dozens of articles for my clients, created many videos for our YouTube channel, and wrote a book, *How to Sail with Dogs.* Each day, I would download movies or a television series to watch on the boat at night.

I had learned to live with the loneliness, but life in the sailboat tree house was difficult. All the other sailors were in the marina or at anchorage. They all had partners and families to keep them company at night. I was the only human in the boatyard at night.

I walked to the local market and purchased cheap wine, keeping it cool in the new fridge. I treated myself to a glass some nights while the movies and shows kept me company.

When I closed the laptop to sleep, it was very quiet and eerie in the boatyard. I used the fans to keep the air circulating and to provide relief for the dogs. I could hear other critters running around the boatyard.

The days were busy with the ongoing paint job. Christoph's crew had scraped all the paint, sanded, and had begun the priming stages. Removing the paint was not as easy as it sounds. Our ship had four decades of paint layers. Heavy rain occasionally delayed the project and only increased the thickness of the mosquito soup.

After all painting was finished, we applied the copper coat antifouling on *Seefalke's* bottom and then gave that coating a harsh sanding.

We lived in the sailboat tree house in the boatyard for 45 days, and it took every single one of them to get the paint job completed. During that time, the skipper returned for a few days, and then left again for another two weeks while *Seefalke* was stripped to the bare bones, sanded, and primed with four layers of gray primer. She looked like a huge gray battleship.

Meanwhile, welding was required to repair some of the rusted areas of the keel and then a leaking fuel tank had to be repaired. *Seefalke* was then painted with two layers of white paint before four coats of orange paint returned our ship to her former beauty.

For 45 days, I used the crane to lower the dogs every morning, worked in the lobby all day, then loaded them back on the crane to return them to the boat at night.

I'll never forget the day the last coat of paint was applied. That's the day I met Des. He was a South African solo sailor who had sailed into the marina a few days before. I saw him in the lobby but hadn't met him yet.

The dogs were leashed in the marina but I was trying to take photos and video of the finishing touches of the longest paint job ever. He saw that I was struggling to manage and offered to watch the dogs for me. He was very friendly, and the dogs warmed to him immediately.

We talked for a while, and he told me that he was a solo sailor because his wife didn't enjoy sailing. He had enjoyed many adventures during his lifetime, including a kayak journey along the entire western coast of Africa. He was also a surfer and was hoping to sail to the Caribbean to find some big waves.

He missed his wife and FaceTimed with her every day in the lobby. I thought it was so sweet. I couldn't even persuade the skipper to send me a text every day. I wondered what it would be like to be loved that much.

While *Seefalke's* underbelly was getting a coat of antifouling and more sanding, the skipper returned just in time for us to get her back in the water. But before we could do that, we had a few more surprises.

More Problems, More Repairs

Sometimes, when you fix one thing on a sailboat, you uncover other problems. After *Seefalke's* paint was scraped, we discovered a leak in the main diesel tank that was in the keel of the boat.

There was a crack in the boat's structure that we later learned was caused by the boat being placed on the support timber in the wrong place when we moved her out of the water. We emptied the fuel tank and flushed it with water many times. The crack had been welded, but the next crucial task would require welding the tank from the inside.

Meanwhile, we finally received the new anchor and chain that we had ordered from Germany two months before. The skipper and I marked the 50 m chain with white paint every 5 m and orange paint every 10 m so that we would know the depth of the anchor as we raised it and lowered it with the windlass.

One of our other ongoing projects was installing our new solar panels, which also had finally arrived.

We realized during our Atlantic crossing that we had not reached energy self-sufficiency. One of the old solar panels was damaged, and the other was covered by the sails most of the time. Furthermore, the wind generator performed well below our expectations.

We decided to significantly upgrade our solar inventory from 90W to 690W. We used the existing massive mast of the wind generator and installed a similar mast on the other side. On the beam between them we installed a 280W solar panel. The support would also serve as davits for the dinghy.

In addition to the big solar panel on the stern, we installed two smaller 160W solar panels on each side of the sea fence. We added adjustable mounts to direct them toward the sun when conditions would allow.

The davits were a great fringe benefit of the structure as we desperately needed more space on the stern deck. Being able to move the dinghy to the davits cleared the stern deck almost entirely. Also, the new configuration would make it much easier to deploy the dinghy.

Then we removed all the rainwater from the engine room, repaired some cracks in the steel cockpit floor, and then refilled the fuel tanks.

By the first week of May, *Seefalke* was back in the water. We finished the work on the rusted steel in the cockpit, painted the cockpit, installed the dinghy davits, repaired the bowsprit that secured the new anchor, and then carefully adhered the vinyl letters of *Seefalke's* name to the side of the boat.

Then, I finally received my new cockpit cushions! I paid Christoph and was overjoyed. The dogs promptly claimed their cushions, and even the skipper remarked that they were "kind of comfortable."

We had already said goodbye to Dieter and Claudia, who sailed away to French Guiana. On that same day, we said hello again to Robin and Philemon, who returned from their month-long break with family in Europe. It was so hard to believe that they had been gone a month, and we were still there.

We were back in the water, but we continued our routine of working in the lobby every day and tried to complete all the boat projects. The skipper had left me alone three times since we had arrived in South America, and he informed me that he would be leaving again.

However, he softened the blow by promising a few days off from work and boat projects to explore some of the Brazilian beaches.

Beach Country Brazil

We rented a car and drove two hours to Praia de Maracaípe, a beach in the middle of the municipality of Ipojuca, Pernambuco, about 75 km from Recife.

With its sprawling fields of coconut trees on one side and a gorgeous ocean with gigantic waves on the other, it was a local hangout that looked like French Polynesia. Open-air dune buggies could be rented for transport along the sand-filled roadways along the beach.

It was not uncommon to see a local casually climbing a coconut tree as easily as a monkey to retrieve the refreshing green coconuts that locals sold to tourists for only 2 Real each (about 50 cents USD).

Local peddlers sliced open the top with a sharp machete and then popped in a straw. Tourists like us drank the milk directly from the coconut. It was delicious and refreshing.

Then we went to Tabatinga Beach, which I believe was possibly the most beautiful beach I have ever seen. We unleashed the hounds and let them run and play for hours while we walked and explored the multi-colored mountains and exquisite tropical nature surrounding the beach. It was secluded with very few people—the absolute antithesis of touristy.

The next day, we went to Praia de Pipa, which was the opposite of Tabatinga. It was incredibly touristy until we made it past some of the major rock formations that looked like lava fields, making it visually unique. With all the graffiti and art galleries, we easily saw that this was where the local artists peddled their talents.

On the way back to the marina, we drove past Tambau Beach, a popular, palm-fringed city beach featuring bars, eateries, and craft vendors.

The next day, I wanted to see a bit of history.

If you ever wondered what graffiti looked like 6,000 years ago, drive about two hours from Cabedelo to the famous Ingá Stone.

Way off the beaten path, the Ingá Stone (*Pedra do Ingá* in Portuguese) is in the middle of the Ingá River near the small city of Ingá, about 96 km from João Passoa in northeastern Brazil.

It's a gneiss rock formation of approximately 250 square meters with entries whose meanings are unknown. Several figures are carved in low relief, and they look like a representation of animals, fruits, and constellations like Orion and the Milky Way. Scholars think it was created at least 6,000 years ago by indigenous people who lived in the area until the 18th century.

I enjoyed the few days of adventure. Those were always the times when the skipper and I were in our happy place.

But his flight was booked, and he was scheduled to leave in a couple days for the fourth time since we had been in Brazil—but not before I would suffer a very serious injury.

CHAPTER 27

AMAZON DELTA, DONKEY & ANGRY BIRDS

15–25 MAY 2019

T he sun was setting as the seadogs and I casually walked out of the marina lobby after a full day of work. The skipper had left the marina about two hours before us and was already on the boat.

A stray donkey stood near the marina entrance—not an unusual sight on the dirt streets near Marina Jacaré Village.

I didn't see the animal at first, but Cap'n Jack and Scout sure did. They went charging so abruptly and so forcefully that they pulled me to the ground. I felt my left pinkie toe bend all the way backward, and I heard a loud pop. The dogs dragged me several meters until I was finally smart enough to let go of their leashes. The donkey never moved or reacted in any way to the two beagles howling directly in his face.

I yelled the skipper's name, hoping he would come help me. But even the howling beagles combined with my screams couldn't get his attention.

Another sailor came out of the lobby and helped me to my feet. It was Des. My entire left foot began to swell, and the flesh from the top of my right foot and right knee had been completely ripped from the skin. Blood was gushing, stinging the hundreds of mosquito bites on my legs and arms.

I could not put any weight on my left foot as it continued to swell to more than twice its size. Des helped me to the boat, and we finally got the skipper's attention. I was crying and in desperate pain, which embarrassed and unnerved the skipper. He demanded that I stop crying. "Adults don't cry," he reminded me.

"Just shut up and help me onto the boat," I begged.

I asked him if he would go to the local market and get me a bag of ice. He agreed and left on the errand while I cleaned away the blood and treated the open wounds with antibiotic ointment. The pain was intense. Des brought the harbor master to the boat. In addition to being the harbor master, chef, and bartender, Jean Pierre was also the marina medic.

Even without an official x-ray, he felt certain that I had broken my fifth metatarsal. He gave me a make-shift splint, bandaged my wounds, and recommended that I see a doctor.

I was conflicted. In the skipper's efforts to reduce my expenses by selling my car and other personal items, he had also suggested that I cancel my expensive U.S. health insurance. I did, and then purchased a cheaper international health insurance. The new insurance policy was not yet valid.

When Des and Jean Pierre left, the skipper had still not returned with the ice. I noticed he had already packed a bag for his trip. He was scheduled to leave the next morning for the fourth time since we had arrived in Brazil.

When the skipper finally returned with a small bag of ice that was already melting I told him about Jean Pierre's diagnosis.

"You're fine," he said.

"Is there any way you can postpone your trip?" I pleaded. "I'm in a lot of pain. I don't think I'll be able to leave the boat to walk the dogs or take a shower or use the bathroom by myself. Jean Pierre said I probably need to see a doctor. I need you. Please, stay and help me."

The tears flowed, even though I knew crying aggravated the skipper.

"You're fine," he repeated.

"If you tell me that sailing is not for sissies, I will not be here when you get back." I meant it. Even though I'm sure he was thinking it, he resisted saying the phrase that always struck a nerve with me.

The next morning, my left foot was badly bruised and swollen to about three times its usual size. My entire right leg was also swollen and deeply bruised. Blood continued to gush through the bandages. The flesh on both my arms and hands was ripped apart and bruised. I asked the skipper one more time to stay with me.

"I'll see you in two weeks," he said. Without getting me more ice or even walking the dogs for me, he left.

One thing about living in a very small space was that there was always something to hold onto. For that reason, I was able to maneuver around the boat and avoid putting weight on the swollen, sore foot. But for the first week, I couldn't leave the boat at all. Des came by every morning to check on me and to walk the dogs—a generous act of kindness.

I was grateful to have my new cushions and tried to work in the cockpit during the day. I was just close enough to the marina WiFi to get a very weak signal. I couldn't download movies, but I was able to entertain myself by reading books at night.

It was lucky that the boat was back in the water so I could use the onboard head. Had we still been in the boatyard, it would have been impossible for me to climb up and down the ladder.

I sent the skipper a few photos of my swollen foot, the bruises, and open wounds on my right leg. He never acknowledged receiving them and never once asked me how I was feeling.

After a week, I finally forced myself to leave the boat and go into the marina for a shower. I rigged the boat hook to use as a cane. It was still painful to put weight on my broken left foot, and I was not yet stable enough to walk the energetic dogs.

The skipper was scheduled to return in a few days. I needed to have a serious talk with him. However, serious talks between us generally resulted in me pouring out my heart to him followed by him giving me the cold, cruel silent treatment.

I decided to write him a letter. That way I could say everything I needed to say without any gaslighting interruptions. Perhaps he would have time to think about it and maybe reply with a written response if he didn't want to talk to me.

It was worth a shot.

My love,

So much has happened in the 18 months since you climbed that fence, knocked on my door, and showed me true, deep love like I've never known before. I'm trying to remember what it was like to be loved by you as much as I felt your love that night and in the couple months that followed. Thinking about it makes me smile, but I must admit, it's been a while since I truly felt your love.

I know pressures are high right now. Insurmountable, really. We are still trying to adjust to living in such a small space—just the two of us—away from all the other people in our worlds. At times it feels like a dream, and at other times, if I'm being honest, it's very difficult. It is lonely and isolating and kind of sad for me a lot of the time.

I want to feel your love again, and I want you to feel mine. I'm not sure how we get back to that place. But it would be nice if we could at least try. I'm sorry that I push you so hard. I don't know why I do that.

I'm struggling a lot with being so far away from home. I'm struggling with not being needed by anyone anymore. When you are upset and silent and short with me—whether you are upset with me or with something else—I try to be understanding and patient. I really do. I know it doesn't seem like I am trying, but I am. It just hurts me that you don't need me. It hurts me that you keep secrets from me.

I will try to give you your space when you are sad and silent and short with me. It would be helpful if you could assure me it's not something I did wrong, or something I said, or something bad that you feel toward me. Maybe we can both work on this?

I suspect that you still give a lot of positive attention to other women...tell them they are beautiful, have sexually-focused conversations, etc. That hurts me more than I suppose I'll ever be able to express. Even if the comments or conversations are innocent in your mind, or ironic, or not meaningful, it still hurts me deeply. It crushes me, in fact. I think there is something that you need from other women that I just can't seem to give you...even though I want to. Or you just don't want it from me. I still can't figure that one out.

I can't even remember the last time you told me I was beautiful, so it really crushes me that you find a way to make other women feel beautiful. Maybe you just don't think I am anymore. I can't remember the last time you initiated physical intimacy with me. I feel like intimacy is always my idea and you just physically respond. I don't feel very attractive or sexy or desired by you anymore. It's my fault. I have gained weight and am out of shape and never fix myself up or take care of the way I look. I guess I can understand why you are not proud for me to be your girl anymore. I suppose this is why you still need the interaction with other women?

Sometimes I think you would prefer to be sailing forever with someone else. And sometimes I think you would prefer to be sailing forever alone. Sometimes I just want to go home and let you be happy without me. Sometimes I just don't know what to feel. If you don't want me here with you sharing this sailing forever dream with you, I would appreciate it if you would respect me enough to tell me. If you do want me here, well... it would be nice to hear that, too.

I shouldn't have doubts about that, but I do.

I feel really alone right now. I am disconnected from Shelby and my family and friends. And I feel disconnected from you. I have felt this way for many months. I'm just lost. What can we do to feel the love from each other again? Do you even want to try?

You may not even read this. And even if you do, you may just get mad and not respond. I need you, and maybe this will help me to write to you if

I can't talk with you directly. I love you and want to be with you forever. I want us to be happy and deeply in love again, so much that we show it and feel it every single day – falling asleep in each other's arms, talking intimately, and supporting each other in everything we do. I want that back. If you want it, too, how can we get it back, my love? I want to feel the love again. Don't you?
—Michelle

Reading it back now I can see how desperate, lost, and confused I was. I can see how tortured I was and how little confidence I had—blaming myself for all that was wrong with our relationship. The skipper never responded to the letter or even acknowledged receiving it. I asked him a few times if he had read it and if he had a response, but he never answered my questions. Just silence.

Amazon Delta Disappointment

The skipper returned, and I continued to nurse my injuries. We were laser focused on boat projects and planning the sailing passage through the Amazon Delta. We pored over the charts, talked to locals, planned the route, and studied the weather and currents.

I was excited about the voyage, completely aware that most casual cruisers like us would never attempt itI. Because of warnings of pirates and dangerous currents (it was the rainy season), we decided it would be a good idea to enlist a few other boats to caravan with us through the Delta. Having other skilled sailors nearby would help if there were boat troubles or issues with hooligans.

We organized a meeting with Des and another German couple we had recently met, Ingo and Andrea. We showed them our detailed plan. I remember the meeting vividly. Often, it was so hot in the mosquito soup that I would hop into the marina shower with all my clothes on and let the cold water cool me off. It would only take a few minutes for my clothes to dry in the intense heat, and I would generally already be sweating before my hair even had time to dry.

Unable to bear the heat, I left the meeting briefly while the skipper was making his presentation. By the time I returned from the cold shower, the other sailors had decided they would not risk the voyage. We had a steel ship, but the other boats were made of fiberglass.

Because of the heavy currents and high water, locals told us that large tree limbs and other debris could easily damage a plastic boat. They were also concerned that motor sailing through the murky waters could cause damage to their propellers and engines. In addition, the locals had spooked them about the possibilities of pirates in the area.

I gave my sales pitch and tried to counter their concerns. I had no idea what the skipper had said while I was cooling off in the shower, but it had completely turned the other sailors off. The skipper told me he wasn't confident enough to make the trip without them.

I was so disappointed.

"So, we are not going?" I asked.

"I'll keep thinking about it, but I don't think so," the skipper said.

"I thought sailing was not for sissies." I felt defeated.

I could see he was also disappointed, but he remained silent. The decision was made. All that time and energy had been wasted on a bucket-list dream that I now had to accept was not going to happen. I felt crushed.

When the Sea Legs Begin to Itch

26 MAY 2019

The day we arrived in Cabedelo on February 27, we met Ellen and Felipe, the proprietors of our favorite local restaurant—a small tent underneath which they grilled meat on a stick and mixed caípirinhas. Ellen was deep into her seventh month of pregnancy then and beginning to get uncomfortable carrying around the extra weight in the unbearable heat.

So much time had passed that now I saw my lovely friends in the lobby every day with their gorgeous baby girl, Elizabeth, who was already two months old.

That's how long we had been in Cabedelo.

Other sailors had come and gone—venturing off to fabulous destinations around the world. We were still there.

Seefalke had been stripped down to her bare bones and repainted to look like new. We had installed new solar panels and no longer needed the electrical land connection for energy. We had sanded and painted the cockpit and built a structure on our stern for the dinghy. We had ordered, received, and installed a new anchor and chain. We were still there.

The locals all knew our names, our dogs' names, and our kids' names. We were practically fluent in Portuguese, a language we had first begun studying during our sail across the Atlantic. I had traveled to the U.S. for two weeks, while the skipper had traveled abroad four times. We were still there.

We endured life on the hard for six weeks and craned Cap'n Jack and Scout in and out of the boat twice a day, every day, for 45 straight days. We were still there.

While in Brazil, I researched and wrote 20 articles for various clients. I wrote a 102-page book and created 14 videos. We were still there.

It had been fun. It had been long. It had been hot. I had grown to like it there, but trust me, I didn't want to stay any longer. No offense to the lovely people, the beautiful landscape, the relaxed culture, and the billions of mosquitos that would certainly miss my tasty blood, but it was time to GO!

We completed our boat projects and prepared for the next sailing passage. I was still recovering from my foot injury, so I worked in the cockpit rather than the lobby.

One morning, I noticed several birds hovering around the end of the main sail boom. They flew frantically in and out of the opening of the new lazy bag, taking twigs, grass, and sticks in with them. I shooed away the birds, opened the lazy bag, and found a huge nest inside. There were no eggs, so I removed the nest and tried to close the bag and fill any openings.

The birds returned and tried to get in, but I kept shooing them away. I felt like I was playing a real-life game of Angry Birds. I love birds and all animals, but they needed to find a home elsewhere.

One thing is certain. When birds build a nest on your boat, you've been sitting in port too long. Our sea legs were itching. It was time to go.

3 JUNE 2019

After three months in port, we checked out at customs and immigration—an all-day procedure—and prepared for departure. We had plenty of time on our visas because we had both left the country during our stay in Brazil. However, we had no time left on our ability to keep the boat in Brazil any longer—the legal limit was 90 days.

So, we made the decision—or rather the decision was made for us—to sail straight to French Guiana rather than stopping along the way at some of the coastal Brazilian islands that we wanted to see. It also solidified our decision to skip the Amazon Delta.

4 JUNE 2019

We stocked up on food, water, and supplies, secured the cabin, and said goodbye to the Cabedelo locals who had become our family for the past 90 days.

Around 16:00—high tide—we untied the lines and moved to an anchorage just outside the marina. That way, we could depart early the next morning without worrying about the tides and without needing to coordinate with marina staff to release us from the mooring buoys.

We planned to spend our final evening with friends aboard *Redemption*. Des had sailed solo across the Atlantic but hooked up with a crew in Cabedelo—20-somethings Isabelle, an American from Washington state, and her boyfriend Tory, an Australian. Neither Izzy nor Tory had ever sailed before.

Redemption was a very cool ship. It was about the size of *Seefalke* and was once used by Des as a charter boat in South Africa. Another sailor who was definitely no sissy, Des had many comfy cushions in the cockpit and on the deck of his ship.

The next morning, we set sail toward French Guiana. I was disappointed about missing out the Amazon Delta adventure but looked forward to being at sea again.

However, my body had something different in mind. My many injuries began to get the best of me. Combined with a few new unexpected health issues, it became the most miserable sailing passage of my life.

CHAPTER 28

NEPTUNE WILL MAKE YOU PAY

PASSAGE TO FRENCH GUIANA

Day 1–WEDNESDAY, 5 JUNE 2019

Departing from anchorage was a good idea. The departure was smooth as we cruised casually down the river. I crawled out onto our freshly-repaired bowsprit to unfurl the genoa as we were passing the wind shadow of Cabedelo and entering the Atlantic.

With waves crashing the bow as I balanced on the new bowsprit boards, I could already feel the uneasiness settle in. No surprise after three months in port—my sea legs were wobbly. It was inevitable that I would once again feel the pit of my stomach begin to rise.

I was seasick all day. The skipper wasn't feeling well either. We were also forced to spend some time in the engine room, and the smells of the fumes were unbearable. It accelerated the queasiness for both of us, but it was unavoidable. The main fuel tank was overflowing.

The skipper crawled down into the engine room and sponged out the extra fuel into a bucket. Then I poured the fuel from the bucket into empty 8-gallon water jugs—not an easy task in heavy conditions. We were both covered in diesel and puking our guts out.

The only way to get to the engine room was by removing the cockpit floor and lowering ourselves down into the pit. It felt like going down the small porthole of a submarine. The movement of the sea was intensified down there, and it was HOT. In addition, it was a very tight squeeze, which forced us to work while twisted like a pretzel. It was a miserable but necessary task. I refused to take seasickness medicine, but I began to consider it. I had no idea at that time that the seasickness would be the least of my worries.

Day 2

THURSDAY, 6 JUNE 2019
  82.7 NM – 17:33 HOURS AT SEA

During my early morning shift, around 02:00, I continued retching. This time, I reluctantly took some Dramamine, hoping it would help a little. Dramamine can be effective, but it causes severe drowsiness. It's not a good idea to take it if you cannot immediately sleep it off for at least four to six hours.

Just two hours into my sleep shift, the skipper went into the engine room to bail more fuel. He woke me to help. It was difficult because I was still drowsy and loopy. When I finally got back to sleep an hour later, the skipper suddenly switched the sails from port to starboard, and I slid off the bed right onto the floor. I regretted taking the medicine.

Later that day, I felt better. I settled into the cockpit with my new comfy cushions, cuddled with Cap'n Jack and Scout, and began reading *Adrift*. It's an amazing story of one woman's miraculous survival at sea. I felt inspired. Understanding what they went through made battling through a little seasickness seem insignificant. But unfortunately, that wasn't all I was battling.

Day 3

FRIDAY, 7 JUNE 2019
232.2 NM – 41:35 HOURS AT SEA

My foot was still swollen, bruised, and sore. My right leg and foot had been stripped of several patches of flesh. The wounds were still open and oozing, and I treated them with antibiotic ointment. Scout loved to lick the open wounds when I wasn't paying attention. I noticed a red ring forming near the area of the large open flesh wound on my right foot, and also noticed the same red ring on Scout's belly and on her foot. She had been licking her own wounds and then licked mine.

The rings bubbled around the edges and itched like hell! We both scratched uncontrollably. I had no idea what the rings were, but it was obvious that it was contagious. We had no access to the internet or any medical books that described anything similar, but the term ringworm came to my mind. I had no way to verify the diagnosis and didn't know how to treat it.

Since the rings itched so badly, I treated them with hydrocortisone cream and continued to treat the flesh wounds with antibiotic ointment. I later learned that was a bad idea. I mentioned the rings to the skipper, but he was flippant and showed no concern for Scout or for me.

Meanwhile, we recorded our fastest one-day distance ever at 148.9 nm in 24 hours. We normally clocked around 100 nm each day, so it felt like warp speed for *Seefalke*.

Thanks to the Dramamine that I wasn't able to sleep off, I had a bad headache all day. But at least the retching had stopped. I finally took some ibuprofen, which helped with the headache and other ailments, including the broken foot I was still battled.

However, the itchy rings began to spread. Soon, I noticed a few rings in my genital area. I suppose I scratched the ring around the sore; then, when I used the bathroom and wiped myself, I transferred the mystery wounds. The rings began to appear on

Cap'n Jack's belly and legs. The skipper finally took notice when they appeared on his legs, neck, and bald head.

That wasn't all. I still struggled with the pain and discomfort from the hemorrhoid that flared while in Cabedelo. I noticed a lot of blood in the toilet. It was scary. There was more and more blood with my bowel movements and a considerable amount of pain. Every time I would poo, it felt like I was passing razor blades.

Conditions remained rocky. I managed to make egg and sausage quesadillas although it was still uncomfortable to cook. The seas smoothed a bit, and we moved the mainsail back to the port side which was more comfortable for sleeping. I was finally getting my sea legs back but still felt dehydrated. I reminded myself to drink more water.

During the early night shift there was a squall. Winds were at 20 knots and we were flying at 9 knots. It was short lived even though we hit a few more rain patches during the night. There were more squalls during the early-morning shift, with heavy rain and huge wind gusts—but I refused to ask the skipper for help. At one point, it got very calm, still, and dark all around us. It felt like we were inside a cone of blackness. I couldn't see a thing, but I could hear the wind whistling and howling and the waves crashing around me even though it felt like we weren't moving.

When the rain stopped, everything was still, black, and eerie.

Day 4

SATURDAY, 8 JUNE 2019
  396 NM – 65:21 HOURS AT SEA

At 164 nm, we beat our 24-hour distance record again. We were flying! Just as I lay down for a nap after a long night shift, the skipper decided to bake homemade bread. Pans and pots were clanking while he furiously stirred. I tossed and turned, moaned and complained, but he didn't get the message. I wondered how he could possibly complain about a few pings from the satellite communicator while he was trying to sleep.

He did things like that: demand complete silence while he was sleeping but make considerable noise when I needed to rest. He often played audiobooks during his shift. I begged him to use earphones or at least lower the volume, but he ignored my requests every time.

I had a pounding headache, but the bread was delicious.

It was a rough and rocky day. I finally managed to get a deck shower (my first of that passage) and it felt good to be clean. I felt queasy all day but managed to fend off the retching for another day. Even with some uneasiness, we settled into a good routine. My sea legs felt stronger. However, my physical ailments wore me down. I lost a scary amount of blood with every trip to the head, and none of us could find any relief from the itchy rings.

Day 5

SUNDAY, 9 JUNE 2019
   561 NM – 89:31 HOURS AT SEA

We passed the 6,000-nm mark for the entire voyage, which was strange because we thought it would take us 6,000 nm to sail all the way from Stralsund to Gulf Shores. We were still about 3,000 nm away from Alabama.

Scout, my ever-faithful night-watch companion, stayed by my side as my night shifts became "our" night shifts. Cap'n Jack preferred to cuddle in the cabin and sleep soundly while the girls stayed on watch. We all enjoyed the cockpit cushions. I caught the skipper sleeping and relaxing on them several times.

I can't remember the last time I slept as hard as I did during my sleep shifts that night. Usually, I woke up on my own just before my shift. At midnight, the skipper had to physically shake me to wake me. On my next sleep shift, it took both beagles licking my face and pouncing on my tummy to wake me from the deep sleep.

Around sunset, we crossed the Equator again and entered the Northern Hemisphere. Without much fanfare, I sat alone in the cockpit and popped one of my mini champagne bottles. I toasted to the sea and dropped a sip overboard for Neptune. As I sipped the remainder of the refreshing treat, I admired the sunset as it melted into the deep blue waves.

I thought about how far we had traveled and how different that equatorial crossing was from the first one just a few months before. First, it wasn't nearly as devastatingly hot! Also, we had been there before, so it was a less exciting—although it was still special in its own way.

I noticed on the chart that as we sailed over the Equator, the Amazon River was directly west of us. We were about 300 nm offshore so, of course, we couldn't see it. I'm sure the skipper made the right decision to forego sailing the Amazon, but it was a bummer to be so close to something I wanted to do so badly and not be able to touch it.

Day 6

MONDAY, 10 JUNE 2019
  703 NM – 113:29 HOURS AT SEA

As we entered the doldrums, we began to lose speed. However, it wasn't quite as miserable as the last time. We had a consistent cool breeze and enough wind to make an average of 4.5 knots all day—a considerable improvement from the the last time through the Intertropical Convergence Zone, but not nearly as speedy as the past several days.

It was one of those uneventful, mundane days. We made home-made bread and homemade pizza dough. I was so bored I was actually excited about the opportunity to wash the dishes—just so I had something to keep me busy.

We worried about the engine overheating, so we did a trial two-hour test and it passed with a steady 78°F temperature. That was a big relief. Plus, it seemed like we had the fuel leak under control.

Scout lounged on the deck almost the entire day. She rarely wanted to be in the cabin. She loved being in the fresh salt air with her velvety ears flopping in the wind. I took a couple of my cushions onto the deck and cuddled with her while I read.

The skipper joined us a few times—with a cushion of his own. Perhaps he was beginning to appreciate that I had forced the issue to purchase the new cushions from Christoph, but of course, he would never admit it out loud.

Day 7

TUESDAY, 11 JUNE 2019
805 NM – 137:27 HOURS AT SEA
Passages could get very mundane and boring.

I relished a shower and more rest. It was a hot sailing through the doldrums. I wanted to jump in and take a swim in the sea, but the swells made that a dangerous proposition. I continued to read books and didn't even try to start conversations with the skipper—I had moved on from needing his company. Of course, I would talk to him if he engaged me in conversation, but he rarely did.

We played Scrabble on the iPad for a little while, but it made the skipper queasy, so we stopped. For some reason, I was better able to handle looking at a screen or reading while at sea than he was. Those two things made him especially uneasy, so he mainly listened to audiobooks—never with earphones. Sometimes, I would use earphones so I could concentrate on my book since he refused to wear them as a courtesy to me. It would have been nice to perhaps listen to the same book together, but he preferred listening in German.

Around sunset, we began to pick up wind and speed—a clear sign that we had moved north of the doldrums and into the northeastern trade winds. We had a bright orange sunset directly in front of us, but the sky and water behind us were pastel pink.

Day 8

WEDNESDAY, 12 JUNE 2019
 917 NM – 161:29 HOURS AT SEA

I continued to read book after book and was grateful for the smooth and steady conditions. I embraced the boredom but was eager to reach our destination and find some relief for all the many ailments that made an otherwise pleasurable sail so miserable.

I looked at the charts and realized that the passage from Brazil to French Guiana put us a third of the way to Alabama from Brazil. It would be our second longest passage to date and not much shorter in terms of distance (about 1,400 nm) than the Atlantic crossing (just under 1,700 nm).

Day 9

THURSDAY, 13 JUNE 2019
 1,058 NM – 185:28 HOURS AT SEA

I made a huge breakfast—bacon, eggs, and sausage. We didn't have much wind, which meant we felt the blazing heat more. We used the motor for a few hours, just to give the boat and the air some movement. We both took late afternoon showers to wash off the layers and puddles of sweat. Once the brilliant orange sun set over the horizon, the evening was nice—cool and breezy.

Just When We Thought It Was Boring–Day 10

FRIDAY, 14 JUNE 2019
 1,173 NM – 209:30 HOURS AT SEA

It never fails. Sailors always pay for it when they complain about being bored at sea. It's almost as if Neptune says, "You're bored? Fine. I'll give you something to do."

It was about 22:30 when the skipper yelled down from the cockpit, "Get up here. I need your help!"

I bolted out of bed and went straight to the cockpit. The skipper was already in the stern cabin trying to maneuver his way to the locker that contained the hydraulic steering system. The rudder wasn't working. He had heard a sound that he thought was a motorboat in the distance. But it was the hydraulic pump trying to move the piston. The piston was moving, but the rudder wasn't moving. He saw that the connection had come loose. The rudder is crucial—it controls the steering of the boat.

The skipper first thought he had sailed over a fishing net that may have blocked the rudder. He checked to see if anything was in the water—any kind of debris that could have blocked it. When he turned the wheel, the tiller didn't move at all.

His second thought was that we had lost oil in the hydraulic system. Perhaps one of the hoses had come loose. He opened the box to check on that and to switch from hydraulic steering to mechanical steering. There was a bypass valve that allowed the oil to move freely when the hydraulic system was not moving it.

That's when he saw that the rudder quadrant had come loose from the piston. For some reason, a board was blocking the movement and caused the piston to break loose from the quadrant. It could have been a sudden movement or something that happened over time.

I went to the stern deck so I could hold the tiller securely in the neutral position, allowing him to line up the piston to the connector.

We swirled around slowly in circles but since conditions were calm and there was hardly any wind and no traffic, it was not a dangerous situation. We were in 1,000 m deep waters with no ships in sight. There was plenty of room to maneuver.

I moved back to the cockpit to guide the steering wheel into the center position so the skipper could attempt to join the two pieces. He was in the stern cabin, flashlight in hand, trying to make the connection. I transferred back and forth from the stern tiller to the cockpit wheel about four or five times until he was able to connect the two parts.

During the chaos, dozens of large ants had surfaced from somewhere in the stern and crawled all over the skipper while he worked.

Once all was secure, we checked to see if the manual hydraulic steering would work. It was working, so we re-engaged the autopilot. The process took about an hour and 15 minutes in the black of night.

We vowed never to complain about boredom ever again!

It was another scorching hot day. We were beginning to see signs of life—lots of birds, which usually meant we were not far from land.

At one point, I went to the deck to douse myself with a bucket of cool seawater. In the distance, off the bow, I saw a huge pod of dolphins swim toward us. Another pod came from the south on the port side.

The dolphins leaped into the air showing off their acrobatics. Then I noticed another group of dolphins coming from the starboard side. They were coming from all directions as if they had never seen a ship before and they all wanted to congregate at our bow.

We saw many dolphins at sea, but we agreed we had never before seen that many at one time. There were hundreds of them. They stayed with us for a while until we found ourselves on an island of seaweed. The dolphins disappeared, and we slowed to a crawl as we worked our way through the thick debris.

About an hour later, we noticed a squall on the horizon, so we battened down the hatches and prepared for another storm. We were happy to have the cool rain, so we both showered on the deck using the fresh rainwater and enjoyed the refreshing downpour.

I struggled with all my ailments, but as I distracted myself with books I felt less lonely. A significant change was happening. I relied less and less on the skipper's company or on his approval.

Day 11

SATURDAY, 15 JUNE 2019
1,275 NM – 233:27 HOURS AT SEA

In sharp contrast to the blistering heat of the last few days, it became rainy and almost chilly. What little wind we had was swirling, so we had to motor sail most of the day.

It was difficult to believe that we were entering our 12th straight day at sea. It only took us 15 days to cross the entire Atlantic Ocean from Cape Verde to Ilha Fernando de Noronha.

I continued to worry about my blood loss and the itchy red rings. I looked forward to picking up an internet signal as we approached landfall to try and find some relief.

Day 12

SUNDAY, 16 JUNE 2019
1,357 NM – 257:20 HOURS AT SEA

The early morning shift was calm and serene. It seemed as if nothing was moving—not the air or the water or even *Seefalke*. It was as if we were frozen in time. I settled in, cuddled with Scout, and with the help of a small flashlight, read another book and enjoyed the relaxing, beautiful stillness.

I looked to the port side, and the huge glow from the moon revealed a massive storm cell heading directly toward us. I closed all the hatches as a light sprinkle quickly became a downpour.

As the storm cell crossed over from the side of the boat to the bow, all of a sudden, I had zero visibility. The rain pounded, and the wind gusted forcefully. It was short lived, as these offshore squalls generally are, but I woke the skipper a little early ... just in case.

Four hours later, when I awoke in the early morning, we had made landfall. We saw the islands of French Guiana in the distance, formations that would guide us for the next eight hours.

Soon, we got a weak internet signal. I did some research and easily identified that the rings were ringworm—a highly contagious fungus that should be treated with antifungal cream immediately (and never hydrocortisone). We had dealt with it for eight days and spread it throughout the entire boat onto all of our clothes, sheets, towels ... and each other. I learned that the rings in my genital area had become good old-fashioned jock itch.

I learned online that we had a few home remedies onboard we could have been using—limes, coconut oil, and garlic—all of which would have worked to fight the fungus. I covered all the rings on all of us in a lime-coconut-garlic concoction that helped temporarily.

The approach was long, slow, and hot! After starting the passage with warp speed, it felt like we were moving in slow motion. We drifted for several hours waiting on high tide and then motor sailed into the channel that would guide us to the port in Cayenne.

At 15:40, we dropped the anchor. I popped a mini champagne bottle to celebrate our second longest passage ever. It always felt gratifying to reach our destination, but as *Seefalke* settled into her anchorage, I felt a bit wobbly and nauseous.

This time ... land sickness.

However, my most urgent mission was simple—finding relief for all my ailments.

CHAPTER 29

THAT WHICH DOES NOT KILL US

16–17 JUNE 2019

F ollowing our 1,400 nm, 12-day passage from Cabedelo to Cayenne, we settled into a small secluded anchorage in the Mahury River, completely tucked away from any civilization except for about a dozen local fishermen and a handful of other exhausted, anchored sailors. It felt odd to be back in French territory and yet so far away from Europe.

While the skipper went ashore to check out the infrastructure and to check us in with customs, I got on the phone to connect with my clients.

Before we set sail from Cabedelo, I had a long conversation with my biggest client—the editor of a major industry trade magazine. He had given me several assignments to work on once we made it to French Guiana. I had reached out to the subject matter experts and arranged several interviews so I could get busy on the articles as soon as I had internet again.

When I opened my email, I had an urgent message from my editor asking me to contact him. He informed me that while I had been at sea the past 12 days, an investor had bought the magazine and then shut it down. All the employees were fired without notice. That meant there was no freelance work for me, either.

It wasn't my fault that I lost my biggest client, but it was a devastating blow to my financial situation. That client accounted for two thirds of my business. The setback made me even more dependent on the skipper.

I decided to switch my focus to my health. I contacted my longtime medical doctor in Alabama. He was also a close family friend and had delivered both my children. I explained to him in tremendous, bloody detail my issues with my bum, ringworm, and my broken toe. My foot was still swollen to twice its normal size. He suggested I return to Alabama immediately if I couldn't find a doctor in French Guiana.

I was exhausted, miserable from my ailments, and now wondered whether I would have enough money to purchase another international flight. I knew the skipper would not help me, but perhaps on this occasion he would have empathy. I didn't want to ask him just yet.

Instead, I called several of my other clients and asked for work. Many of them came through for me and a couple offered to pay me to cover a major industry trade show in September. They would pay for part of my travel expenses, and that would get me back in the U.S. However, I wasn't sure whether I could wait three more months to get medical treatment.

While I was trying to solve my problems, the skipper spent half a day walking more than 3 km to get to the immigration office to check us into customs. Then he walked another 10 km for a few provisions. However, he could find no antifungal cream or anything that could help my other pain and discomforts.

The marina "office" was a small metal container (like on container ships), and it was only manned in the mornings. There were no taxis, no Uber, no trains. The skipper was able to hitch a ride part of the way with a friendly local on a motorbike.

When he returned, we inflated *Nela* and took the dogs ashore. They were thrilled to have a huge open field to run and play to their hearts' desire. They played and sniffed every scent and rolled in all the stinkiest stinks they could find. The local fishermen allowed us to use their water faucet on the pontoon, which we used more to hose off the filthy dogs than to replenish our supply.

The port had no infrastructure, and we soon realized we could only use the stop as a resting spot to replenish our energy. We spent the evening with a sailor we met who was from Clemson, South Carolina—sailing on *Pawsitive Latitudes*. I always found it fascinating when we would meet a sailor from the United States.

While it was nice to rest a bit, I was ready to set sail again and desperate to find a pharmacy so I could get some relief. I was also ready to find stronger internet so I could get to work.

Passage from Cayenne to Kourou

18–19 JUNE 2019
48.7 NM – 11:43 HOURS AT SEA
Our two-day sail to Kourou was uneventful except for my own pain and anxiety. During the passage, I explained to the skipper what had happened with my client. I had already sold my car, the contents of my storage unit, and other personal items. All that money earned was immediately invested right back into the voyage, and I had nothing left to sell—except for my condo and my boat. I wasn't ready to give up my land home. The skipper refused to understand or help in any way—reinforcing my theory that he was a man incapable of empathy.

I asked him if he would at least help me with mortgage and expenses on the condo—about $3,000 USD per month. He told me that he was paying for the apartment in Germany—the equivalent of $400 USD per month. In fairness, he also paid for most of the expenses and repairs for *Seefalke*. But I paid more per month, and he was able to travel, work on his business, see his clients, and earn more money. I wasn't.

"I realize we are not married," I pleaded with him. "But I was under the impression that we were partners in life. If you needed help, I wouldn't hesitate to help you if I could."

"The difference is," he said coldly. "I would never ask you for help. Asking for help is a weakness. You have to be stronger. The only way to solve your financial problems is to work more."

"That's great advice, but we are in the middle of nowhere French Guiana—in the middle of the fucking ocean," I was desperate, fighting to keep the water from trickling from my eyes. "I will find more work, but it will take time. Can you at least help me with a flight to Alabama so I can see a doctor?"

"You're fine," he said. "I need to plan another trip, so we'll see how you are feeling when I get back."

I allowed the tears to fall.

We settled into our anchorage in Kourou, a small river spot with muddy brown water and not much scenery. It was depressing. There were about eight other anchored sailboats on mooring buoys. There was no marina, no shower facilities, no restrooms, no WiFi, and no space on the small pier to moor. For the first time in a while, we were forced to be fully independent of any modern amenities.

There were two small pontoons, but we couldn't moor there. One was reserved for local fisherman and the other belonged to the members of the Spaceport Yacht Club. Those crusty, salty sailors were interesting and kind. They allowed us to moor our dinghy on the pier, fill our jugs with fresh water from the faucets, and dispose of our trash and recyclables.

The Spaceport Yacht Club was nothing like you might imagine. The rickety pontoon had room for about 10 small sailboats. Two spots were reserved for tourist catamarans that took daily sails to Îles du Salut (home of Devil's Island). At low tide, at least half the boats were sitting on their keels in thick mud—floating a bit during high tide.

The local sailors were friendly and helpful. The boats were rusted and weathered with decks that looked like trailer park rummage sales. In fact, every time we passed by with trash or debris from our boat, they stopped us and wanted to know what they could have of our throwaways to use on their ships. A couple sailors benefited from the used batteries we later replaced.

It wasn't until we found a pharmacy in Kourou, about two miles from the anchorage, that we were able to find effective antifungal cream, antifungal soaps and lotions, and all types of home remedy medical supplies, just in case. I got some extra treatment for my hemorrhoid and continued to worry about the excessive blood loss every time I passed those painful razor blades.

I spent the next three full days washing all our clothes, sheets, and towels by hand because we couldn't find any laundry services in Kourou. I was forced to boil hot water on the stove to pour into the laundry buckets because steaming hot water was required to kill the fungus.

Ringworm can live on clothes, bedding, and other surfaces, so the entire boat had to be completely disinfected and scrubbed. I worked so hard washing and wringing out sheets and clothes with the boiling hot water that my hands were covered in blisters.

Soon, the rings on our bodies disappeared for the most part, but the pain in my ass remained.

We had access to a solid infrastructure of markets, pharmacies, and restaurants within walking distance, and there was a bakery that stayed open from 05:30 to 19:30 every day including weekends and holidays. No dogs were allowed in the bakery, but they offered free, yet very slow, internet—emphasis on slow.

The skipper had purchased a data card that he allowed me to use occasionally on the boat when he wasn't using it. It was slightly stronger than the bakery internet, but regardless, I was having difficulty completing my work with my limited access.

We were able to take the dogs into the city center for exercise each day and found a gorgeous beach where they ran and played unleashed.

With every trip ashore, we filled three, 10-liter water jugs. We slowly replenished our 200-liter freshwater tank. I washed clothes by hand every day. Daily rainfall allowed us to collect fresh rainwater to use for laundry and deck showers.

To collect rainwater, we used the lazy bag on the main sail and set out all our buckets and laundry basins. We opened an umbrella and placed it upside down in the biggest basin—a brilliant idea to direct as much rainfall as possible into the container.

I scrubbed the cabins and swept out all the dog hair. Even though it was such a small space it could be difficult to keep it clean. I completed my book, *How to Sail with Dogs*, and it required a full eight hours to upload it onto Amazon using the slow bakery internet.

Several of our friends from Cabedelo were in our anchorage, so we invited some of them onboard for dinner. We had a lovely evening with South Africans Janine and Rob of *Matangi*. Janine and I became close friends while Rob and the skipper got along great.

One evening, Rob was talking about a long passage and commented about how Janine was not a real sailor. He had to do most of the sailing, but she did take some watches when the conditions were smooth. She agreed. "I don't want to learn how to sail," she said. "I'll cook and clean and help when I can, but Rob is basically a solo sailor."

The skipper chimed in and said the situation was exactly the same onboard *Seefalke*.

I didn't let him get away with it.

"Now, wait just one minute," I interrupted. "I have been sailing for six years. I am the captain of my own boat in Alabama, and I go solo sailing regularly. I have sailed this ship all the way from Germany 50% of the time—the exact same amount of time as you!"

I was furious.

"Don't you ever again say that I haven't pulled my weight," I continued. "I have sailed alone through storms and squalls and taken watches when you were too seasick to stand on your own two feet! I AM A SAILOR! I've earned that title. I won't let you take it away from me or minimize my contributions."

The skipper rolled his eyes but remained silent. He did not confirm nor deny. Even though I felt good about defending myself, I knew he would make me pay for it.

The next day, there was a live space rocket launch scheduled in Kourou. We invited Rob and Janine to join us on the local beach for the launch of Ariane 5 Mission VA248. The dogs played on the beach, and the four humans settled into our spot while hundreds of locals gathered to witness the launch at sunset. We heard the oohs and ahhs of the crowd and looked up just in time to see the rocket decorate the sky right at sunset.

Janine and I talked about our children and our lives back home. She and Rob had been together for about a decade at that time. While she enjoyed the sailing and traveling, she told me she missed her young daughter and was considering returning home soon. She knew Rob would never return to land life, so it was a struggle for her to make the decision.

The next morning, the skipper implemented his own brand of torture—his punishment for challenging him in front of Rob and Janine.

Every day, the skipper would leave before I awakened, taking the dinghy and the data card with him. He would not ask if I needed anything, nor would he invite me to come along.

Without access to internet, it was impossible for me to work. I was also shut off from any contact with family, friends, or social media because I had virtually no cell signal.

I sat on the boat, all alone except for the dogs, every day without any connection to the outside world. I suppose I could have jumped into the muddy water and tried to swim to shore, but how would I have taken my laptop, my phone, or the dogs with me?

One day, the skipper decided to go into town and purchase some fishing equipment. Throughout our entire journey, he had refused to fish or let me fish because he felt that the fish were his "comrades of the sea." He had no problem with eating fish, but he didn't want to be the one to kill them. I could respect that.

Rob fished every day, catching yummy dinners for him and Janine. With Rob's encouragement, the skipper decided to try to learn the craft. I was excited because I had grown up fishing with my father and loved to fish. I had some experience, but of course, he didn't want my help and wouldn't allow me to join the activity.

While the boys were down the river fishing in our dinghy, Janine came by *Seefalke* in her dinghy and invited me to come to *Matangi* and watch a movie with her. I couldn't jump in the dinghy fast enough. I was desperate for human interaction.

Onboard, they had a pull-down movie screen and projector with tons of movies and TV series available to watch. She made popcorn and we turned on a movie, but mostly we talked.

She remarked that I must love to stay on the boat because she noticed that I never went ashore.

"No," I corrected her. "He leaves every morning before I can get myself or the dogs ready to join him. It is not my choice to be stranded on that boat all day, every day, with no connection to the outside world. I hate it, and I would love to go ashore every day. But he doesn't give me that choice."

I told her how I would love to have her movie screen on-board—or anything to keep me entertained. I had already read all the books onboard. I explained to her how I sat on the ship all day with nothing to do—in complete isolation.

She seemed timid and uncomfortable about discussing it with me. Perhaps I had shared too much, so I changed the subject.

But my personal torture continued.

I couldn't work. And because we were not connected to onshore electricity, the skipper would not allow me to use the onboard energy to charge my laptop or use the fans, even though it was broiling hot in the mosquito soup that followed us from Cabedelo to Kourou.

Each evening when the skipper returned to the boat, he would check the energy usage to be sure I had not disobeyed his rules. He was punishing me. I tried to stay strong, but I felt trapped and helpless.

One morning as he was fleeing the ship, I ran out onto the stern in my skivvies and asked him if he would at least take the dogs with him so they could have a walk. "I need to work, and there are no dogs allowed in the bakery," he said coldly.

"I need to work, too," I reminded him. "But regardless, even if you won't be kind to me, at least don't take it out on the dogs."

"They are your dogs and your responsibility," he said.

"Don't you even have a human, beating heart?" I yelled at him as he cranked the outboard motor and sped away to the shore without us.

He didn't respond, and he didn't need to—I knew the answer.

26 JUNE 2019

After several weeks of that excruciating routine, the skipper finally invited me and the dogs to join him on an errand. He was unhappy with our battery life and decided it was time to invest in new batteries. He rented a car, and we shopped around Kourou for a while with no luck.

Then one of the local sailors on the pontoon told us about a battery shop in nearby Cayenne. We made the one-hour drive to the shop. He found exactly what we needed and loaded the extremely heavy batteries into the small trunk.

On the way home, he decided to reward Cap'n Jack and Scout with a trip to the beach for playtime. I was relieved that he at least showed a little mercy toward the dogs.

A couple of days later, we waited for the catamaran to leave on its daily tour to Îles du Salut and then took *Seefalke* to the pontoon to install the batteries. Rob met us there to help.

We rigged the puppy crane to load the ridiculously heavy batteries into *Seefalke's* engine room for installation. While the boys were doing the heavy lifting, I used the pier hose to fill our water tank.

Following the one day ashore, the skipper returned to his routine of leaving the dogs and me alone onboard every day. Without any exercise, the dogs and I were gaining weight. The extra pounds added to my already depleted self-esteem.

I continued to battle with blood loss and pain whenever I went to the head. The pain was so intense with every bowel movement that I would force myself to hold it as long as I could.

It resulted in unbearable bloating and further discomfort. I knew that it was probably not helping my situation, but the pain was too severe.

I began a daily practice of leaving the blood in the toilet until the skipper returned in the evenings. He would flush it but never acknowledged that he saw it.

One day, he finally spoke.

"This is not making me feel sorry for you, if that's your intention," he told me.

3–4 JULY 2019

It had been a year since Cap'n Jack and Scout had their necessary shots required to travel in and out of the various countries. They needed everything, including a new rabies shot and rabies titer, as well as updated health certificates.

The skipper agreed that we should take care of it.

We found a veterinarian in Kourou who spoke English. We didn't have an appointment, so we walked over to the office to make one.

They invited us in and immediately took us to a room where the vet took care of all the shots and all the details. Because the titer test had to be administered in a laboratory within 24 hours of drawing the blood, we needed to return to the vet the next morning to draw the blood and then ship it overnight to France.

There were no labs in French Guiana that could perform the required tests. Since I was responsible for all the dogs' expenses, I put the $724 USD charges on my credit card.

We had another important errand. The boat was infested with ants and cockroaches. We purchased a full supply of ant and roach poison and more mosquito spray to deal with the mosquito soup.

We bought traps and sprays and pretty much anything they had available to combat the problems. We planned to sail to Suriname soon, and decided to wait and try to find an exterminator there, hoping our temporary remedies would help in the meantime.

I tried to stay strong, but my confidence and my will dwindled rapidly. The isolation forced me to fall into a deep, dark depression.

I spent most days hidden in the dark cabin because when I went outside onto the deck, the idea of jumping overboard and slowly sinking to the bottom of the muddy river was too tempting.

Then one day, I got a text from my daughter, Shelby. I believe it was a gift from God. I had no internet, no cell signal, and my phone was not charged. In fact, I'm fairly certain my phone wasn't even turned on. But nevertheless, I heard a ping.

I didn't have enough signal to make a call, so I couldn't hear her voice. But somehow we were able to text for about an hour. It was so nice to finally have a long conversation with her after months of no contact. She had broken up with her boyfriend after a difficult long-distance relationship. She felt stronger and more confident and was ready to move forward positively.

I didn't tell her anything about my medical, financial, or relationship problems. I only focused on her.

I think it's possible that Shelby saved my life that day. She reminded me what I have to live for.

I found photos of Shelby and Bo in my backpack. Against the skipper's strict orders, I taped them to the wall next to my bunk so I could see their faces every day. He had made it clear that I was not allowed to hang anything on the walls but maps and charts.

Defying his cruel rules made me feel better.

I found a blank notebook and started a gratitude journal. I vowed to write down something every day that made me happy.

That day, I wrote my first entry:

I am so grateful to have beautiful, smart, kind children who love me unconditionally. Somehow, I will survive this and find my way home to them. Then, I will be surrounded by love.

I added one of my favorite quotes:

"That which does not kill us makes us stronger."
Friedrich Nietzsche

CHAPTER 30

THE DARKNESS & DEVIL'S ISLAND

T he skipper continued to punish me with cruel isolation. He had immediately noticed the photos of Shelby and Bo on the wall and ordered me to take them down. I refused, which only angered him further.

"Don't look at them, if they bother you," I told him. "Just look at all your maps and charts. I'm not taking them down."

Even though I was defiant and firm about the photos, my confidence and my will were shriveling. It was difficult to find any light in the darkness of my deep depression.

Some days I forced myself to sit in the cockpit or on the deck to get a glimpse of fresh air and sunshine. If I saw any other sailors on their decks or onshore, I quickly moved back into the cabin. I didn't want them to see me stranded there all alone.

Most of the time, I stayed in bed all day in the dark cabin—a place that seemed even more like a dungeon now. I continued to fight the depression by writing daily affirmations in my journal. I tried to find positive reflections of gratitude, but the gloomy feelings were impossible to ignore.

I wrote them down, too.

The loneliness is overwhelming, but I am grateful that I can see the faces of my beautiful children. I am so proud that they made me a mother, and I'll find a way to be a better example for them.

I forced myself to take a shower on the deck today. The sun almost blinded me, but it felt warm on my skin. It felt good to wash away all the sweat. My hair is not so oily now. I let it dry in the sun and was grateful for the light breeze.

I made myself go on the deck to see the sunset tonight. It gave me hope. I can always remember the details of every sunset and am so grateful that they are all unique. Tonight, the sky was magenta, deep purple, and lavender with a brilliant splash of sunflower yellow. I thanked God for the few moments of beauty and prayed that he would help me find happiness again.

I'm trying to find something positive to write, but today is a bad day. How did I get so lost? Where did that strong-willed, determined, adventurous, happy woman go? Where is the Michelle I knew six years ago? I miss her.

6–7 JULY 2019

Des was anchored at Iles du Salut with engine trouble. We told him we would sail to Devil's Island to help. Even though the skipper wasn't speaking to me, I was excited for the break in the gloomy routine.

It took 2.5 hours to sail the 9.9 nm to Devil's Island. I felt exhilarated to finally be sailing again after sitting still for so long. When we arrived, it felt like paradise! The three small islands were covered in gorgeous wildflowers, natural swimming coves, curious wildlife, and lush coconut palms. The water was crystal blue, which was a spectacular change from the muddy brown river in Kourou. We anchored about 50 yards from Des's ship, *Redemption*, and there were no other boats in the alcove.

Des had already repaired his engine and had caught a huge Spanish mackerel. He had a bottle of wine, so I grabbed some potatoes, cheese, crackers, and olives and we joined him onshore for an open-fire fish fry. Cap'n Jack and Scout were happy for the opportunity to run, play, and explore the secluded island. They had been stranded onboard the boat for as long as me. I took a long walk with them and enjoyed the feeling of freedom—an emotion I had not felt in a very long time.

It was stimulating to have a conversation with another human being. The skipper was always charming and engaging when other people were around—a gentle reminder of why I fell in love with him so many years ago. The mood, the meal, and the scenery were positively perfect.

The next day was my 52nd birthday. I loved the islands and didn't want to leave. I asked if we could stay another day and celebrate my birthday there. The skipper was in a good mood, so he agreed. We awoke the next morning to a breathtaking view, hoisted the hook, and took a 30-minute motor sail to Bora Bora Cove at Ile du Diable—better known as Devil's Island, the Alcatraz of the Atlantic.

It was hard to believe that the three stunning islands had once been the site of one of the world's most notorious prisons. The French penal colony of Cayenne operated in the 19th and 20th centuries in the Salvation Islands of French Guiana. Opened in 1852, the Devil's Island prison system received convicts deported from all parts of the Second French Empire and was infamous for its harsh treatment of detainees. The death rate was 75%.

The waters were filled with hundreds of sharks that made it almost impossible for prisoners to escape. The prison guards kept the sharks well fed with dead bodies and equally well fed with prisoners who broke the rules. They were thrown to the sharks while still alive.

The prison was closed in 1953. In 1969, Henri Charrière brought attention to the prison when he published the autobiographical novel, *Papillon*. It detailed the torture he and other inmates endured and his 1945 escape.

The prison system stretched over several locations, on the mainland and in the off-shore Salvation Islands. Ile du Royale (the largest of the three islands and where we anchored the first time) was the reception center for the general population of the penal colony. Prisoners were housed in moderate freedom due to the difficulty and unlikelihood of escape.

Ile Saint-Joseph, also known as the *Reclusion* island, was where inmates were sent to be punished by solitary confinement in silence and darkness.

As I learned more about the island of solitude, I thought about my own plight. I wondered if the skipper would continue to punish me with silence and isolation.

Once settled at our anchorage in Bora Bora Cove, we took the dogs to Devil's Island to explore. Des easily made his way onto the island using his kayak, but we had trouble navigating our little blow-up dingy against the crashing current and huge, sharp boulders that bordered the island.

The skipper was able to drop off the dogs and me, but he was unable to come ashore himself. There was no way to tie off the dinghy.

Enjoying the tiny, secluded island, the dogs ran, played, and explored. Des and I climbed the huge boulders to the top and found dilapidated stone buildings that looked like forts. They must have once been quarters for the prisoners.

There was not another human on the island while we were there. We later learned that it was illegal to be there.

The views were spectacular, but getting in and out of the dinghy was a challenge as the waves continued to crash onto the shoreline rocks. It wasn't easy, but we managed to get back into the dinghy and returned to our anchorage.

Without even a trace of internet or cell signal, Des returned to the main island so he could call his wife, but we decided to stay at Bora Bora Cove.

It was a fun day for me. The skipper was in a happy place and practiced his fishing skills while I swam in the cool, clear water and relaxed all day in our own private island paradise.

I didn't want to leave, but the skipper said he felt lost without internet and wanted to go back to Kourou.

The thought of returning to the muddy waters and the possibility of more isolation completely deflated me. I asked him if we could return and spend more time on the islands. He agreed to my simple request.

8–14 JULY 2019

After two lonely days in Kourou, the skipper kept his promise to return to Devil's Island. Des, who was sailing alone, planned to meet us there. We spent an entire day going through the process of checking out of customs, provisioning, and preparation for our departure to Iles du Salut. We planned to sail to Suriname from there. I was ready to leave Kourou and prayed I would never have to return.

With the wheel in his hand and the wind in his face, the skipper was happy. At one point, I took the helm while he tried to catch dinner with his new fishing rod. He had spent more than $300 USD in Kourou on fishing equipment, but he struggled to get the feel for the craft. Since I had fished as a young girl, I offered to help him.

"I can show you a few pointers that my dad taught me," I said.

That one comment changed the entire mood of the day. "I can do it," he snapped at me. "I don't need your help."

It was an unnecessary reaction.

"I was just trying to help," I said, throwing my hands in the air. "I have fished all my life and you are just learning, so I'm sure you know more than me." My sarcastic remark was also unnecessary, I suppose.

A few minutes later, his line got tangled in the dinghy. I couldn't help but laugh, but of course, my reaction angered him. He immediately inflicted his greatest weapon—the silent treatment.

This time the passage took about 3.5 hours. We struggled to find any speed and wondered why it took much longer to get there the second time. When we arrived, Des was already anchored and settled in. The sun had already set, so we were losing light quickly.

A strong current entered the alcove, forcing us to miss the mooring buoy a couple times. While the skipper steered, it was my job to stand on the bowsprit and hook the line through the loop on the mooring buoy. In the darkness, he wasn't getting me close enough to make the connection. When I failed to hook the line the third time, the skipper screamed at me, placing the blame solely on my shoulders for our inability to complete the task.

Then I saw the skipper toss one of my beautiful blue cushions overboard in frustration.

"Did you just throw my cushion overboard?" I screamed at him.

"It got in my way!" he said.

I was pissed, but I tried to maintain my composure. I focused on getting the line hooked and helped the skipper secure the anchor. Then I let him have it!

"You need to go in the dinghy right now and get that cushion!" I screamed at him.

"I'm not doing it," he said. "It's a stupid cushion."

"Well, it's not stupid to me!"

I marched to the stern and deployed the dinghy. I tried to crank the motor, but the skipper's fishing line was tangled in the propeller. It was almost pitch black and the current was strong, but I wasn't giving up. I tried frantically to untangle the line as the fishing hook punctured my fingers. Des paddled over in his kayak and asked if he could help.

"No," the skipper quickly stated emphatically.

"Yes!" I overruled him. "He is acting like a spoiled rotten child and just threw a hissy fit. He dumped my cushion overboard, and I am going to get it!"

Embarrassed, the skipper ordered me to get out of the dinghy and said he would try to retrieve it. He grabbed a flashlight and paddled around for about 30 minutes with Des's help, but they couldn't find it.

It was just a cushion, and I had three others just like it. But that wasn't the point. When he returned to the boat, I didn't let it go.

"Why did you have to throw it overboard? Why couldn't you just throw it into the cabin if it got in your way? It was mine. I worked hard to earn the money to pay for it. It was one of the few things on this boat that I owned, and you had no right to throw it overboard!"

"You'll get over it," he said, flippantly.

I had no cell signal, so I grabbed the skipper's phone and texted Christoph. I ordered another cushion and told him to send the bill to the skipper. The next morning, I was still pissed, but I tried to find gratitude in the stunning surroundings of the Salvation Islands. I looked out into the water and saw something blue and square floating near the shore. It was my cushion! I jumped in the dinghy, rowed to shore, rescued the cushion, and brought it back onboard. I texted Christoph and canceled the order, but I was still furious.

Realizing it was just a cushion, I asked myself why it made me so mad. But I knew it wasn't really about the cushion. It was about the way the skipper treated me and how he loved to make me feel insignificant.

I thought about the weeks of torture and isolation. I thought about the times he abandoned me in Iceland and Italy and when he left me alone to battle the storm while crossing the Atlantic. And I couldn't help but think of all the acts of infidelity.

I let the thoughts of all of his horrible treatment marinate. Usually, thoughts of all the bad times would bring me to tears. This time, it made my blood boil.

Something began to change in me. I was finding my strength again.

Without telling the skipper or inviting him to come with us, I leashed the dogs and got them safely into the dinghy with me. I rowed to shore, leaving him behind alone on the boat.

Let him feel what it's like to be stranded for a change.

For several hours, the dogs and I walked every square inch of the small island. With each step, my still-broken foot ached, but my self-esteem began to grow. Cap'n Jack and Scout were captivated by all the wildlife on the island—monkeys, red-rumped agoutis, and exotic birds.

The irony did not escape me. On an island that was once a prison, I finally felt free.

I made it to the highest peak and found a small café for the local tourists who would visit daily on the ferry from Kourou. I ordered a refreshing lemonade with lots of ice and a bowl of water for the dogs. Then I went to the veranda to enjoy the view. That's where I found Des and the skipper sitting at a table. Des was video chatting with his wife, while the skipper was booking a flight on his laptop.

The skipper ignored me. But when Des finished talking to his wife, he asked me if I wanted to go swimming in a natural cove he had discovered on the island. I accepted the invitation and handed the leashes to the skipper.

"Can I trust you to take care of the dogs for a little while?" I asked him. He nodded but wouldn't look at me.

Des was a very kind and caring man. As we walked to the swimming cove, I could tell he was concerned but didn't really know what to say to me. "What exactly happened last night?" he asked me. "It's okay if you don't want to talk about it."

I wanted to confide in him. I felt that I could trust him. "We have a lot of issues to work out," I said, afraid to say much more. "He has a temper and doesn't always treat me with kindness."

"Are you safe?" he asked me. The direct question startled me.

I didn't realize it at the time, but often victims of abuse are thrown a life ring from a caring person who sees something that the victim is not ready to see yet. The victim can either grab it and hold on, or they can continue to drown.

I allowed the life ring to float away and continued to gasp for air.

"I'm okay," I said. "He just has these moods."

We jumped into the swimming alcove and splashed around in the cool, soothing, crystal clear water. It was refreshing and just what I needed. Des told me he had offered to take the skipper fishing that afternoon and asked if it was okay if he had a talk with him. A feeling of desperation overwhelmed me. "Please don't say anything to him," I begged. "He will make me pay for it later."

He promised he wouldn't say a word but reminded me that he was there for me if I needed a friend. I was grateful and wrote in my journal as soon as I returned to the boat.

I am grateful for my friend Des. He has such a kind soul. I can feel him reaching out to help me, but I'm afraid to tell him too much. Janine pulled back and seemed uncomfortable when I tried to confide in her. What would these people think of me if they knew the truth? Would they understand why I continued to go back and take more abuse? Of course not. How could they? I don't understand it myself.

The skipper was busy gathering his supplies and loading the dinghy for his fishing outing with Des. As he got into the dinghy, I decided to lay the groundwork for an important conversation.

"We really need to have a serious talk about our future," I said. "I just can't do this anymore. You obviously don't love me anymore, and I think it's best if the dogs and I just go home."

He became enraged.

"Why do you have to bring this up now?" he screamed. "I wanted to have a relaxing day fishing."

"Well, that's too bad," I said. "You obviously don't want me here. I thought you would be happy if I left."

Maneuvering the motor-powered dinghy, he began circling the boat like a shark stalking its prey. He yelled and screamed at me loudly, for all the world to hear. "You get on my nerves!" he screamed. "I need to be away from you sometimes, but I don't want you to leave. You said you would love me forever and stay with me forever."

As he became more enraged, I became more calm. He continued to circle *Seefalke* in the dinghy, and I went from side to side on the deck following him around, trying to reason with him.

"I can understand that I get on your nerves sometimes, and that's fine," I said calmly. "We live in a very small space. But when I get on your nerves, maybe let me leave and take a walk with the dogs and get away from the boat. Why do you continue to leave me stranded all day without any access to the outside world? It's cruel."

"You can leave the boat anytime you want." It wasn't true, and he knew it. But he quickly changed the subject. "You said you would love me forever." He sounded like a child.

"Yes, but you can't treat me like shit and then expect me to stick around," I said. "I can't live like this for the rest of my life. God help me, I probably will love you forever. But I cannot live with you anymore. I cannot be left stranded alone on this fucking boat another day."

His rage escalated. "Why couldn't you just let me go fishing?" he screamed.

His childish fit intensified. He stood in the wobbly dinghy and threw the tackle box overboard. Then he threw both brand-new fishing rods overboard. An expensive fishing knife that was attached to his belt was the next item that was slung to the bottom of the sea. There was a bucket in the dinghy. He threw that overboard, too. Losing complete control, he urgently rowed toward *Seefalke's* stern and boarded the boat.

Afraid of the sudden outburst, I slouched into the corner of the cockpit and held Scout close to me. Cap'n Jack placed himself between me and the skipper and began to howl loudly, barking directly at him. The alpha-male beagle was loyally protecting the leader of his pack. Scout was trembling and whimpering in my arms.

"Shut up, Cap'n Jack!" the skipper screamed at my protector. Then he whacked my dog in the head. But nothing could silence my fearless pup.

The skipper's eyes looked dead and cold. He was in a complete state of rage and on a mission. He marched down into the cabin and ripped the photos of my children from the wall. Then he made sure I saw him tear them into a million pieces. He threw some of the torn pieces in my face and then threw the scraps overboard. He then went back into the cabin and began emptying the lockers. He broke every dish, emptied every food locker, ripped pages out of every book, and violently threw anything he could grab across the cabin.

Cap'n Jack stayed in front of me and continued to bark, while Scout and I trembled in the corner.

The skipper wasn't finished. He completely trashed the cabin. He emptied the bins that stored all my clothes and personal toiletry items and scattered them throughout the cabin. Even after every item had been tossed or broken, he still didn't stop.

I don't remember all the hateful things he was screaming at me, but it was loud and horrible. Then, I heard a sound coming from the VHF radio.

Sailing Vessel Seefalke, Sailing Vessel Seefalke, this is Redemption. Come in Seefalke.

It was Des.

"Don't you dare answer him!" the skipper warned me. I didn't move a muscle.

Then Des abandoned all radio protocol. "Michelle, this is Des. Are you okay?"

The message further infuriated the skipper. He grabbed the receiver and tried to sling it across the cabin, but the attached cord boomeranged it right back to him, almost hitting him in the face. He flipped the switch to shut off the radio.

There was nothing left to break, but the skipper's fit continued. He took the hat off of his bald head and threw it overboard. Then he took off his own shirt and slung it into the water. He was obsessed. He took off one of his boots and then the other, throwing them both into the sea.

Then he unbuckled his belt and slipped it quickly through the loops of his jeans. He brandished it like a whip. I was terrified and braced myself for a beating.

"You never loved me!" he screamed at the top of his lungs.

Cap'n Jack continued to bark, howl, and growl directly at him. I said nothing.

He slung the belt into the sea and then jumped into the water. He began swimming to shore, which was about 200 yards away. When he got about halfway there, I grabbed the receiver and turned the radio back on.

Sailing Vessel Redemption, Sailing Vessel Redemption.

Screw protocol. "Des, it's Michelle. Please answer if you can hear me."

He quickly answered. "What the hell is happening? I can see him swimming to shore."

"I have no idea," I said. "I made him mad, so he completely trashed the boat, threw all the fishing supplies overboard, tore up photos of my kids...he's just out of control. He's acting like a big fat baby."

We both watched as he made it to shore, climbed the ladder, and then ran as fast as he could to the other side of the island—shirtless and in his bare feet. Des continued to talk to me on the radio in his sweet, calming, voice.

"Michelle, he is on the other side of the island," he said. "What if you just pulled in the anchor and sailed away."

I considered it for a split second. But all my confidence was stripped from me in the past six years.

"I could probably sail the ship back to Kourou, but I'm not sure I have the confidence or the skills to sail by myself all the way to the U.S. I think it's something like 3,000 miles away. And besides, knowing him, he would probably report me to the authorities for stealing his ship."

Then Des threw me another life ring. "Ok, how about this," he said. "Pack a bag, grab whatever the dogs need, get in the dinghy, and come over here to my ship. We can leave right now, and I'll take you and dogs to Key West."

I wanted to say yes. *Why didn't I say yes?*

"That's so sweet, and I can't thank you enough," I said.

Then I began to gaslight Des as I gaslighted myself. "Don't worry. He's just throwing a hissy fit," I said. "He will calm down and come back to the boat when he is ready. He'll be fine. He does this sometimes."

"Okay, but the offer stands." He meant it.

There was no way for the dogs or me to maneuver through the mess in the cabin. And there was no way in hell I was going to clean it. We spent the night in the cockpit. The mosquito soup was bad that night. I thought about the skipper walking all over the rocky island in his bare feet and without a shirt. I tried to feel sorry for him but couldn't muster any sympathy after he had thrown his own clothes and shoes overboard.

I couldn't sleep. I occasionally looked through the binoculars to see if I could see him, but he was hiding. I finally drifted off around 2 or 3 in the morning, but I was as unsettled as I had ever been. When the sun rose, I looked through the binoculars and saw him lying on the ground near the shore, in full view. He wanted to be seen. I called his name loudly, but he didn't respond. So I blew on the ship's horn. He looked at me, and then stormed off to the other side of the island again.

Des called me on the radio. He had seen him, too.

"I guess I'll go ashore and see what's going on," I said.

"I'm right here if you need me."

The dogs and I went ashore, and we almost immediately found the skipper sitting on a bench. He was covered in mosquito bites, but I found it impossible to feel sorry for him. "What the hell is going on with you?" I asked him.

"You said you would love me forever, and now you want to leave me," he whined. He still sounded like a frightened child.

"When you treat me like shit, it gives me the right to break that promise," I told him. "I need to book a flight home to go to a trade show and earn some money. And by the way, I need to see a fucking doctor!"

My foot was still broken and swollen. The constant loss of blood and the pain that came with it were ever present. "After what happened yesterday, don't expect me to come back," I added.

"I'm not stopping you from seeing a doctor," he said coldly. "I already booked a flight from Suriname. You can go when I get back." It was mid-July. I would have to wait until the end of August. Six more weeks. I wondered if I would make it that long.

I looked him directly in the eye. "I'm not going to take this cruel punishment anymore," I said. "I will not allow you to continue to isolate me on the boat without access to my family and friends."

"I think your advisors give you bad advice," he said. I ignored the comment.

"And there better not be any more rendezvous or flirty conversations with other women," I was firm. "I'm serious. I've put up with this shit for six years, and trust me, if it happens again, I will not hesitate to leave you forever. I'm not kidding."

I had made the same threat many times, and he knew it.

He said nothing. Silence.

"You need to believe me," I was firm and desperate for some type of reaction. "I'm guilty of giving people more chances than they deserve, but when I'm done, I'm DONE!"

I tried to calm down, but I needed to make one more plea. "Can you at least explain to me why you lost all control yesterday?"

Silence.

I reluctantly went back to the boat with him, something I have regretted every day since. I have asked myself so many questions since then.

Why didn't I just sail away while he slept on the island? Why didn't I leave with Des? Why didn't I accept his life ring? Why was I allowing myself to continue to drown?

I continued the dangerous pattern of gaslighting myself.

He won't do it again. He was just mad. I should have let him go fishing. I shouldn't have instigated the serious conversation. The timing was wrong. It was all my fault.

People rarely change. I understand that now but couldn't accept it then. I let myself believe that the fit of rage was isolated—a one-time thing. But I later realized that his rage had been escalating for a while. I just couldn't see it clearly yet. Soon, I would.

CHAPTER 31

I AM THE MASTER OF MY FATE

13–14 JULY 2019

The chaotic mess left behind from the skipper's fit of rage was an unsettling reminder of his dangerous outburst. However, as we boarded the ship, he glanced down at the trashed cabin and seemed unfazed—barely any reaction at all.

He sat down on my comfy blue cushion in the cockpit and tried to make peace with Cap'n Jack. It had not escaped his attention that the larger beagle had defended and protected me. He must have also noticed how terrified Scout was during the dramatic episode.

He gave both dogs a few treats, along with plenty attention. In that moment, two things occurred to me. First, in addition to being a master manipulator of humans, particularly me, the skipper was also skilled at manipulating canines.

The second thing that became clear to me—an ironic revelation—was that it was my cushion on which he and the dogs sat. My four cushions were the only objects in the entire cabin that he had not destroyed or thrown overboard during the fit of rage.

As if nothing unusual had happened in the past 24 hours, the skipper went down into the cabin and rummaged through the mess. For a quick minute, I thought he might be cleaning the evidence of his juvenile fit. But I was wrong. He found his scuba mask and jumped into the water.

When he surfaced, he announced that the reason our last sailing passage was so slow was because the hull was covered in barnacles, preventing *Seefalke* from sailing smoothly through the water. It was essential that we dive below and manually scrape them, he told me.

He walked through the trashed saloon to the bow cabin—stepping over broken glass and other obstacles as if the mess was completely normal. He foraged through the spare parts locker. He found some flat pieces of metal that we could use for the scraping task and began rigging lines around the ship to aid in the diving efforts.

"Before you start a new project," I said, "don't you think you should clean up this mess that you made?" I was completely confused, frustrated, and irritated by his inability to take responsibility for the mess or even to acknowledge that it existed.

"It doesn't bother me," he said in his usual flippant tone. "If it bothers you, you can clean it up."

"So, you are honestly going to just leave all this shit everywhere and not clean it?"

He knew I would not be able to live in the cluttered mess. I knew he would rather continue to walk over the broken glass in his bare feet than give me the satisfaction of cleaning it. I didn't have the energy for the battle of will.

"You are an asshole," I said. Of course, he most likely took the insult as a compliment. That was the point, after all. "Ok, fine. I'll clean up the mess *you* made while throwing *your* insane and ridiculously juvenile hissy fit. But I'm not going to help you scrape the barnacles until this task has been completed."

I grabbed a large Hefty bag and began filling it with broken items.

"Take your time," he said. "Scraping the hull is such a brutal task, you won't last five minutes."

I thought he knew me better than that by now. I ignored the mean comment, but it was obviously meant as a challenge.

As I continued to work my way through the rubble, I remembered another time he threw a challenge like that at me.

Several years before the voyage, I was learning to sail my little wooden boat, *Protagonist*. The skipper and I were in the middle of one of our many breakups, and he was flooding my phone with ugly text messages. One of them read, "If you break up with me, what are you going to do with your boat? There is no way you can sail it without me."

The message lit a fire in my soul.

I marched out to the marina like a warrior on a mission. I wasn't sure whether I could handle it, but I tried to find the courage.

Today is the day! Today I'm going on my first solo sail. Screw that arrogant asshole! I'll show him that I don't need him to sail my own boat!

As I prepared *Protagonist* for departure, Sailboat Bob—my patient, kind sailing instructor, neighbor, and friend—walked onto the pier. He could easily see that I was angry, yet determined.

"It's a beautiful day for a sail!" he said.

My emotions got the best of me, and I burst into tears. I told him of my latest breakup with the skipper. He was aware of our many relationship challenges but didn't know all the details. I told him what the skipper said about my inability to sail the boat without him.

"Do you want me to go with you?" Sailboat Bob generously offered.

"Yes," I said, truthfully. "But this is something that I need to do alone. I don't care if he knows I did it or not. It's just something I need to do for myself. Today, I'm going on my first solo sail. That's it. Today is the day."

"You can do it," he said with sincere confidence. Then he gave me a few tips. "Go ahead and untie the sail ties now. That way you won't have to fiddle with them when you are ready to hoist the sail. Make sure you have the main sheet and the tiller in one hand when you raise the sail. That way, if the sail catches a heavy gust of wind, you can make an adjustment."

I listened carefully and soaked in his wisdom and advice.

"Don't forget to get the boat into the wind before you raise the sail," he reinforced the lessons he had already taught me. I was grateful for the reminders. "Go ahead and hoist the sail when you get into the canal so you can benefit from the wind shadow, but only if there are no other boats nearby. If there are other ships, wait until you get into the bay where you have room to maneuver."

My confidence was growing.

"I'll sit on my boat with the radio on," he continued. "If you get into trouble, call me and I'll talk you through it. You can do this, Michelle. You are a good sailor—a great sailor."

He untied my mooring lines for me. Then I cruised through the marina and into the Intracoastal Waterway. I remembered his advice. There were no other ships in the canal, so I turned *Protagonist* into the wind, and hoisted her huge tabernacle sail. Then I turned my boat toward the bay and found the perfect wind angle to glide her into the open water.

I screamed with glee as I tacked my way farther out into the bay. I was free and happy. I remembered my favorite quote from William Ernest Henley: "I am the master of my fate. I am the captain of my soul."

That's exactly how I felt.

After a couple hours of exhilarating solo sailing, I returned to the marina. Sailboat Bob was still there, ready to help if needed. "Come aboard!" I said. He jumped in, and we returned to Bon Secour Bay. We enjoyed a lovely sail together, celebrating my milestone.

When I returned home, I took great pride in sending the skipper a response to his message. "I took my first solo sail today. Fuck you!"

In his typical fashion, he didn't believe me. But it didn't matter. I knew the truth.

As I filled the fifth Hefty bag with the skipper's mess, I was ready to prove him wrong again.

"Start the clock," I challenged him. "Let's see if I last five minutes."

He was working on the port side, so I took the starboard side. He had our only mask, so I worked on what I could reach while remaining above water—just under the side to the top of the keel.

Large swells were coming in, and the current pushed me with great force. I swallowed so much salt water I was choking almost every other breath. I couldn't see anything so I had to feel may way around the hull. The barnacles cut my hands, arms, shoulders, feet, and legs as the seawater stung my eyes.

After about an hour—clearly longer than five minutes—I decided to get back on board and rig some more lines to hold onto so I wouldn't have to work so hard treading water between dives and scrapes. I also wanted to rig a longer tool. My arms were not long enough to reach the deeper angles of the hull. I found a metal spatula in the galley and attached a ponytail holder to the end so I could wrap it around my wrist in case I dropped it. That proved many times to be a good idea.

I had no long pants onboard, and my legs were getting ripped apart by the sharp edges of the barnacles. So I put on a pair of the skipper's jeans and went back in. We both worked for many hours. My eyes burned badly from the saltwater. The loose, sharp barnacles scratched my eyes and face. There were millions of them.

I wore gloves, but before too long they were shredded.

After about four hours, Des paddled over in his kayak. I asked him if he had a mask that I could borrow. He loaned me one, making the task more manageable. It protected my eyes and allowed me to see what I was scraping.

The water was not as clear as it had seemed from the surface. To see anything, I had to be only inches away from the hull. If I got close enough, I could see all the spots I had missed. My spatula scraper was much more efficient than the small metal scrap I had previously used.

I took 20- to 30-second dives and wished I was in better shape so I could hold my breath just a little longer. I knew I could do such a good job if I could just stay down there a few more seconds each time. With each dive, I took a few seconds to drop deep enough and then another few seconds to feel my way to the top without hitting my head on *Seefalke's* steel hull. That allowed only a few seconds for the actual scraping in between diving and surfacing. The skipper could stay underwater a little longer than me and also had longer arms and legs, so he could make fewer dives.

I remembered my American friends, Molly and Baxter of *Terrapin,* told me that they would scrape their hull wearing bicycle helmets. I understood now why that was such a great idea. With every resurfacing, I felt the boat above me with one hand and pushed my way outward to avoid hitting my head on the steel hull.

I don't know how many times I dove, scraped, and surfaced. We were both in the water for nine hours that day.

We were exhausted and decided to take a break. The sun was setting. We had originally scheduled to depart the next day, but we both were too tired to get back in the water to finish the job. We had scrapes and cuts all over our bodies, and our legs, backs, and shoulder muscles were sore from working in the water so long. It was a good kind of sore—the kind of satisfying sore that comes from a hard day's work.

The skipper was doing a good job of drinking a lot of water during the day, but I was not so diligent. It was tricky. The sun was broiling hot and intense. But since I was in the cool water, I didn't feel hot or thirsty. And since it required a lot of extra effort to climb the swimming ladder to get back on the boat, I didn't take many breaks out of the water. I was dehydrated, although I didn't realize it at the time.

We decided to start early the next morning to finish the job, then depart the next day. With the relief of the smart decision, we crashed.

The next day, it took about two more hours to complete the barnacle scraping task, and then we decided to take one more walk around the main island, Ile de Royale. I wanted to let the dogs run and play some more before setting sail to Suriname.

We walked to the natural pool where Des and I had gone swimming. I wanted to cool off in the water, but the skipper said he had had enough swimming. He rested on the water's edge in the shade with the dogs while I jumped in and floated a while. For me, there was a big difference between swimming for work and swimming for fun. The water seemed magical—maybe even medicinal. I floated peacefully and soaked my sore muscles, allowing the cool saltwater to sting all my cuts.

Passage to Suriname

MONDAY, 15 JULY 2019
Departure 07:00
I had gotten too much sun the past two days and was roasting the entire night before departure. I spent most of that night in the cockpit because I felt like I was suffocating. I needed the fresh cool air that barely made its way through the mosquito soup and into the cabin. The massive amount of time spent scraping barnacles in the salt water, combined with the lack of hydration, had dried me from the inside out.

Des was ready early, so we rushed to prepare the ship in an effort to convoy with him.

There was a refreshing early rainstorm and then no wind at all for about six hours. The heat was unbearable, and I felt like my skin was sizzling from the inside out. We motor sailed for a while, and I was roasting in the intense sun with no wind to provide any relief.

Around 14:00, we caught a little wind. We turned off the engine and hoisted all five sails. We finally felt a cool breeze and cruised at about 4.8 knots. We could feel the reward of our barnacle-free hull reflected in our increased speed.

It was a relaxing day, but I didn't feel well. The skipper showed rare concern and told me that perhaps I was suffering from heatstroke and dehydration, which was probably correct. My skin sizzled, and I was panting like a dog. Late into the afternoon as the sun set over the horizon, I cooled down from the boiling heat and could breathe more easily.

Days 2 and 3

TUESDAY–WEDNESDAY, 16–17 JULY 2019
71 NM – 17 HOURS AT SEA

I woke up with the sunrise and relieved the skipper from his morning shift an hour early. There was absolutely no wind. The smooth swells rolling in looked like a soft watercolor painting with hues of blue, gray, and silver.

It was already blazing hot by 08:00, and with no wind to cool the air, it was once again stifling. We had communicated with Des all night via the VHF radio. He was itching to turn his motor back on. We motor sailed for a while but later turned the engine off and slowly drifted. Des was not patient with our slow, steel battleship. He cranked his motor and took off without us. He never looked back.

It wasn't until about 15:00 that we finally got some wind.

I felt horrible most of the day. I couldn't cool down, and I couldn't drink enough water. My body struggled to recover.

Uncharacteristically, the skipper offered to take my early-evening shift, but I wouldn't let him. I had never missed a shift, and I refused to start now. Fortunately, as the sun went down and the wind picked up, the cool air gave me some relief.

In Port at Suriname

17–19 JULY 2019

We made it into Domburg, Suriname after nightfall. Des had arrived four hours earlier and reserved a mooring buoy for us. We anchored on the buoy and crashed after a 3-day, 228.5 nm, 61-hour passage.

We had sailed 7,173 nm total. After an excruciating two-day customs and immigration process, our early impressions of Suriname were positive. We were definitely in the rainforest, anchored on fresh (but muddy) river water, with plenty of solid infrastructure available to replenish our supplies and our bodies.

There was a pool at the marina, and I looked forward to refreshing daily swims. However, we learned quickly that the marina restaurant was infested with ticks. The pests immediately attached themselves to Cap'n Jack and Scout on the first day. I spent several hours hand picking at least 100 ticks off each dog that day. The infestation appeared to be isolated at the restaurant, so we decided to steer clear of that space while in Domburg.

We split the cost of a rental car with Des and began exploring the area. We replenished supplies, and I found a pharmacy to help with my ailments. It was not any better, but I was learning to live with the pain. The loss of blood continued to concern me, however.

One day, we were in the car running errands. I was in the back seat with the dogs while Des and the skipper were having a heated conversation about international politics. It was a healthy, intelligent debate for the most part, until something hit a nerve with the skipper.

He snapped.

He screamed at the top of his lungs and insulted Des. I knew exactly how it felt to be the victim of one of the skipper's outbursts. I had seen him snap around his children, but I had never seen him lose his cool in front of another adult besides me.

Des didn't take it.

"Look, man," Des said calmly. "This is not cool. You cannot talk to me like that. We can have a conversation, and we can disagree, but it's not cool to yell at me like that."

The skipper fell silent.

Then he deployed his most powerful weapon. He inflicted the silent treatment on Des.

Des tried to change the subject. No response from the skipper. He tried to chit-chat, talk about the scenery, engage in small talk ...

Nothing from the skipper—no response whatsoever, even to direct questions.

His ability to give a cold shoulder was chilling. I was as uncomfortable as I had ever been. I tried to have a conversation with Des to distract him from the skipper's deplorable behavior. But it was impossible to ignore.

The skipper stopped at an outdoors shop and went inside. He wanted to replace the expensive fishing equipment he had thrown overboard. *It must be nice to be able to just throw away money like that and then spend more money to replace the items,* I thought, as I wondered how I would afford my plane ticket home to see a doctor.

While the skipper shopped, Des and I stayed in the car with the dogs. He turned around and expressed his confusion about the skipper's behavior.

"Michelle, what is going on with this guy?" Des asked.

"It's his M.O.," I tried to explain. "If he doesn't like a conversation or especially a confrontation, he just doesn't speak. It's so rude, and I'm so sorry. I know exactly how it feels, and it's disgusting."

"Man, this is just not okay," he said. "I'm going to talk to him about it."

"It won't do any good," I told him. "It will just make him happy that he was able to get under your skin. That's the whole idea. He can be really cruel at times."

The skipper loaded hundreds of dollars of new fishing supplies into the car and drove to the marina in silence.

Once we were parked, I got out to walk the dogs. That's when Des confronted the skipper. I watched from afar, but within hearing distance. Des was gracious and kind and asked the skipper why he was acting so rudely. The skipper just stared at him, rolled his eyes, and laughed under his breath. He said nothing—no excuses and no apologies. As suspected, he was proud that his behavior struck a nerve with Des.

When we got back to the boat, I calmly tried to explain to the skipper why Des was so upset. I knew he wouldn't get it, but I tried to explain how terrible his actions were and how they made people feel small and insignificant.

"Des has been a good friend to us," I said. "He's a kind man. He didn't deserve to be treated that way, and frankly, neither do I."

The skipper heard what he wanted to hear.

"Whose team are you on?" the skipper asked me. "You should take my side."

"There are no sides here," I tried to explain. "You treated him badly and owe him an apology. That's it. If you can't understand why, then you should just trust me and apologize anyway. Be a better man."

The next day, we went into the marina to work and saw Des sitting alone in a corner video chatting with his wife. I encouraged the skipper to extend an olive branch. When Des was finished with his call, the skipper walked over to him, shook his hand, and, I assume, apologized. I had never seen him apologize for anything.

We invited Des to join us for lunch, our treat. We drove to another nearby marina that had a small café and a water view.

It was slightly uncomfortable at first, but I tried to be the positive and happy mediator. I asked Des about his wife, his life in South

Africa, and his worldwide travels. We were having a lovely conversation, and the vibe was more pleasant.

When our food was ready, the skipper grabbed a fried chicken nugget from his plate as he was telling a story. He moved his hands around in an animated way while he told his tale. He let his hand linger in the air just a couple seconds too long, right in front of Cap'n Jack's face. The hungry beagle snapped the nugget from his fingers.

Cap'n Jack knew better, and it was appropriate to scold him.

However, the skipper's reaction was the opposite of appropriate. He completely snapped.

He jumped out of his seat and slapped Cap'n Jack hard across the face. Everyone in the café stared at us in disgust.

The skipper wasn't finished. His rage surfaced again, and the cold look in his eyes sent a chill down my spine. He held Cap'n Jack's leash tight and slapped him forcefully across the face several times—back and forth with the back of his hand then his open palm—again and again—at least 20 times.

"I can't take this," Des said. He got up, left his food on the table, went to the bar to pay for his own meal, and called a cab.

Scout whimpered in fear underneath my chair.

I couldn't take it either. I leaped from my seat and went to Cap'n Jack's rescue. I got between them, not caring about being in the path of the strikes. I pulled my dog from the skipper's grasp. Then, I turned to him and yelled in his face. "That's enough!" I screamed.

I tried to comfort my loyal dog, but he was focused on the skipper—growling at him. He wasn't backing down. I petted him and loved on him and tried to let him know that it was going to be okay. Cap'n Jack had protected me at Devil's Island. It was my turn to protect him.

There were about 15 other people in the café, and all eyes were on us.

I was mortified, but the skipper was unfazed by his own unforgivable behavior. He sat down and began calmly eating his meal.

"He won't do it again," he said coldly.

I grabbed the rental car keys off the table, loaded the dogs, and drove back to the marina. I took the dinghy to the boat, grabbed my backpack where I kept my laptop, and then took the dinghy back to the marina café where I would have a strong WiFi signal.

I noticed that Des had returned and was already moving his boat to the other end of the anchorage, as far away from us as possible.

The skipper had already booked a flight for July 20, the next day. He would be gone for two weeks.

I searched for flights, but the earliest one I could find was two weeks after he would return. It was expensive, but I didn't care about the money anymore. I had a credit card.

I researched ways to take the dogs with me. I had sworn I would never again put them on an airplane and make them fly in the cargo in a kennel. But I had to find a way to get them home.

I couldn't ask Des for help. I was too embarrassed.

Why didn't I leave with him when I had the chance at Devil's Island?

That question still haunts me.

Through a little research, I learned that airlines would not let dogs fly in the cargo if the temperature outside was above 85°F. I looked at the gauge on the wall. It was 104. If I put them in the cargo of a plane when it was that hot, they would roast to death. They were too big to fly with me in the main cabin. I couldn't claim they were support animals—only one was allowed per person.

The only way to get them home from equatorial South America was by boat.

I was stuck.

I couldn't leave Cap'n Jack and Scout. They were my faithful and loyal companions. They were my family.

I didn't trust the skipper to take care of them, and I definitely didn't trust him to sail them safely to the U.S. if I finally ended the relationship.

I had no choice but to return after my trip and then sail back to the States with the skipper. I wondered if I could endure it. His recent outbursts proved to me that he was a ticking time bomb.

But maybe I could just stay out of his way and try not to get on his nerves.

I had already begun to separate myself from any loving or romantic feelings I had once had toward the skipper. At that point, the only thing I felt was loyalty and a competitive drive to finish what I had started. I was not a quitter.

But even the feelings of loyalty were fading fast.

Maybe I could return and just be the first mate. I could take care of the dogs and find a way to survive until we got to Key West. Then I could rent a car and drive to Alabama.

It was the only plan that seemed doable. I would have to dig deep to find the courage and the strength. But first, I needed to see a doctor and take care of my health. The soonest that could happen was in four weeks.

Knowing I had no choice but to return, I booked the ticket to Alabama—round trip.

CHAPTER 32

TRUST THE GUT OF A WOMAN SCORNED

The skipper left on Saturday, July 20, 2019 for Germany, but he planned to stop in Madrid on the way. The pain in my bum was unbearable, and the daily loss of blood frightened me. In addition, the equatorial heat was suffocating. With the skipper gone for two weeks, I decided to ignore his rules and use my electric fans. The dogs and I needed some air circulation in the 104° steamy heat.

I called my U.S. doctor again. His advice was the same. "You need to see a doctor, and the sooner the better," he told me. "It's possible you need surgery."

I updated the skipper, whose response was repugnant. "Stop complaining," he said. "If you are so worried, take yourself to a doctor."

I researched doctors in the area, but few of them spoke English. I was unsure about the quality of healthcare in such a remote location, and I honestly wasn't sure if I could get myself to one alone. I asked the skipper if he would take me when he returned.

"I'm not asking you to feed me, pamper me, take care of me, or to wipe my ass," I said. "But it would be nice if you would at least pretend to care."

He reluctantly agreed to take me, but I would have to wait two more weeks.

As a bonus, the creepy-crawling cockroaches that had infested the ship were multiplying. At night, I would lay out large swatches of duct tape—sticky side up. In the morning, there would be dozens of them caught in my homemade traps. But there were more than I could manually kill that way. I found a local exterminator who spoke English and asked him to come to the marina.

I met him at the pier and gave him a ride in *Nela* to the ship. Within seconds, he confirmed they were German cockroaches and treated the entire ship with a gel that was safe for people and dogs. If it didn't work, he said, we would have to empty all the contents of the ship, stay away for at least 12 hours, and bomb it with a poisonous gas.

I continued to wrestle with the effects of the heatstroke that I suffered on the passage from Devil's Island to Suriname. I took daily swims at the marina pool, which cooled me temporarily and also gave me the opportunity to get a little exercise. However, the mosquito soup was thicker than ever, and the temperature hovered around 104° all day and night.

One day, I didn't have the energy to go ashore and decided to work on the boat. I had one fan blowing directly on my face, and the other blowing directly on the dogs. I felt my skin start to sizzle, and then I had a sudden rush of dizziness.

It was so disorienting I couldn't even finish typing the sentence I was writing. I closed my laptop and crawled to the bunk, where I collapsed. I awoke to two loving beagles licking my face. I don't know how long I was passed out, but it was obvious to me that I had a very high fever along with nausea and chills. I could barely move and felt paralyzed.

I texted the skipper and got his usual response. "Stop complaining and take yourself to a doctor."

I texted Des and asked if he could check on me. Within a few minutes, he was climbing onboard *Seefalke's* stern. He took my temperature. It was 101. There wasn't much he could do, but he brought me a cold wet towel and a cold drink and promised he would continue to check on me. I didn't move from that spot for the rest of the day.

I awoke the next morning when I felt a cockroach crawling on my face. I screamed at the top of my lungs—letting out all the frustration of all the many things that were causing me pain and discomfort.

After another razor-blade bowel movement that resulted in another toilet full of blood, I looked in the mirror. My hair had turned bright green from the chemicals in the marina swimming pool. When I was a little girl, my hair had always reacted to chlorine in that way, but it had been more than 40 years since I'd had green hair. I could only chuckle at that point.

I always kept my primary necessities in my backpack—laptop, phone, chargers, passport, credit card—carefully packed to protect the valuables from the salt air and the heat. I grabbed the bag and took the dogs ashore. I called the exterminator to order the poisonous gas bomb, but he wasn't available to do it for another couple weeks. He did, however, deliver some more gel for me, even though it obviously wasn't working that well.

I worked a few hours, walked the dogs, and took a refreshing swim. I was too exhausted and frustrated to care much about my green hair. The thought of returning to the blistering hot, dark, depressing, cockroach-infested boat made my stomach turn. We stayed onshore until almost sunset.

With about 30 minutes of daylight remaining, the dogs and I reluctantly got into the dinghy. With every trip onshore, I always brought along three empty 10-liter jugs to fill with fresh water. It required a constant effort to keep the freshwater tank filled. The tiny dinghy was barely big enough for the three jugs, my backpack, Cap'n Jack, Scout, and me.

The outboard motor generally worked, but sometimes it gave us problems. I tried several times to crank the motor, with no luck. Another sailor came out to the pier to help me. He tried several times as well. I decided I would just paddle to *Seefalke*, which was anchored about 200 yards from the pier. It was high tide, which made the strong current even more forceful.

As the sun set, I paddled my heart out and got within about 20 yards of the stern ladder. I was paddling with all my might, but the current pushed me backward faster that I could paddle forward. I couldn't quite reach the ladder. My arms were tired, but my legs felt strong. A good swimmer, I decided to jump into the muddy river water and pull the dinghy to the ladder.

Big mistake.

I completely underestimated the current. It continued to push the dinghy and me backward at a much faster pace. I swam as hard as I could for about 10 or 15 minutes, but it was no use. I climbed back into the dinghy as we were being washed away from *Seefalke* quickly and forcefully. We passed *Matangi, Redemption,* and all the other boats in the anchorage. I screamed for help. The dogs were howling too, but no one could hear us. It was dark, so no one could see us either.

I looked at the three jugs of fresh water and calculated how long 30 liters of water might last for a human and two dogs. Then, in the dark, I saw a fishing boat. I screamed for help and the two local fishermen turned on their motor and came to my rescue. They tied the dinghy to their boat and gave us a tow back to *Seefalke*.

They asked me why my clothes were wet. I told them about how I jumped into the water and tried to swim and drag the dinghy to the boat.

"Don't ever do that again," they warned me. "These waters are full of piranha."

The experience was so harrowing we didn't leave the boat again until the skipper returned more than a week later.

Each day, I boiled water on the stove and poured it into a laundry bucket to create a homemade sitz bath to relieve some of the pain in my ass. I continued to search the internet trying to find a local doctor who spoke English. I finally found one and made an appointment for the day after the skipper would return.

One day, Des told me he was going to South Africa for a family funeral. He would be gone a month and asked me to keep an eye on his boat. He paddled over in his kayak to tell me goodbye and gave me $50 in U.S. cash that he owed the skipper for his share of the car rental. I put it in my backpack fully intending to give it to the skipper.

As he paddled away, I wondered if I would ever see my friend again.

I battled the pain, heat, and cockroaches until the skipper finally returned. We had not spoken much since the cruel beating he gave Cap'n Jack in the restaurant the day before he left.

He gave me an olive branch in the form of an electronic picture frame.

"This way, you can load as many pictures as you want and look at them all the time," he said.

It was a sweet gesture, and I truly appreciated that he finally understood how much I needed to see the faces of the people I loved and missed. However, it didn't make sense.

"I really appreciate this," I told him. "But it doesn't run on batteries. It looks like it must be plugged into an outlet, so that means it requires onboard energy. You won't let me charge my laptop or run the fans onboard, but are you going to let me keep this plugged in using constant energy?"

"No, but you can use it when we are connected to marina power," he said.

I knew there was a catch.

"So, I can't use it at all here in Suriname, or while we are sailing, or at any other anchorage?" I asked.

"That's right," he said, as if that were not a problem.

"It was a nice thought, and I suppose that's what counts, but it's not much of a solution if I can never use it."

I taped another photo of my kids on the wall next to my bunk. I made sure he saw me do it.

"When we are connected to marina power again, I'll take the photo down and use the electronic frame," I said. "Thank you very much for getting it for me."

The next day, we went into the city center to see the doctor.

She was very sweet and seemed competent. She took one look at my bum and then quickly looked away, practically covering her eyes. I'll never forget the look on her face. She made a gesture that was kind of like, "talk to the hand," as she grimaced and then said she had seen enough.

She informed me that I had a grade 4, prolapsed, active hemorrhoid and three anal fissures. She made a comment that she couldn't believe I was able to walk into her office because of the unbearable pain I most certainly must have been experiencing. Of course, the skipper was not in the room to hear her say it. She said there was not much she could do for me except to prescribe some ointments and stool softeners. I needed to see a surgeon.

The first ointment burned so badly I could not bear it. It was so bad, we returned to see the doctor again the next day. We had to go to two pharmacies to find the right ointment that would relieve some of the pain and hopefully begin the healing process. My flight was still two weeks away.

Meanwhile, we scheduled our date with the exterminator. This time, we spent an entire day removing everything from all the cabins and lockers while the exterminator filled *Seefalke* with airborne poison.

The meds from the Suriname doctor began to help relieve some of the pain, but the loss of blood continued. I told the skipper I was genuinely worried, but not surprisingly, he did not express much concern.

I got organized for my trip home. My flight would arrive in Atlanta, so I planned to rent a car and drive to Birmingham where I had an appointment with my longtime hairdresser who was prepared to give me my first haircut in a year and hopefully do something about my green hair. After that, I would see my doctor and then meet Shelby for her birthday dinner.

When I went online to book the car rental, I realized that I didn't have a valid driver's license. I had renewed it when I was in Alabama in March, but I left before the new license had arrived in the mail. I asked Trisha to send it in the mail to my ex-husband, Doug, in Birmingham and then I found a shuttle that had service from Atlanta to Birmingham.

I called my parents and told them there was a possibility that I needed surgery. I asked if they could come to the hospital with me and then take care of me in Guntersville during the weeks of my recovery. Of course, they were happy to help.

My mom asked me why the skipper would not be there to support me during the surgery and recovery. To avoid sharing too much, I told her he needed to stay in Suriname with the dogs.

In her typical problem-solving nature, she sprang into action and began searching the internet for a place to board the dogs in Suriname. "He should be here with you if you have surgery," she insisted.

Still not wanting to tell her the whole story, I made more excuses for him and reminded her that no one could take care of me like my parents.

Everything was in order. I would only have to keep peace with the skipper and then dutifully return to the ship to help sail the dogs to Key West. Then I could make a clean break with the skipper and drive the dogs home with me to Alabama. It was a solid plan.

The skipper returned to his routine of leaving early each morning and stranding the dogs and me alone on the boat. I mentally fought the loneliness and depression and tried to stay strong, content with my plan of action.

Every day, I could see Janine and Rob socializing with our friends Dan and Mer.

They laughed and played cards in their cockpit and cooked dinners together. It looked like so much fun. I wanted to invite myself to join them, but I was too embarrassed.

I worked as much as I could, wrote in my journal, and tried to stay mentally strong.

I was counting down the days until I could get out of there.

Always Trust Your Gut

26 AUGUST 2019

It was two days before my flight. The skipper still had his rental car, so he volunteered to take a few newly anchored sailors into the city center to help them check into customs. He would be gone for several hours.

I was battling boredom and loneliness but felt confident about my ability to last another two days. Then, I noticed that the skipper had left his laptop open on his navigation table.

I didn't want to look. Maybe I shouldn't have looked, but my gut told me to look. I couldn't help myself.

The linked text chats from his phone were in full view. I didn't even have to look around or open anything. It was almost as if he wanted me to see it.

The chat that was open was a conversation with Kimia, a gorgeous Iranian woman. I knew her very well. She was the skipper's business colleague, and I considered her a friend. Very quickly, it became apparent that they had met in Madrid, and she was the reason for the stopover.

There were photos, but I wasn't upset about the ones you might think.

One was a photo of a plush king-size bed in a five-star hotel. The message the skipper sent to Kimia, along with the photo, read "I just got here. Come see me."

There were photos of rooftop cocktails, an elegant dinner, and fun activities like sightseeing around the city on electric scooters.

My reaction was strange. I didn't even care that they obviously had sex. Instead, I was jealous of the comfy, plush bed. I wanted the rooftop cocktails and the delicious meal cooked by someone besides me. I wanted the fun day of sightseeing and electric-scooter riding. Instead, he gave all those things to another woman while I was in unbearable pain—literally bleeding—with cockroaches crawling all over me in the devastating, steamy heat. He was wining and dining her while I suffered all alone on his fucking ship!

It was the ultimate betrayal. At least that's what I thought before I moved on to the next conversation. This time it was a sexual conversation with Kerstin, a German woman the skipper claimed was only a friend. A few months earlier, she had befriended me and asked if she could join our voyage at some point. She was a good sailor, so the thought of an extra hand onboard was intriguing.

But I wanted to ensure there was no romantic history between them, so I had asked the skipper if he had ever had sex with her. He had emphatically said, "No. Never." She never joined us, but the text conversation clearly revealed they had sex many times as they reminisced and relived all the details. He even mentioned the possibility of a rendezvous in Cape Verde during the Christmas holidays. The affair was apparently a long time ago, but it didn't matter. He had lied right to my face, again.

My blood was boiling.

I decided to read one more chat. It was shocking.

It was with a friend, another business colleague that I knew. It was innocent enough until I began to scroll up to read older messages. Apparently, a couple months before we set sail from Stralsund, she had informed him that she tested positive for HIV and told him he should get tested. I checked the dates of the messages. I was apparently on a business trip in Omaha when he received the news. He was staying in my condo in Gulf Shores and apparently got tested at a local clinic. A few days later, after I had already returned from Omaha, he had reported back to her that he was negative. He had never told me about any of that.

I was furious! That's when the worst occurred to me. I thought about all the blood loss and the pain. What if my health problems involved more than just a broken foot, heat exhaustion, a hemorrhoid, and anal fissures?

I closed the laptop and sat still in that spot for what seemed like a very long time.

I was in shock.

My phone rang, snapping me out of my catatonic state. It was the skipper. I didn't answer, but he left me a voice message. He and the other sailors were going to lunch, so he asked me if I wanted to meet them.

I just sat there.

Then he texted me, several times. I refused to respond. He tried calling again. I let it ring through.

After maybe 10 minutes, I sent him a text. "When you get back, I need you to watch the dogs for a little while. I need to go into the marina and work on something alone."

He knew something was wrong and seemed desperate. He continued to text and call, but I refused to take his calls or respond to his messages.

His desperation made me curious. I decided to open the laptop again. He had deleted all the messages with Kimia and Kerstin. Of course, it was too late. I had already seen them and taken photos of some of them with my phone.

When he returned to the boat, I grabbed my backpack and without saying a word, got into the dinghy, and went ashore.

I sat in the marina café and ordered a glass of wine. I thought very carefully about my next step. I was so close to leaving—just two more days. I knew that if I confronted him, he would only gaslight me and tell me none of it meant anything. Or he would inflict the silent treatment. I wasn't in the mood for either.

For me to gather my thoughts and say all the things that needed to be said, I needed to write him a letter. That way he couldn't interrupt me with lies and excuses. I opened my laptop and began to write.

I simply can't continue to do this anymore. Period. I will not make you endure a conversation about it. And frankly, I'm not interested in hearing any more lies.

You have an addiction, and there is nothing I can do to give you what you so obviously need. Having these sexual conversations with other women is your heroin. I cannot love you enough or give you good enough sex or love or support or companionship, apparently, to replace this addiction. Even fulfilling your lifelong dream of sailing the world cannot compete with it. You simply can't help yourself, and I feel so sorry for you.

You have a loving woman lying next to you in your bed every single night. But she will never be enough for you. You won't touch her or kiss her or anything else. You would prefer to instead have these ridiculous text conversations with all the other women you have fucked in your lifetime, which is, by the way, too many to count. You would prefer to arrange countless booty calls all over the world than to love an amazing woman who has given up her entire life and everything she knows and loves to be here with you.

I can't do it anymore. I won't do it anymore.

What pisses me off is that YOU are turning me into a spy. YOU have turned me into an untrusting, skeptical, paranoid woman because of your countless sexual encounters and lies. It's a horrible crime to continue to give these other women the attention I so earnestly ask you for and need, but it's unforgivable to continue to lie to me about it.

Did it ever occur to you that maybe I would love to sleep one night in a five-star hotel with a comfy bed and have rooftop cocktails and a fun afternoon on a scooter? But you gave those things to another woman while I was literally bleeding on your boat with cockroaches crawling all over me. WHY????????

You deserve the world's record and the Olympic Gold Medal for cheating! To accomplish this from the middle of the fucking ocean is really something, I must say. You should NOT be proud of this!!! However, you definitely win the prize.

I must leave you forever. I can no longer live like this. And I HATE YOU for this! You are making a quitter of me, and it's NOT FAIR. I have been wrestling the past couple weeks about whether I just don't come back from Alabama or if I stick it out and sail to Alabama with you. I don't want to be a quitter. I want to complete our mission to sail this boat to Alabama. But frankly, I cannot stand the sight of your face for another four months.

I can't continue to let you leave me alone on that boat bleeding and with severe pain and fever so that you can go have a fun booty call in Madrid. What a SNAKE you are for doing that to me!!!!

And having sexual conversations with another woman...planning long-distance booty calls with Kerstin to Cape Verde over Christmas when you should be with your family is just disgusting! Is that why you wanted to start a business in Cape Verde? You just love to humiliate me for your own gratification. Does it make you feel that satisfied to relive those sexual encounters with someone else when I'm sitting right next to you????

The bottom line is that I must quit, and this is NOT FAIR!!! I HATE YOU FOR THAT!!!!

But I cannot and will not stay with you. You have an addiction that I have tried to deal with for the past 6 years, and I will not do it one more day!

So, until my flight leaves on Tuesday, I will stay out of your way so that you can have all the sexual text marathons with all your many women that you desire. You can plan all the long-distance booty calls to Iran and Madrid and Berlin and Frankfurt and Cape Verde and Poland and Kaliningrad, and only God knows wherever else you have them planned. You will no longer have to worry about me finding the messages or "nagging" you for a simple good night text. You are free.

My only request is that you please return my dogs to me safely. As soon as you make landfall in the U.S., I will come to get them and then you will not need to ever see the sight of my ugly face again. You will never again have to worry about me looking at your precious phone.

Meanwhile, while I am at the doctor in a couple days, I will get the complete round of STD and HIV tests that I should have gotten back in June of 2018 when [...] told you of her HIV status. It's nice that YOU took the tests to protect YOU, but did it occur to you that perhaps YOU may have infected ME????? I suppose we will soon find out.

I'll be out of your life as of Tuesday. Goodbye and good luck.

I sincerely hope that the sexual text conversations and endless stream of long-distance booty calls make you happy. Without a heart and soul, it's all you will ever have!

Michelle

It all just poured out of me. I didn't even re-read it. I attached it to an email and hit the send button. Then I sent both Kimia and Kerstin email messages letting them know what a sorry son of a bitch the skipper was and told them that they could have him.

Within ten minutes, the skipper responded to my email.

Michelle,

I don't want to stop you from what you are obviously set to do. And I really don't know what has come to my mind when I texted with Kerstin. I felt bad about it while I was doing it. It was wrong and I knew it. And I will also not make you feel bad for spying after me. But I want to set a few things straight that you may or not may believe me:

1) I have not touched another woman since I came back to you. Period. There was no booty call in Madrid and nowhere else. I was faithful to you ever since I came back to you. I have not touched neither Kimia nor Kerstin nor anyone else. Period.

2) There was no booty call planned. I don't know what you mean by a booty call on Christmas on Cape Verde. I had no Plans on becoming unfaithful again.

3) The last time I had sex with Kerstin or had a relationship with her was many years ago. Just in case you were wondering.

4) Of course, it occurred to me that I could have been infected, long before we even started dating. The fact that I am not means you are not, too.

I have been faithful since our re-start and only I know this is the truth. I am sorry for those flirting or sexual messages. I really have cut them down to almost zero, and there is no woman I have feelings for or have a physical relationship with.

I love you.

It was the closest he had ever come to giving me an apology. But I knew it was all bullshit. I didn't believe any of it and chose not to respond.

I sat in the café for at least two more hours. There was no communication between us during that time. I wondered how I could possibly endure two more days on the boat with him. But then I realized that he would most likely leave me alone all day anyway. My plan was to just stay away from him, not say a word to him, and get through the next two days. Then I could board my flight, go home, take care of my health, and make a plan to get the dogs back home to me.

I didn't love him anymore and certainly didn't care about the affairs anymore. But enough was enough! Even if I had separated myself from the relationship, it was not okay for him to humiliate me.

I was beginning to feel calm. It was almost over. What I didn't realize was that while I was calming down, the skipper was reaching a boiling point. He was a ticking time bomb that was about to explode.

CHAPTER 33

WHAT'S LOVE GOT TO DO WITH IT?

"For anyone who's in an abusive relationship, I say this: nothing can be worse than where you are now. Nothing. If you get up and leave, if you rise from the ashes, life will open up for you again."—Tina Turner

Feeling calm and resolute about my plan, I got into the dinghy and cruised toward *Seefalke*. As I got closer, something didn't seem quite right. Usually, the dogs would hear the motor and meet me on the stern, barking and howling with glee. This time, there was an eerie silence.

I boarded the ship and set my backpack down on the stern deck. I don't know why I did that because I never left it there usually.

There was a ghostly, spooky stillness in the air.

I walked the few steps to the cockpit. The skipper sat on the bench on one of the blue cushions. He stared catatonically at nothing. On the seat next to him was the photo of my children I had taped to the wall when he returned from his trip. It had been ripped into a million pieces and left in a pile on the blue cushion as if an animal had marked its territory.

"Where are the dogs?" I asked.

Without saying a word or losing his targeted stare, he pointed in the direction of the stern. The wooden doors to the companionway of the stern cabin had been closed, the latch bolted. I opened the doors and let the dogs out. They greeted me with their usual enthusiasm as I petted them and loved on them. But they were not barking.

Scout was trembling. I could not and cannot let my mind imagine or guess the reasons why.

I did not ask him about my photo of Shelby and Bo that had been ripped to shreds. He obviously staged the strange scene and wanted a reaction from me. I refused to give it to him.

I glanced toward the stern. My backpack was sitting there. In it was my laptop, my phone, my chargers, my passport, and my credit card. I could easily grab it and jump into the dinghy.

But I didn't.

Without saying a word, I went down into the main saloon. I grabbed a small bag and began packing a few items of clothing. I could see that the skipper could snap at any minute, and I did not want a confrontation.

After a few moments, he broke the silence.

"You annoy me," he said, without looking away from the nothing that he continued to stare toward. "I hate it when you make me coffee in the mornings. I feel pressure to drink it."

It was bizarre. I didn't know if it would help or hurt to respond.

"I don't give a shit whether you drink it or not," I said. "It's just coffee. I make it for you because I'm making it for myself and that's the sort of thing kind people do for each other. It's no big deal. I don't care if you don't drink it."

He continued to stare at nothing. I continued to pack.

"You never loved me, and I never loved you," he said.

He was trying to get a rise out of me, and I took the bait.

"It's quite obvious that you never loved me, or you would never have treated me so horribly. But I certainly loved you," I said very calmly. "Otherwise, why would I have put up with all this bullshit all these years? You can feel whatever you want, but don't tell me what I feel or don't feel."

"You pressure me to have sex with you," he said, still refusing to look in my direction.

"That's hilarious," I said. "And since we only had sex five times in the past year, you probably need to rethink that theory."

I continued to pack. He continued to stare.

"I guess I just miss the picture hunting," he said, like it was the ultimate sacrifice. "You know, I gave that up for you. I don't even like sex that much."

That did it. He got the rise out of me that he was after.

I went up into the cockpit and looked him right in the face. I grabbed his face in my hand and forced it in my direction so he would have to look at me.

"If you don't like sex that much, then why did you use it as a weapon to hurt me and humiliate me so many times for six solid years?" I was trying to stay calm, but it was difficult. "Why did you risk our relationship time and time again because of your need to have sex with all these other women?"

"It wasn't that many," he said flippantly. "It was only, like, one a month."

ONE A MONTH?

"Are you fucking kidding me? You had sex with one other woman a month, every month, for six solid years? I know that's just your warped sense of self-worth talking, but to even say a lie like that out loud makes you the worst kind of jackass! I can't wait to get away from you!"

I should have left at that moment.

Why didn't I just leave?

I went back down into the saloon to finish packing—just a few more personal items to throw into the bag.

With my back turned, I heard a loud crash. He had thrown something across the room, almost hitting me with it. I don't know what it was, but it shattered into a million pieces.

I turned around and saw him standing in the doorway.

His eyes were dead, black, lifeless.

The dogs began to bark and howl.

In a calculating, intimidating way, he slowly walked down the four wooden stairs.

"See what you make me do!" he screamed.

I said nothing.

He began to trash the cabin, throwing anything he could find. Breaking anything that could be broken. I slinked into a corner, trying to stay out of his way. Cap'n Jack and Scout stood in the doorway of the cockpit—barking, howling, growling.

The next item he picked up he threw toward them, barely missing them as they scattered to avoid the flying debris.

I charged toward the companionway. "I'm out of here," I said as I whisked past the enraged skipper.

I made it up two stairs, then I felt a forceful tug of my ponytail. I fell backward onto my back and banged my head hard on the wooden floor. I remained conscious but I could feel my head throb with pain. I wasn't sure whether it was from the wooden floor or from the skipper's forceful yank of my ponytail that nearly scalped me.

Then the skipper stood over me. The look in his eyes was chilling.

He put both of his hands around my throat and lifted me from the floor by the neck.

He slammed me against the wooden wall, not letting go of his grip.

My feet were not touching the floor. I kicked and fought and hit him with closed fists. I tried to pry his hands away from my throat, but his grip tightened as he continued to squeeze. I tried to scream, but no sound would come out.

Everything began to get fuzzy.

There is something especially cruel and sinister about being strangled. It forces you to look your abuser directly in the eye while you feel the oxygen slowly leave your body. There was no aquamarine left in his eyes. They were black. It was like he was possessed by a demon—like he wasn't even there.

I could hear Cap'n Jack barking and howling. Scout was crying.

I thought of Shelby and Bo. No matter how many pictures of them the skipper ripped to shreds, I would always be able to see their faces staring back at me. I prayed that they would always know how much I loved them.

I thought of my parents. They would never understand. I prayed they would never have to know what was happening to me in that moment. There are just some things that a momma shouldn't have to know.

I could still see my precious dogs in the doorway. Through blurry eyes, I saw Cap'n Jack take a few steps backward to get a running start. Then he leaped through the air, avoiding the four wooden stairs. He landed directly on the skipper's back. The skipper let go of his grip just long enough to sling my dog across the cabin.

But that didn't stop my loyal protector.

He came right back at him—biting his legs, barking in his face. He pinned the skipper on the ground, freeing me from his grip. Then Scout stepped in to help her brother.

I knew it was my chance.

Trying to catch my breath, I crawled through the broken glass to the companionway and stumbled on all fours into the cockpit. Scout's howl sounded like a wounded animal crying. I could hear Cap'n Jack growling and attacking.

Without looking back, I crawled as fast as I could to the stern, grabbed my backpack that was still sitting there, and slung it into the dinghy. Then I jumped in. I untied the line and pushed myself away from the boat, letting the strong current propel me toward the pier.

I could still feel the squeeze of the skipper's cold hands on my throat and realized that he had essentially been strangling me for years.

I looked back at the boat. I didn't see the skipper. I only saw my loyal dogs, Cap'n Jack and Scout, standing on the stern howling and barking, watching me drift away.

I didn't want to leave them, but it was the only way I could save myself.

"I will find a way to get you home," I screamed at them. "I love you, Cap'n Jack and Scout. I'll get you home! I promise!"

CHAPTER 34

PIECE BY PIECE

With great urgency, I ran into the marina café. Unable to hold back the tears, I asked the bartender to call a cab. Then I sat on a bench outside the café and waited.

I had no idea where I was going, but I knew I had to get out of there fast. I sobbed uncontrollably while I searched on my phone for an Airbnb near the airport. I found one for $20/night and used my credit card to book it online. Then I remembered that the Suriname cabs only accepted cash.

Like a gift from God, I reached into my backpack and pulled out the $50 Des had given me for the rental car. It was an honest oversight that I had forgotten to give it to the skipper, but I figured he owed me.

As I was waiting for the cab, I continued to sob openly and struggled to breathe. My throat felt constricted. It hurt to swallow. I could still hear the dogs barking and howling—a sound that would haunt me for months. I felt selfish and guilty for leaving them but vowed I would find a way to safely get them home.

I felt a hand gently touch my shoulder. It startled me, so I jerked away. Through teary eyes, I saw a friend. It was Janine.

With her arms wrapped around me, she let me sob and tried to comfort me. I told her I was leaving and not coming back. "He cheated on me, many times," I told her, feeling like I owed her an explanation. "I've had enough and just can't put up with it anymore."

I was too embarrassed and ashamed to tell her anything else.

She continued to hold me and comfort me but didn't say a word.

"Will you please keep an eye on Cap'n Jack and Scout for me?" I asked her. "He has a temper, and I just want to make sure they are safe. Can you please promise me that you will let me know how they are doing?"

"Of course, I will," she said. "Where are you going?"

I didn't want to tell her too much. I didn't want the skipper to find out where I would be for the next two days.

"I already had a flight scheduled," I told her. "I have some health issues to attend to. I'm going home."

The cab arrived, and I gave my friend a hug knowing I would most likely never see her again.

"Thank you, Janine. Please look out for my dogs."

As far as she knew, I was going straight to the airport. The cab driver asked me if I had any bags. I shook my head and got inside with only my backpack and the clothes I was wearing. I gave him the address of the Airbnb. "Please go now," I said urgently.

As he drove away, I looked back out to the water. The dogs had stopped barking, and the skipper was sitting on the stern petting them and making peace with them. I'm not positive, but I assume he saw me get into the cab.

During the 20-minute drive to the Airbnb, I received a text from the skipper asking me if I was ready to come back to the boat. *Unbelievable.*

I paid the $20 fare, then checked into the small room. There was a bed and a small bathroom with a shower, something that felt like a luxury to me. I asked the sweet lady if there was a market within walking distance. She pointed in the direction of one and told me it was only a mile down that road. I could easily walk it.

With some of the $30 I had left, I purchased a toothbrush, a hairbrush, soap, a couple bottles of water, and a few food items—just enough to get me through the next two days.

When I got back to the room, I went inside and locked the door behind me. I took a long shower. I was so trained to conserve water, I used the same shower water to wash out my panties, my sleeveless t-shirt and my tennis skirt so that I could re-wear the only clothes I had with me. Then I looked at myself in the mirror. The red marks on the sides and back of my neck were in the shape of fingers. I could see exactly where his hands were positioned around my throat.

I pushed all my hair forward to see if it would help to hide the red marks that were already bruising. It helped a little, but that's when I noticed that a huge chunk of hair was missing from the back of my head, leaving a noticeable thin patch of green strands barely covering my bloody scalp.

I didn't leave that room again until it was time to go to the airport two days later.

The skipper continued to text me—saying mean, awful, ugly things. Each text was more and more bizarre—random musings similar to the coffee complaint. I texted with Trisha. I didn't tell her that he physically attacked me, but I told her of the latest infidelities and about some of the other abuse. She already knew some of it and was not surprised. Each time the skipper texted me, Trisha helped me find the strength to not answer him or take the bait.

In one especially cruel text, he said he was only going to feed the dogs every other day. I prayed it was only a bluff—another attempt to get a reaction from me.

The owner of the Airbnb offered to drive me to the airport. I was grateful, and since I only had about $9 cash left, I offered her the money. A kind woman, she refused to take it. I feared the skipper would be at the airport, but fortunately I didn't see him. I rushed through security and went straight to my gate, just in case. I couldn't wait to get the hell out of there, but I was worried about Cap'n Jack and Scout.

I texted Janine and asked her to send me a photo of my precious dogs. A group of sailors, including the skipper, were all having lunch together in the marina café. She told me the skipper told the other sailors that I went home to take care of some health issues but would be back in a couple weeks. He probably believed it. She sent me a photo of my sweet dogs sitting under the table. They looked fine, which gave me some relief as the plane took off.

I said goodbye to Suriname forever.

As soon as I got to Atlanta, I used my credit card to buy a few t-shirts, a couple pairs of clean underwear, some toiletries, a large hoodie, and some makeup to cover the marks that the skipper left on my neck. The makeup, hoodie and strategically pushing all my hair forward masked the bruises and marks almost completely.

I took the shuttle to Birmingham where my ex-husband offered to let me stay at his house with him and Shelby. Doug and I had remained close friends and co-parents following our amicable divorce in 2010. He also gave me a ride to the doctor.

After a quick examination, my doctor recommended I see a rectal surgeon immediately. He gave me a referral and was able to book an appointment for an hour later. In the meantime, I told the man who delivered both of my children that I needed a full round of STD tests, including HIV. It was humiliating. A true professional, he didn't react or ask questions. He calmly walked me down the hall to the lab.

I was too embarrassed to ask him to examine the marks around my neck. And since his focus was on the other end, I don't think he noticed them.

The rectal surgeon urgently scheduled surgery for the next morning. I called my parents. Pops said he would be there, and my mom sprang into action, shopping for the best donuts for me to sit on, sitz baths, medicine, new pajamas, and any other supplies she thought I might possibly need. I had no doubt I would receive excellent care and love during my recovery.

My next stop was to see Miranda, my sweet friend who had been cutting my hair for 20 years. She gave me a much-needed cut after more than a year of neglect, and worked some magic to remove most of the green. She asked about the missing patch of hair but reasoned that it was probably the result of a year of saltwater and sun damage combined with months of wearing ponytails. If she saw the marks on my neck, she didn't say anything about them.

Then, I had a lovely dinner with Shelby to celebrate her 24th birthday. Bo was in school at Auburn but promised to visit me during my recovery in Guntersville.

The next morning (Friday, August 30, 2019), I was put under full anesthesia and underwent three procedures—a hemorrhoidectomy, a fissurectomy, and a sphincterotomy. When I awakened from the surgery, Pops was right by my side.

I didn't realize the seriousness of the surgery or the difficulties of the recovery. I spoke to my aunt who had recently undergone the same procedure. She told me the suffering prior to the surgery and during recovery was the worst pain she had ever experienced. She had previously had two back surgeries, so that got my attention. But I also knew that I would finally feel much better on the other side and that the surgery would be worth it. I just wanted to feel healthy again.

I spent the next few weeks at my parents' house on gorgeous Lake Guntersville. I never told them about what had happened in Suriname, nor did I tell them about the previous months of my cruel isolation. As far as they knew, I would be returning to the voyage after my recovery. They took such good care of me. It had been a long time since I had felt loved.

I was relieved to finally get a call from my doctor's lab. All my STD tests came back negative, including a negative HIV result. I also received the bill of more than $400 for the lab work. The cheap international health insurance the skipper convinced me to get in Brazil didn't cover any of it. It also didn't cover any of the costs of the surgery. That bill was more than $40,000, so I negotiated a payment plan for both.

For the benefit of our social media followers, the skipper continued to post photos of the dogs. They looked healthy, happy, and well fed. His daughter was visiting him in Suriname for a few weeks, and I knew he would never hurt them in front of her.

Occasionally, he would send me a photo or video of the dogs. I always zoomed in tight to be sure they looked healthy.

He also continued to send me hateful messages. One day, he insisted that we should delete our Sailors & Seadogs website, social media channels, and YouTube channel. We had been documenting our voyage the entire time, but of course, we only revealed the happy times to the public.

"I don't want any evidence that this voyage ever happened," he said. "Delete all the videos and photos and erase it all from existence."

I thought about what I had been through—all the seasickness, the long night watches, and fighting through all the storms. I had survived the Bay of Biscay and sailed across the Atlantic Ocean on a tiny sailboat. I didn't do any of those things alone, but neither did he. And even though I had to live through all the abuse, neglect, isolation, and more, I was proud of my accomplishments and not willing to let him take them away from me.

He was so insistent about deleting my connection to the voyage from the public domain, I decided to use it as leverage.

"I'll delete the videos when I get the dogs back," I told him.

Returning Home to Gulf Shores

Recovery from the surgery was slow and painful. After about a month, I finally felt well enough to return to Gulf Shores. My friend and neighbor, Lisa, was visiting family near central Alabama and offered to drive me home.

Trisha had cleaned my condo was right there to fill my prescriptions, bring me food, and continue the excellent care that my parents had started. But I struggled to settle in and find comfort in my own home. Land life still felt strange. Without the dogs there with me, it didn't quite feel like home yet.

The skipper harassed me with horrible messages. To make matters worse, family and friends would often ask me when I planned to return to the voyage. I would burst into tears. The scars and the pain were still right on the surface.

I began therapy and, in doing so, truly began my recovery.

In the first one-hour session, I gave my therapist the condensed story of the entire past year. For the first time, I revealed every detail to another human being—including the cruel isolation and the events of my last moments on the boat.

My therapist's use of the word "captivity" caught me off guard. It didn't sit well with me at first. "I was not held against my will," I told her. "I wanted to be there and kept going back voluntarily. I was not held captive. He wasn't even there most of the time."

She explained to me that even when I wanted to leave, I was unable to. I had deep loyalty to the skipper, and I couldn't leave the boat or the dogs. I was held psychologically and emotionally captive, and truth be told, she explained, I was held captive by a narcissist's virtual grip around my neck for six years.

I began to see her every week. She helped me understand that even though until the very end there were no bruises or blood, I had suffered from abuse for six years with cruelties that amplified during the past year.

It was no different than what a battered woman goes through, she explained. He would abuse me with the infidelities, then reward me with the gift of a fun adventure. He would abuse me with neglect, then reward me with the gift of a Christmas tree. He would abuse me with the silent treatment and isolation, then reward me with the gift of an electronic picture frame.

It was all a game—a cruel game of psychological warfare. He wanted to control me and was successful for many years. However, as I became stronger and began to stick up for myself, the abuse accelerated. When he saw there was a real chance that I would leave and he might lose complete control of me, that's when he became physically abusive.

I began to get stronger as I realized with each session that none of it was my fault. I reminded my therapist that I was guilty of getting on the skipper's nerves and thought that perhaps I provoked him.

She explained to me that she got on her husband's nerves all the time, but he didn't abuse her because of it. She also helped me to understand that it wouldn't have mattered if I were prettier, or thinner, or a better sailor. He would still have manipulated me and abused me for as long as I stayed with him.

She gave me great tools to help with recovery. For example, she suggested I get regular massages from a female masseuse. "Humans need to be touched by other humans," she told me. I had not been touched in a loving way in more than a year. I told that to my friend, Krista, and she immediately booked a massage for me and paid for it. I have such wonderful friends.

Trisha was right by my side the entire time. She would let me cry on her shoulder and listened to my many unsettling stories. It was hard for her to hear. She could feel my pain. But she listened to every word and supported me completely as the skipper continued to harass me with text messages.

I couldn't understand why my emotions were still so raw and right on the surface. I would burst into tears every time I said the skipper's name. My therapist helped me understand that while I had no romantic or loving feelings for him anymore, I still needed time to grieve the death of the relationship. Tears were a good thing, she told me. "Don't keep it all inside. The tears are a sign that you are healing."

Since saying his name made me cringe and actually produced a negative physical reaction, my therapist suggested that I stop using his name. She recommended giving him a label instead. I called him "the jackass" for the longest time but felt "the skipper" was more appropriate for this book.

She recommended that I block him from every possible communication. I took her advice.

Within an hour, I received a text from the skipper's teenaged son. "Dad said if you don't unblock him, he's going to throw the dogs overboard." I unblocked him and continued to take the abuse.

"Okay," my therapist said. "But as soon as you have the dogs, block him."

One day my therapist asked me what I would do if I found out that my daughter Shelby had been treated by a man the same way the skipper had treated me. "I would kill him," I said without hesitation. "He would be so dead it would be as if he had never lived! It would be such a bloody and painful death that I would surely go to prison for the rest of my life, and I would be fine with that."

"So why is it okay for someone to treat *you* that way?" she asked.

It wasn't okay, and I finally realized it. I knew that I had to do a better job of modeling what a healthy relationship looks like. If not for me, then for my daughter.

I went to Guntersville for Thanksgiving and was grateful to be with family. I had already told Trisha and a couple close friends that I was not returning to the voyage and had turned my focus toward working hard to get the dogs home safe. I didn't want to be a quitter, but my life was worth more than completing the voyage.

I told my family I was home to stay.

"I'm so happy, but what happened?" my mom asked.

I still didn't want to reveal all the details to my parents. I can't say this enough—there are just some things a momma shouldn't have to know.

"He cheated on me again," I told her. "My wise momma once told me that I deserve to be with a man who will honor me. I finally believe that."

"You've gone back to him many times before," she reminded me.

"Please tell me I won't ever have to welcome that son of a bitch in my home again," Pops chimed in. The crime of being unfaithful was enough for them. They didn't need to know any more details.

"You won't," I assured him. "I'm guilty of giving people more chances than they deserve, but when I'm done, I'm done. And trust me, I AM DONE!"

I continued my recovery with weekly therapy.

As the months went by, the skipper had made it as far as Cuba but continued to delay his sail to Key West. He started social media channels touting his skills as a solo sailor and taking ownership for the entire sailing voyage that I had helped him accomplish.

We made arrangements for the handoff several times, but he canceled each one for various reasons. Knowing that Bo was graduating from Auburn mid-December, he scheduled a delivery for the exact same day as the graduation—forcing me to choose. I chose my son's graduation. He reluctantly rescheduled, not expecting me to call his bluff.

He still had the leverage of the dogs, but I still had the leverage of the videos which clearly proved my sailing contributions. We both used our weapons strategically.

I continued my weekly therapy sessions and grew stronger. But it was still a challenge for me to leave the house and be around other people, especially men. After several months, my therapist suggested I try dating casually. She wasn't pushing me into anything serious, but she felt it was time for me to ease into spending time with other men. She advised me to take it slowly, but she also explained that it was important to avoid closing off any future possibilities of finding a healthy relationship.

I reluctantly got on a dating app, but only had a few flirty conversations. It felt good to get attention from men who would tell me that I was pretty or smart—compliments I would have never received from the skipper. I guess I needed to hear that, even if I knew it was all superficial. I agreed to go on a couple of very casual lunch dates, but it was uncomfortable for me. Midway through one meal, I burst into tears and realized I just wasn't ready. The man was kind and understanding.

After that, I decided to delete the app. That's when I saw that I had a message from an old friend, DJ. He was the kind fisherman whom I had dated briefly when the skipper and I were broken up in 2017. I had accidentally sent the photos of our date to the skipper—a mistake that (I'm convinced) was the reason he boarded a plane from Germany and then hopped the fence at my condo gate.

I told DJ about my recent breakup and insisted I wasn't ready to date yet. However, he offered me his friendship and a male point of view. We became close friends and began spending time together. He was a great listener and offered a strong shoulder for me to cry on. I probably told him more than he wanted to hear, but he was understanding and patient with me.

I went to Guntersville to be with my family for Christmas. Of course, the skipper decided that December 25 was the perfect day to meet in Key West to hand off the dogs. I called his bluff again and spent the holiday with my family.

While watching *Christmas Vacation* for the hundredth time with my sister-in-law, Kelly, we began to talk about the voyage. With the benefit of months of therapy and healing, I started to open up to her about what had happened during the past year. I felt safe with her in that moment and told her the details of my final day on the boat. I asked for her confidence and begged her not to share the story with Mom or Pops, but I told her she could tell her husband, my brother Tim.

"Do you think he would drive down to Key West with me to get the dogs?" I asked her. "I don't think I can do it alone. I have no idea what state of mind he will be in, and frankly, I'm afraid."

My brother was an athlete all his life and to this day is in excellent physical shape. He's not a tall man, but he's stocky, muscular, and strong—and most important, he's fearless. The skipper had always been intimidated by all three of my brothers. I knew I would be safe with him by my side.

"We will make that happen," she assured me.

Knowing a lot of the history already, and now with the new information, Tim was pissed. He was willing to help me but needed advance warning so he could plan around his four active sons' athletic and school schedules.

I continued to try to coordinate with the skipper, and he continued to make it difficult. One of my oldest and dearest friends, Lisa, volunteered to drive down and pick up the dogs for me, but I didn't want her to be in harm's way.

Then I got a call from my longtime friend, Pamela. We had grown up together. As kids, she lived across the street from me. She and her partner, Michelle, were planning a trip to south Florida for New Year's. "We are going to be right there and would be happy to pick up Cap'n Jack and Scout and drive them back to Gulf Shores," she kindly offered.

It was perfect. She would already be in the area, could coordinate directly with the skipper, bring the dogs home safely, and I wouldn't have to face that monster again.

When I told the skipper of the plan, he sent me a sarcastic text. "It must be nice to have a friend available for everything."

I didn't respond, but thought to myself, *Yep, it is nice. Most humans have friends willing to help them when they need it.*

For half a second I felt sorry for him. I knew he didn't have friends like that and probably never would.

With the plan in place, I anxiously waited for the handoff. Pamela coordinated with the skipper, who continued to delay. She had a short window before they needed to drive back home. The skipper made sure he missed that window. Pamela and Michelle were forced to return without the dogs.

I can't confirm it, but Pamela and I believe that the delays were deliberate. He was going to make me face him.

CHAPTER 35

TWO TICKETS TO THE GUN SHOW

In the following weeks, we continued to try to coordinate the trip to Key West to get Cap'n Jack and Scout. The skipper was not going to make it easy.

One day, he sent me an incredibly bizarre email.

I want an answer from you to the question I asked. I think it's a straight-forward simple question and the answer should be easy. So, do you want to come back onboard?

A) Yes, absolutely.

B) No way.

C) I don't know.

I don't need an explanation, just a clear answer.

I showed it to my therapist, who suggested I make it very clear with a short, simple reply. I sent him a one letter response—B.

Apparently, it hit a nerve.

He flooded me with cruel messages. "I'm keeping the dogs! You don't deserve them! You abandoned your boat and your captain and your crew!"

I wanted to respond and tell him I had only abandoned the captain, but my therapist reminded me that a narcissist's worst nightmare is to be ignored.

I coordinated with Tim and the skipper to secure a firm date. But delays went on for another excruciating month.

I was working hard to rebuild my business and scheduled a trip to see a client in Indiana. As I was boarding the plane, the skipper sent me a message that he would be in Key West the next day. If I didn't show up, he threatened, he would either throw the dogs overboard or leave them alone on the pier.

"You will have to wait another week," I told him firmly. "I'm in Indiana on a business trip, and then I have a medical procedure in Birmingham. But I can drive down there on Saturday."

Then he sent a message that chilled me to the core.

"Perhaps you should bring a personal guard."

I snapped a screenshot of the message and sent it to my brother and to my friend, DJ. Tim told me he couldn't go with me over the weekend. He was the pastor of a small church and couldn't be back in time to preach his sermon on Sunday. The timing was bad for him.

DJ stepped up to the plate. "I'll drive down there with you," he said. "Don't worry. We will get the dogs back and he won't lay a hand on you."

DJ is a large man—6-foot-2 and 250 pounds of pure muscle. A former University of Alabama defensive end, he is athletic and strong. A good ole' southern country boy, he also is not the kind of man to back down from a fight—a perfect personal guard. After all, it was the skipper's idea for me to bring one along.

I packed the car and included new collars and leashes for the dogs, huge bones from the butcher, and plenty of treats. I was a nervous wreck as we set out on the 16-hour drive. The plan was to meet the skipper and make the handoff as soon as we arrived in Key West, which would be during the very early morning hours. He was also bringing all my clothes and personal items that I had left on the boat. But I didn't care about all that—I just wanted Cap'n Jack and Scout.

It was a long, stressful drive for me. DJ continued to talk me down from many ledges and helped to calm my nerves. I expressed to him all the fears that I had about what could happen. I couldn't help but anxiously mull over the possible outcomes of the upcoming encounter.

The first fear was simple—he might not show up. It was possible we could drive all the way down there, and he just wouldn't be there.

I also feared that he would show up but try to incite an altercation. DJ assured me that he would handle it if that were the case.

My greatest fear was that he would show up but make me get in the dinghy and go with him to the boat to collect the dogs. The thought of stepping foot onboard *Seefalke* made me shake with fear. I could still feel his cold hands on my throat.

"I won't let that happen," DJ assured me. "You will not have to go alone to that boat. I'll either go with him and get the dogs myself, or I'll go with you. I can assure you he won't do anything if I'm right next you. I'm your personal guard, remember? I won't leave your side."

We arrived in Key West around 5 a.m. and I texted the skipper to let him know I was there. I gave him no indication that I brought a friend with me. He responded and told me that because of the tides in the anchorage, he would not be able to meet me until 8 a.m.

Damn, another delay. This is not a good sign.

He sent the coordinates.

"I'll be there," I responded.

I was shaking—more nervous and anxious than I had ever been.

We got some coffee and tried to wait it out. The various scenarios kept going through my head, and DJ kept trying to reassure me that everything would be okay.

"You need to stay hidden until I have the dogs' leashes safely in my grasp," I told him. "Maybe it will just be a quick handover.

Please don't provoke him. Let's just make it quick and smooth. Once I have the dogs, I'm going straight to the car. I don't care if I don't get all my personal items. None of that matters. I just want to secure the dogs in the car and drive away."

"It's all going to be okay," he continued to reassure me. "Don't worry."

I wanted to freshen up a little, so we stopped at a convenience store. I went into the restroom and washed my face. I brushed my hair and applied some makeup—something I knew the skipper hated. I wanted to feel confident.

I went back to the car, and as soon as DJ pulled the handle to reverse, I had a full panic attack. I was sweating, shaking uncontrollably, and burst into tears. "I can't do it," I told him. "I can't face him. Can you just go get the dogs for me?"

I felt desperate.

"Michelle, you can do this," he said calmly. "You are so strong, and I know those dogs are going to be so happy to see you."

It had been almost six months since I left them howling and crying on the stern—a sound that still haunted me. Not a day had gone by that I didn't worry about their safety. I missed them so much and wondered if they would even remember me.

We waited a few more minutes so I could gain my composure. I tried to fix my face again, but I was still shaking.

We drove to the marina and parked about 40 yards from the pier.

It was 08:00 exactly, and I still wondered if he would even show up. I couldn't see *Seefalke*.

"I see him," DJ said as the skipper maneuvered the dinghy around the corner and toward the pier. "The dogs are in the dinghy with him."

I looked out onto the water and saw my sweet Cap'n Jack and Scout on the front of the dinghy, their velvety beagle ears flapping in the wind.

"Okay, stay hidden until I get the dogs," I reminded my personal guard. "Hopefully, you won't even have to show your face. I'll get the dogs and go straight to the car. Let's get this over with."

I walked to the pier. As the skipper tied off the dinghy, the dogs saw me. They charged toward me at full speed, gleefully barking and howling. They definitely remembered me. They smothered me with sticky kisses right on my face, and I grasped their leashes in my hands with clenched fists. There was no way I would ever let go.

The skipper had all my things packed in Hefty bags. He began to unload them. "Just leave all that on the pier, and then you can go," I told him. "Thanks for getting the dogs here safely."

I wanted to keep the peace.

I stood at the end of the pier to see what he would do. I had packed a bag with his belongings that he had left in my condo. In the bag were expensive suits, his German navy sweater, some other clothes, several photos of his kids, and other personal items. I set the bag down on the pier.

He grabbed a couple of my bags and began to walk toward me.

"Just drop them there," I said. "I'll get them. And this is your stuff." I pointed to the bag.

He ignored me and walked right past me. I put myself between him and the dogs. I didn't want to take any chances. I could only assume he was going to take my things to the car. But then he ran into DJ.

"I got that," DJ said calmly.

The skipper stopped in his tracks. He looked the big burly man up and down, as all the color left his skin. He turned white as a ghost. That's when I noticed that DJ was wearing a sleeveless tank top that emphasized his broad shoulders and gigantic biceps. Printed on the shirt was a clear message, "Get two tickets to the GUN SHOW." Nice touch, but I did NOT want a confrontation.

Like a spoiled teenaged girl, the skipper dropped the bags at DJ's feet, then turned on his heels and marched away from him and toward me. Cowards only pick on people smaller than them.

I stood my ground and guarded the dogs from him, still clutching their leashes as tightly as possible. He briskly walked past me and then with his back turned to both of us, shot us the bird and said, "Fuck you!"

I had never in my life seen him flash anyone the middle finger. It was bizarre and juvenile. I just wanted to get the hell out of there. I walked quickly toward the car with the dogs.

"Come on, let's go," I said to DJ as I swiftly passed him. But DJ wanted to make a point.

"Be careful what you wish for," he shouted to the skipper, who was frantically rushing to get into the dinghy. "You shouldn't tell people to bring bodyguards and then not expect them to do it."

"Fuck off!" the skipper screamed, shooting DJ another bird.

"LET'S GO!" I screamed. DJ really wanted a fight, but I did not.

I got the dogs into the car, gave them their bones, and safely buckled them in the back seat. They seemed well-fed and healthy. Then I buckled myself into the passenger seat and locked my door. DJ took his time, slowly loading the car with the Hefty bags. "Come on, let's get out of here!" I screamed at DJ.

The skipper came back to the gate. DJ stood outside my door, protecting me and daring him to come toward us. Without opening it, the skipper grabbed the bag full of personal items that I had brought for him and tossed it into the dumpster. Then he quickly boarded the dinghy and sped away.

We drove away, and I could finally breathe a sigh of relief.

I immediately received a text from the skipper. "I did my part, now delete those videos." I didn't answer him, but the texts kept coming.

"You have no idea what I went through to get the dogs here to you! We were in heavy storms and almost capsized! No one else in the world would have gone through what I did to sail them here for you. I completed this mission, and it wasn't easy. Now you have to do your part and delete the videos immediately."

I couldn't help myself and decided to send a response. "Sailing is not for sissies." I made sure my text went through, and then I hit the block button.

We went to the southernmost tip of the U.S. to snap a quick photo with the famous Key West buoy, then found a restaurant on the beach and ate breakfast. We called Tim, Trisha, Pamela, and a few other people to let them know we accomplished the mission and had safely retrieved the dogs.

Pamela sent me a blog the skipper had posted on social media about how much he loved the dogs and would miss them—painting himself as a hero for the dangerous sailing passage he had endured to get them to Key West.

Of course, he didn't mention his many threats to withhold food from them or to throw them overboard. He also didn't mention isolating them on the boat for weeks at a time without exercise. He certainly didn't mention horrifically beating Cap'n Jack in the restaurant.

DJ wanted to celebrate, but I felt uneasy. I feared the skipper would come into the city and we might run into him. I did not want that. We ate quickly, then began the long 16-hour drive home.

When we got as far as Miami, I felt safe enough to make a stop. We found a dog-friendly beach where I unleashed the hounds and let them run and play. I splashed in the water with them and finally felt free.

CHAPTER 36

HOW I GOT MY LAND LEGS

EPILOGUE

"I am the master of my fate.
I am the captain of my soul."
William Ernest Henley

S ometimes I lie in bed and can still feel the rocking and rolling motion of the sea. I can smell the salty air, hear the waves, and feel the cold wind on my face.

I close my eyes, and with vivid accuracy I can see the brilliant colors of each sunset.

I don't just *remember* the uncomfortable queasiness of my epic battles with seasickness—I can still *feel* it. I think of the Bay of Biscay, and my body has a physical reaction. But then I remember what I went through to get to the other side and what I proved to myself in the process.

The mind is stronger than the body. If I want to do something badly enough, I can do it.

All the memories of a year at sea—the good, the bad, and the ugly—left their imprint on my senses.

My brother, Tim, had encouraged me for almost two years to tell the whole story. It took countless hours of therapy and healing before I felt healthy and strong enough to reveal the truth publicly. Then three things happened that convinced me that the timing was right.

First, I was determined to never let my mother know the extent of the torture and abuse that I had suffered. She knew that the skipper was unfaithful to me, and for her, that was a good enough reason for me to leave him.

When she died unexpectedly in May 2021, I realized that now she knows everything. Something told me she would help me get through it. She did.

I can still hear her voice saying to me, "You deserve to be with a man who will honor you."

The skipper was not that man. He was incapable of loving me the way I deserved to be loved—with honor. I realize now that I was holding on so tightly to what I thought was the great love story of my life. With all the international rendezvous and exciting adventures in exotic places, I was convinced that my love story would have a fairy-tale ending.

What I forgot along the way was that even fairy tales can be bloody and gruesome. Sometimes things are not as they appear. Sometimes, the knight in shining armor is actually the fire-breathing dragon in disguise.

Secondly, a couple weeks after my mom's death, an old friend called to offer his condolences. He had recently read a book that the skipper apparently published about his "solo" sailing adventures. I haven't read the book and never will, but my friend described the skipper as a "hero" for bringing my dogs all the way to Key West for me. "What a great guy," my friend said of the skipper.

I spent the next hour telling him in great detail a little story about what had really happened—including the "great guy's" mistreatment of my dogs and me. Some of the stories, as you now know,

398

are embarrassing and humiliating. But it felt good to unleash the truth.

As I told him the details, I didn't shed a tear and felt like a warrior—strong and mentally healthy.

Then, by coincidence or by fate, a new platform for authors, Kindle Vella, was launched. It allows authors to tell a very long story one episode at a time. There was no word count limit, so I could share all the details and leave no stone unturned. And since readers wanted new episodes every week, I was forced to continue to write until I got to the end.

With the right motivation and timing in place, I hired my 23-year-old son, Bo, to be my editor. He is a brilliant creative writer and humorist, and a gifted content editor. I knew he would always be truthful about whether I was telling a story that was fair and honest.

A strong content editor, he helped me weave in some of the backstory of the relationship to show the history of abuse. He helped me to develop the key characters and encouraged me to reveal my own character flaws as well as the skipper's.

We agreed that my story shouldn't be a skipper bashing. We made great efforts to ensure that I was telling the story of *my* journey—keeping the skipper nameless and staying true to my own experiences. It was important to recount the good times and fun adventures, as well as the darkness and the pain.

I know it wasn't easy for Bo.

Several unsettling things were revealed that he previously didn't know. A true professional, every time I warned him that the next chapter may be tough to read, he always said, "Mom, just keep writing. I'm proud of you."

With the story structure in place, I hired my favorite copy editor—the brilliant Emily Britt. Thanks to her meticulous attention to detail and emotional support, she helped me make difficult cuts and gave the final version the polish it needed.

About midway through the publishing process, something else happened that confirmed that sharing my story was important.

Gabby Petito was found dead, allegedly the victim of abuse. Her disappearance and death became international news. It hit me hard because her story mirrored mine.

She and her boyfriend had documented their adventures on YouTube. So did I. She blogged about her experiences. So did I. Everything she reported to the public was happy and upbeat—just like me. And just like me, there was a deep, dark history of abuse that she never revealed. Just like me, she had been thrown life rings that she allowed to float away. No one else knew about the heartache and terror that Gabby and I both experienced when the cameras were turned off.

But her story didn't have a happy ending. She was strangled to death.

Not a day goes by that I don't think about her last minutes on Earth. I think about her and can feel the skipper's cold hands squeezing my throat. Her fate could have been mine.

I thank God every day that Cap'n Jack saved my life so that I could live to see my children, my parents, my family, and my friends again.

I'm able to share my story in hopes that it may help the next Gabby.

Many people have reached out to me who have been, or currently are, victims of abuse. Some are friends I've known for a long time, and some are strangers. Some have escaped from their abusers, and some still struggle to find a way to leave.

Sharing my story is worth it when others find strength in it.

I've also heard from people who ask me why I was so stupid to stay in such a toxic relationship. It's a fair question. Trust me, I asked myself that same question a million times over the course of six years.

It's easy to say, "Why doesn't he or she just leave?" But it is impossible to describe how difficult that can be. Rather than judging that person for staying, please, throw them a life ring and don't stop until they grab it.

Don't let them drown.

I always said, "If he ever hit me, I would leave him immediately." I know what that kind of abuse looks like. But it's important to understand the coercive control that abusers hold over their victims.

And let me assure you, even if the abuse is not physical at first, it can escalate quickly like it did with me.

It is important that I make it absolutely clear. Neglect is abuse. Gaslighting is abuse. Isolation is abuse. Verbal defamation is abuse. Emotional control is abuse. Psychological brainwashing is abuse. Cheating is abuse.

The silent treatment is cruel abuse.

The victim does not have to be bruised and bleeding to suffer the pain of the deep scars.

When I first met the skipper, I was a strong, well-educated, confident, successful journalist. He broke me down, slowly, piece by piece. He took his time and was strategic and methodical—all while demanding loyalty from me but giving me no loyalty in return.

Gaslighting is a cruel and effective weapon. When someone is able to convince you that what you saw with your own two eyes wasn't real, that's pure power. The skipper was the master.

My therapist helped me see that it wasn't until he began to mistreat my friends and my dogs that I made the concrete choice to leave him and never look back. I needed to see the abuse through a different lens to understand how horribly he treated me.

I hated how he treated Des and Cap'n Jack, but sometimes I wonder if he had not treated them badly, would I still be there with him enduring the abuse? I would hope not, but it's a question I often ask myself.

When you are the victim, it's so difficult to see it. I was the kind of person who wanted to see the good in people. I wanted to believe I had the capacity to forgive. I believed that people could change for the better. I was blinded by love and loyalty.

I'm not so trusting anymore. I'm much rougher around the edges, and I often wonder if that's a good thing or a bad thing.

The skipper was calculating and strategic. He made sure the abuse happened behind closed doors. Around other people, he was the life of the party—charming, engaging, and very likable. When he was around other people, I remembered why I fell in love with him. There were times when he was tender and sweet, but when he was abusive, it was chilling.

And he could brainwash me to believe just about anything.

A Broken Deal

Almost a year after I left Suriname, six months after I brought the dogs home, I looked out the window of my condo and saw a bright orange sailboat with a German flag sailing along the Intracoastal Waterway. It was the skipper sailing on *Seefalke*.

I leashed the dogs and went to the condo below me. My neighbors, Chandy and Ken, gave us a safe place to hide. I had a severe panic attack—shaking and sobbing uncontrollably.

Terrified, I called Trisha because her condo had a view of Bon Secour Bay. He was sailing away toward Mobile Bay. But he made a sharp turn and sailed directly toward the complex.

Apparently, he had reached out to one of my other neighbors and asked her to take photos of him. I'm convinced he wanted to be sure I knew he was there.

Not knowing the whole story, she posted the photos on Facebook and congratulated him for completing the journey. It hurt me deeply.

Completing that voyage meant nothing to him, but he knew it meant a lot to me. He knew I felt like a quitter for not completing the mission, and I'm sure it gave him great pleasure to throw that in my face. He easily manipulated my own friend into publicly tormenting me.

He was still the master manipulator.

I was too afraid to go home that night. The dogs and I hid in fear in Chandy and Ken's condo while the skipper anchored for the night less than 100 yards away from my home on Plash Island.

Several months before that, I had taken his precious videos down with the agreement that he would never again contact me or any of my friends or family in any way.

That night, he broke his end of the bargain, so I reposted the videos. They remain in the public domain to this day.

Time Heals All Wounds

I no longer live in fear of the skipper.

But the scars run deep and will most likely stay with me forever, along with all the good memories. It's been several years since I left Suriname, the skipper, and the voyage behind me. I believe now more than ever that time does heal all wounds.

With time, I've been able to regain my health, although I still have not repaired all of the neglected injuries that I endured while at sea.

With time, I've been able to re-enter society and civilization and have re-learned how to apply makeup, fix my hair, use appliances, drive a car, and be social—although sometimes I still struggle with feeling captive in my own home just like I sometimes felt captive onboard *Seefalke*.

With time, I've regained some of the confidence and self-esteem that was slowly stripped from me for so many years. I've re-established relationships with family and friends. I'll never again take for granted something as precious as the time spent with the people I love.

Some things have been easy. As soon as Cap'n Jack and Scout returned to Gulf Shores they remembered their former routine, their neighborhood, and their home. I thought I would have to retrain puppies again, but they remembered their potty training and had zero accidents. It was as if they had only been gone a few days.

I pray they have healed from their own traumas.

Cap'n Jack still protects me with his life.

My clients and business associates embraced my return and trusted me with projects. I regained my confidence in my professional abilities and talents and have worked on personal writing projects that I wanted to tackle for years.

I've never felt so inspired to work and write.

I'm remembering what it's like to be truly loved and cared for—thanks to loyal friends and loving family.

Important Lessons Learned

My year-long, worldwide sailing journey taught me that can I live without a lot. I can live without air conditioning or ice in suffocating 100-plus degree heat. I can live without refrigeration, a proper shower, or a comfy bed. I can survive in a very small space with no microwave, coffee maker, or hair dryer.

I can live in solitude and survive without internet, television, or conversation. I can manufacture creative rigs and fix things when they break. I can walk sideways, sleep sideways, pee sideways, and cook on a moving boat while heeling on a 20-degree tilt.

I finally learned that disloyalty is not okay. I learned that a person can sacrifice everything she knows and loves to give someone else their lifelong dream, but it still may not be enough to make that person love her, respect her, or honor her.

That has perhaps been the hardest lesson of all.

I've learned that confidence and self-esteem can be recovered even when it has been buried for years deep beneath a heavy blanket of manipulation.

Most important, I have learned that the mind is stronger than the body. I can challenge myself and fight physical, mental, and emotional obstacles to accomplish things I never thought possible.

I can fight gut-wrenching seasickness and stay on watch. I can battle fear and sail at night in heavy traffic. I can withstand severe heatstroke, exhaustion, severe loneliness, and isolation and still find a way to come out clean on the other side.

I sailed challenging bodies of water, sailed across the Equator twice, and crossed the Atlantic Ocean in a sailboat!

I didn't do any of those things alone, but I did them.

Even if photos and videos have been removed from existence, it doesn't change the fact that the voyage happened, or that I was an integral part of it. I never missed a sailing shift or a night watch. I organized and planned, cleaned and cooked, cared for two precious dogs, and carried a significant chunk of the financial burden.

I stayed alone on the boat with the dogs 12 times—once with a broken foot, and another time while bleeding and in torturous pain.

I overcame those and other challenges for 7,194 nautical miles over the course of 372 days. And just like the beautiful memories of gorgeous beaches and fascinating people, I'll never let anyone take any of that away from me.

While the worldwide sailing journey ended early for me, my experiences, the scars, and the memories will live forever in my heart, my soul, and on the worldwide web. I am not and never was a nameless first mate or simply a passenger on board.

I sailed that ship 50% of the time all the way from Germany to Suriname. I was at the helm exactly the same amount of time as the skipper.

I am a sailor!

I have the significant contributions, the experiences, the nautical miles, and the scars to prove it. I will never stop sailing, traveling, or seeking adventure.

The skipper apparently wrote in his book that the reason he is now a solo sailor is because his first mate couldn't handle the seasickness. Let me set the record straight. I handled the seasickness. The skipper is a solo sailor now because he is a man without honor and without character.

The year-long sailing journey changed me. It changed me for the better. But the years back on land have also changed me for the better. I am now a much stronger person—physically, mentally, and emotionally.

For the first time in a very long time, I am happy. I am happy on my own terms, in my own environment, and in my own skin. Life is good. I got my happy, fairy-tale ending after all.

Finally, I am the master of my fate and the captain of my soul.

THANK YOU for reading *Living Life Sideways*!

Please leave an honest review. Reviews are an author's greatest currency, especially those of us who do not have the support of huge publishing houses. Reviews help our books show up in searches and we love them more than anything—even more than chocolate.

About the Author

ABOUT THE AUTHOR

MICHELLE SEGREST

Michelle Segrest has been a professional journalist for more than 30 years. She is the president of Navigate Content, Inc., a full-service content creation firm, and works hard for her clients even while sailing and traveling around the world.

Michelle is a proud Southern girl from Sweet Home Alabama. She sailed for the first time with a longtime friend in Hamburg, Germany in 2013 and was immediately hooked. Sailing became a part of her soul as this journalist found a passion that would burn deeply within her forever. She still delights in researching and learning the finer details of sailing.

In 2018, she embarked on a year-long sailing adventure that included an Atlantic Crossing with passages across the Baltic Sea, the North Sea, the English Channel, the Bay of Biscay, around the Atlantic coast of Spain and Portugal, around the western coast of Africa and across the Atlantic to Brazil and then up the South American coast.

She chronicles her adventures and provides tips and guides for sailors with practical advice on battling seasickness and living on a boat in her award-winning blog, "How to Get Your Sea Legs."

If you'd like to chat with the author and other memoir authors and readers, join the friendly, fun Facebook group, We Love Memoirs. https://www.facebook.com/groups/welovememoirs/

OTHER BOOKS BY MICHELLE SEGREST

Life on a 20-Degree Tilt

Blinded By Love & Loyalty

Captain of My Soul

How to Sail with Dogs

How to Battle Seasickness

Sailing Logbook & Journal

Be Grateful Every Day Gratitude Journal

Adventure is Worthwhile: Travel Journal

Cap'n Jack & Scout's Travel Adventures
A picture book series that teaches children about geography, culture, and wildlife through the adventures of two well-traveled beagles.

www.ingramcontent.com/pod-product-compliance
Lightning Source LLC
Chambersburg PA
CBHW060852120626
46553CB00001B/58